Intermediate C Programming for the PIC Microcontroller

Simplifying Embedded Programming

Hubert Henry Ward

Apress®

Intermediate C Programming for the PIC Microcontroller: Simplifying Embedded Programming

Hubert Henry Ward
Leigh, UK

ISBN-13 (pbk): 978-1-4842-6067-8   ISBN-13 (electronic): 978-1-4842-6068-5
https://doi.org/10.1007/978-1-4842-6068-5

Managing Director, Apress Media LLC: Welmoed Spahr
Acquisitions Editor: Natalie Pao
Development Editor: James Markham
Coordinating Editor: Jessica Vakili

Distributed to the book trade worldwide by Springer Science+Business Media New York, 1 NY Plaza, New York, NY 10004. Phone 1-800-SPRINGER, fax (201) 348-4505, e-mail orders-ny@springer-sbm.com, or visit www.springeronline.com. Apress Media, LLC is a California LLC and the sole member (owner) is Springer Science + Business Media Finance Inc (SSBM Finance Inc). SSBM Finance Inc is a **Delaware** corporation.

For information on translations, please e-mail booktranslations@springernature.com; for reprint, paperback, or audio rights, please e-mail bookpermissions@springernature.com.

Apress titles may be purchased in bulk for academic, corporate, or promotional use. eBook versions and licenses are also available for most titles. For more information, reference our Print and eBook Bulk Sales web page at www.apress.com/bulk-sales.

Any source code or other supplementary material referenced by the author in this book is available to readers on GitHub via the book's product page, located at www.apress.com/ 978-1-4842-6067-8. For more detailed information, please visit www.apress.com/source-code.

Printed on acid-free paper

Table of Contents

About the Author

Hubert Henry Ward has nearly 25 years of experience as a college lecturer delivering the BTEC, and now Pearson's, Higher National Certificate and Higher Diploma in Electrical and Electronic Engineering. Hubert has a 2.1 Honours Bachelor's Degree in Electrical and Electronic Engineering. Hubert has also worked as a consultant in embedded programming. His work has established his expertise in the assembler and C programming languages, within the MPLABX IDE from Microchip, as well as designing electronic circuits and PCBs using ECAD software. Hubert was also the UK technical expert in Mechatronics for three years, training the UK team and taking them to the Skills Olympics in Seoul 2001, resulting in one of the best outcomes to date for the UK in Mechatronics.

About the Technical Reviewer

Sai Yamanoor is an embedded systems engineer working for an industrial gases company in Buffalo, NY. His interests, deeply rooted in DIY and open source hardware, include developing gadgets that aid behavior modification. He has published two books with his brother, and in his spare time, he likes to build things that improve quality of life. You can find his project portfolio at `http://saiyamanoor.com`.

Introduction

This book looks at some useful aspects of the PIC microcontroller. It explains how to write programs in C so that you can use the PIC micro to control a variety of electronics and DC motors. After reading this book, you will be well on your way to becoming an embedded programmer using the C programming language.

The Aims and Objectives of This Book

The main aim of this book is to introduce you to some useful applications of programming PIC micros such as

- Creating header files

- Controlling seven-segment displays

- Using an LCD display with two lines of 16 characters

- Pulse width modulation

- Using driver ICs such as the ULN2004A

- Controlling DC motors, including stepper motors and servo motors

- Using every aspect of the Capture, Compare and PWM, CCP module in the PIC

- Using interrupts

- Writing to the EEPROM

The Objectives of This Book

After reading through this book, you should be able to program the PIC to use all of the above. You should have a good understanding of some of the advance programming techniques for PIC micros. You should be able to download your programs to your PIC in a practical situation where you have the ability to design and build some useful projects.

The Prerequisites

There are none really, but understanding the C programming language will be useful. However, I will explain how each program works as we go through them.

Also, if you understand the binary and hexadecimal number systems, it will be an advantage but there is a section in the Appendix that will help you with that.

However, to get the full use out of this book, you will need to install the following software:

- MPLABX, which is the IDE from Microchip. The version in the book is MPLABX Version 5.25. However, any version later than 2.20 is OK.

- A C compiler for the 8-bit micro. I use XC8 (V2.10) but with some programs I use XC8 (V1.35) compiler software. However, you should be aware that some of the later compilers are missing some useful libraries. This is why I sometimes use version 1.35.

All of these programs are freely available from the Microchip web site.

Another useful piece of software is a suitable ECAD (electronic computer-aided design) software program that supports 8-bit micros. The ECAD software I use is PROTEUS. However, it is not free, so as well as showing you how to simulate the programs in PROTEUS, I will show you how to use a suitable prototype board to run the programs in a practical situation.

If you want to go down the practical route, you will need to purchase a programming tool and a prototype board.

The tools I use are either the ICD3 can (Microchip has now moved onto the ICD4 can) or the PICkit3 programmer to download the programs from MPLABX to the PIC.

The prototype board I use is the picdem2 plus DEMO BOARD and a prototype board from Matrix Multimedia (although Matrix no longer produces the more versatile board that I use).

This book was written based around using MPLABX V5.25. However, the principles of how to create projects and write programs are transferable to earlier and later versions of MPLABX. There may be some slight differences in the details, but they shouldn't cause too many problems.

The PIC that this book is based around is the PIC18F4525. This is a very versatile 8-bit micro that comes in a 40-pin dual-inline package. As long as the PIC you want to use has the same firmware modules, then the programs in the book can easily be used on other PIC micros with some minor modifications. However, you should always refer to the data sheet for the particular PIC you use because some of the SFRs (special function registers) may differ. For example, the PIC18F4525 uses the ADCON0, ADCON1, and ADCON2 SRFs to control the ADC module but the 16F88 uses the ANSEL, ADCON0, and ADCON1 registers.

Throughout the book, I include program listings and I go through an analysis of any new instructions that the listings introduce. With respect to the first listing, I will assume that all of the instructions are new to you, the reader.

INTRODUCTION

Before we move into the book for real, I think it will be useful to you if I explained a bit about what MPLABX is. It is an industrial IDE created by Microchip. The term IDE stands for integrated development environment. It is actually a lot of programs collected together to create a programming environment:

- There is an editor, which is slightly more than a simple text editor. However, in my early days, I used to write my programs in Notepad.

- There is also a compiler program that converts your program instructions from C to the machine code that all microprocessor-based systems use. In the very early days of programming, the programmers used to write in this machine code. This was a bit before my time, although in my early days, I wrote all my programs in assembler. Assembler is the closet language to the actual machine code that all micros use.

- There is also a linker program that will bring together any include files that we wish to use in our projects.

- As well as these programs, there are a range of programs that we can use to help debug our programs or simply simulate them.

So this IDE is a very large collection of programs that make our job of writing code much more efficient. Yet it's free; well, I use the free version, which is not as efficient as the paid version but it is more than good enough for us.

I therefore hope that you not only learn how to program the PIC micro but you also enjoy going through my book and that you produce some useful projects along the way.

CHAPTER 1

Creating a Header File

In an effort to reduce the amount of text in the program listings and reduce the amount whereby I simply repeat myself, let's create and use a series of header files. Header files are used when your programs use the same series of instructions in exactly the same way in all your projects and programs.

In this book, you will create three header files. The first will be concerned with the configuration words you write for your projects. The configuration words are used to configure how the PIC applies the essential parameters of the PIC. They have to be written for every project and program you create. Therefore, if you are going to write the same configuration words for all of your projects, you should use a header file.

The second header file will be associated with setting up the PIC to use the ports, the oscillator, the timers, etc. You will set them in exactly the same way in all of your projects, so it's useful to create a header file for this. However, in some projects you may need to modify some of the settings, so be careful when using this header file.

The third header file you will create will be used if your programs use the LCD (liquid crystal display) in exactly the same way such that

- The LCD is always connected to PORTB.

- The LCD uses just four data lines instead of eight to save I/O.

- The RS pin is always on Bit4 of PORTB and the E pin on Bit5 of PORTB.

© Hubert Henry Ward 2020
H. H. Ward, *Intermediate C Programming for the PIC Microcontroller,*
https://doi.org/10.1007/978-1-4842-6068-5_1

- The LCD always increments the cursor position after each character has been displayed.

- The LCD always uses 2 lines of 16 characters.

- The actual characters are always on a 5 by 8 grid.

If this is all true, you should create a header file for the LCD.

These are the three header files you will create in this book. There are many more examples of when you should create a header file. The process of creating and using header files makes your program writing more efficient.

Header files can be made available for all of your projects, like global header files as opposed to local header files. Local header files are available only to the project they were created in.

Also, you can split projects up so that different programmers can write different sections of the programs and save them as header files to be used in all projects by all of the company's programmers.

Creating a Header File

Now that I have explained what header files are and why you would use them, let's create one. The first header file you will create will be for the configuration words that you will use for most of the projects in this book. It will also give me the chance to go through creating a project in MPLABX for those readers who have never used MPLABX before. The version I am using is MPLABX V5.25. It is one of the latest versions of the IDE from Microchip. Microchip is always updating the software, but the main concepts of creating a project and writing programs do not change. You will be able to follow the process even if you have an earlier version of MPLABX or a later version.

Creating a Project in MPLABX

Assuming you have downloaded both the MPLABX software and the XC8 (V2.10) compiler software or XC8 (V1.35), when you open the software, the opening screen will look like Figure 1-1.

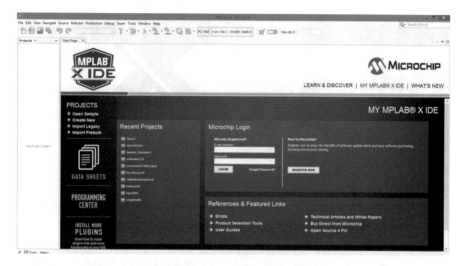

Figure 1-1. *The opening screen in MPLABX*

The project window on the left-hand side may not be shown. If you want it shown, you should select the word Window from the top menu bar. Click the word Projects, with the orange boxes in front of it, and the window should appear. You may have to move the window about to get it in the position shown.

Now, assuming you are ready to create a project, you should either click the word File, in the main menu bar, and select New project, or click the orange box with the small green cross on the second menu bar. This is the second symbol from the left-hand side of the second menu bar.

When you have selected the Create project option, you should see the window shown in Figure 1-2.

3

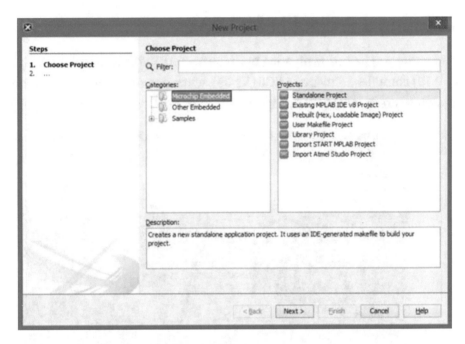

Figure 1-2. *The New Project window*

Most of the projects you will create are Microchip Embedded and Standalone. Therefore, make sure these two options are highlighted and then click the Next button. The Select Device window should now be visible, as shown in Figure 1-3.

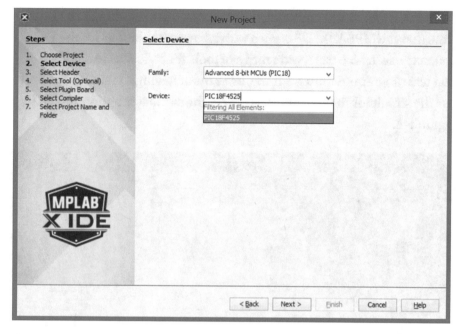

Figure 1-3. *The Select Device window*

In this window, you can choose which PIC you want to use. Select the Advanced 8-bit MCUs (PIC18) in the small box alongside Family, as shown in Figure 1-3. Then, in the Device window, select the PIC18F4525. The result is shown in Figure 1-3. To make these options visible, you need to click the small downward pointing arrow in the respective box. The different options should then become visible. If the device window is highlighted in blue, you could simply type in the PIC number you want, such as PIC18F4525. Your selected device should appear in the window below.

If you are using a different PIC, select it here.

Once you are happy with your selection, click the Next button.

The next window to appear is the Select Tool window. This is shown in Figure 1-4. With this window you can select the programming tool you want to use to download the program to your prototype board. There are a range of tools you can use. I mainly use the ICD3 CAN or the PICkit3 tool.

However, if I am only simulating the program, I use the simulator option.
Note that the MPLABX IDE comes with its own simulations for the PICs
you may use. It also has a wide range of tools that allow us to simulate
and test programs within MPLABX all without having a real PIC. You will
use the simulator in this project, so select the simulator option shown in
Figure 1-4.

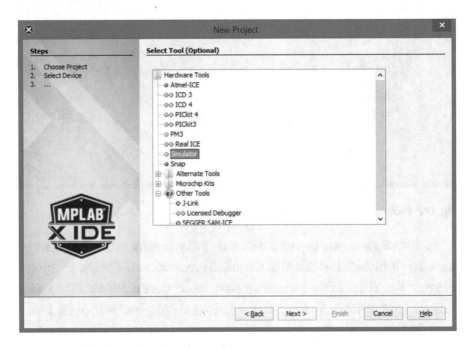

Figure 1-4. *The Select Tool window*

Having selected the tool you want, click Next to move on to the next
window where you can select the compiler software you want to use,
assuming you have downloaded the appropriate compiler software (see
Figure 1-5).

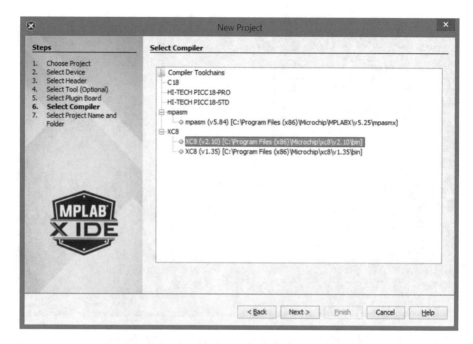

Figure 1-5. *The Select Compiler window*

You should select the XC8(V2.10) compiler software, although with some later projects you will use V1.35, as shown in Figure 1-5. Then click Next to move to the Select Project Name and Folder window shown in Figure 1-6.

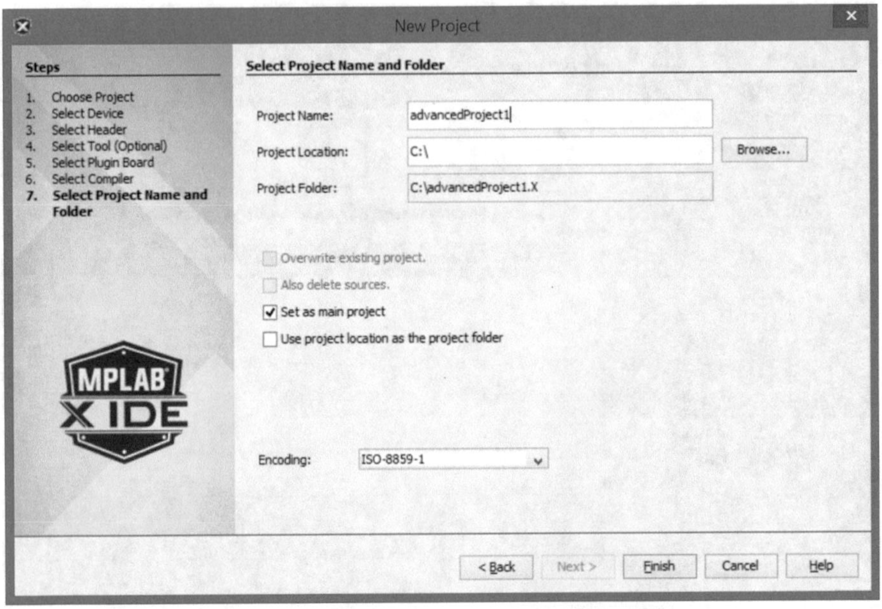

Figure 1-6. *The Select Project Name and Folder window*

In this window, you will specify the name of the project and where you want to save it. The software will create a new directory on your computer with the project name you create here. It is recommended that you don't use long-winded, complicated path names for the new folder so I normally save all my projects on the root directory of my laptop.

I have suggested a project name for this new project as advanceProject1. Note that I am using camelcase, where two words, or more, are combined together. The first letter of the first word is in lowercase and the first letters of any subsequent words are in uppercase. In this way multiple words can be combined together to make one long word.

As you type the name for your project, you should see that the folder is created on the root drive, or wherever you have specified it should be. The folder name will have a .X added to it.

It will be in this new folder that all the files associated with the project will be saved as well as some important subdirectories that are created.

Once you are happy with the naming of the project, simply click the Finish button and the project will be created. The window will now go back to the main window, as shown in Figure 1-7.

Figure 1-7. *The main window with the project created*

You should see the project window at the left-hand side of your screen, as shown in Figure 1-7. Note that you may need to move the window about to get it the same as that shown in Figure 1-7.

Now that you have the new project created, you need to create a header file that you will use in all of your projects in this book.

To create the header file, right-click the subdirectory in the project tree named Header Files. When you do this, the flyout menu will appear, as shown in Figure 1-8.

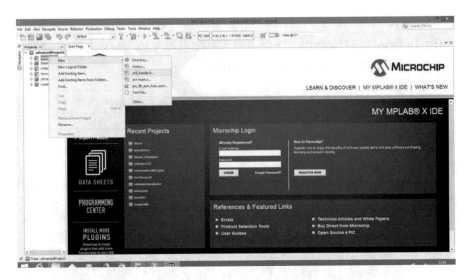

Figure 1-8. *The flyout menu for the new header file*

From that flyout menu, select New. From the second flyout menu, select xc8_header.h, as shown in Figure 1-8.

The window shown in Figure 1-9 will appear.

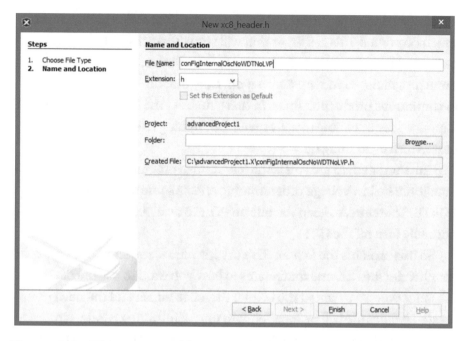

Figure 1-9. *The name and location for the new header file*

All you need to do here is give the file a name. I have chosen the name conFigInternalOscNoWDTNoLVP as it gives a good description of what I want to do in this header file, which is set these three main parameters of the configuration words. Note the configuration words specify how you want to configure and so use the PIC.

The main concern is that PICs have a wide variety of primary oscillator sources and you need to tell the PIC which one you will be using. The oscillator is the device or circuit that provides a signal from which the clock signal, the signal that synchronizes the operations of the PIC, is derived. I prefer to use the internal oscillator block as the primary oscillator source. This saves buying an oscillator crystal. It also saves two inputs that would be used if I used an external oscillator. This is because I would connect the external oscillator to the PIC via those two input pins, normally RA6 and RA7.

The second major item I change is to turn off the WDT, which is the watch dog timer. This is a timer that will stop the micro if nothing has happened for a set period of time. This is a facility that you don't want in these programs, so you must turn it off. Note that the WDT is mainly used in continuous production lines. In that situation, the fact that nothing has happened for a set time usually means something has gone wrong so it's best to turn everything off.

The third item to turn off is the low voltage programming (LVP) function. The low voltage programming affects some of the bits on PORTB. Therefore, to keep the bits on PORTB available for general I/O, I normally turn off the LVP.

So this explains the header file's cryptic name. You should always give your header files a name that relates to how you want to use the file.

Once you have named the header file, click Finish and the newly created header file will be inserted into the main editing window in the software. However, Microchip automatically inserts an awful lot of comments and instructions that, at your level of programming, you don't really need. Therefore, simply select all that stuff and delete it so that you have an empty file ready for you to insert the code that you really want.

Now that you have a clean file, you can control what goes into it. The first thing you should do is put some comments in along the following lines:

- You should tell everyone that you wrote this code.

- You should say what PIC you wrote it for and when you wrote it.

- You should explain what you are trying to do with it.

There are two types of comments in C programs, which are

- **Single-line comments**: They start with two forward slashes (//). Anything on the same line after the two forward slashes is ignored by the compiler as they are simply comments. For example,

  ```
  //these words are just comments
  ```

- **Multiple lines of comments or a paragraph of comments**: This is text inserted between the following symbols: /* */. For example,

  ```
  /* Your comments are written in here */
  ```

So insert a paragraph of comments as shown in Figure 1-10.

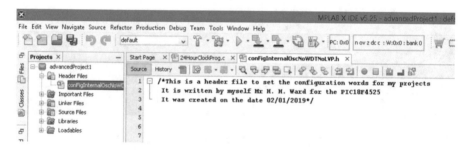

Figure 1-10. *The comments for the header file*

You should insert your own comments into the editor similar to those shown in Figure 1-10.

You will notice that I changed the colour of my comments to black and bold size 14. This is to try and make them more visible than the default grey.

If you want to change the colour, you can do so by selecting the word Options from the drop-down menu that appears when you select the Tools choice on the main menu bar. You will get the window shown in Figure 1-11.

Figure 1-11. *Changing the font and colours*

Click the tag for Fonts and Colours and then select what you want to change. Once you are happy with your choice, click OK. I changed the colour of the comments to black, as shown in Figure 1-11.

Now you need to create the configuration words for your header file. As this is something you must do for all your projects, Microchip has developed a simple process for writing to the configuration words. This can be achieved using a special window in the MPLABX IDE. To open this window, click the word Window on the main menu bar and then select Target Memory Views from the drop-down menu that appears. Then select Configuration Bits from the slide-out menu that appears. This process is shown in Figure 1-12.

14

Figure 1-12. *Selecting the configuration bits*

Once you have selected the configuration bits, your main window will change to that shown in Figure 1-13.

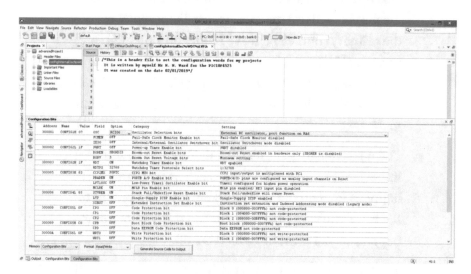

Figure 1-13. *The configuration bits*

You may have to drag the window up to make it as larger as shown in Figure 1-13.

This configuration window allows you, as the programmer, to select some very important options for the PIC, the most important being the primary oscillator type and source used and if you want the watch dog timer or not.

There are three main options you need to change at this point. You should change

- The OSC to INTIO67. This is done by selecting the small arrow alongside the box next to the OSC option. The default setting is usually RCI06, the resistor capacitor oscillator with bit6 on PORTA left as a normal I/O bit. You need to change this. When you click the small arrow next to the OSC option RCIO6, a small window will open. If you move the selection up to the next one, it will be the one you want, INTIO67, which means you will use the internal oscillator block as the primary source and leave Bits 6 and 7 on PORTA as normal I/O bits. Note that when you select this, a description of the change will appear in the description window alongside this tag and it will have a blue colour to the text.

- The next change is simpler. Set the WDT to OFF. It important to turn the WDT off because if nothing happens for a predefined period of time in a program, the WDT will stop the program. You don't want this to happen so you must turn the WDT off.

- The third change is to turn the LVP off.

Once you have changed these settings, you can generate the source code and then paste this code into your program. To do so, click the

Generate Source Code to Output tab shown at the bottom of the IDE. The source code should appear in the output window on the screen, as shown in Figure 1-14.

Figure 1-14. *The source code for the configuration words*

Use the mouse to select this code and the comments but **do not** select the phrase #include <xc.h> because I want to discuss the importance of this include file later in the book. So, once you have copied just the configuration words and **not** the #include <xc.h>, paste the selection into the header file you have in the open window.

I pasted these source instructions and comments into my open file window starting at line 5 and ending at line 62. Yours may differ due to what comments you have put in.

Your screen should look like that shown in Figure 1-15. Note that the #include <xc.h> is not in the file.

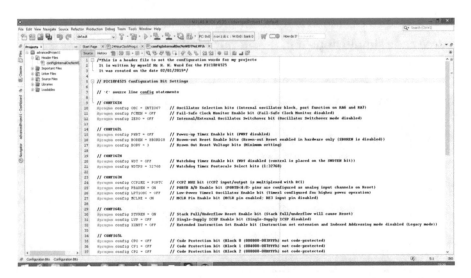

Figure 1-15. *The configuration words inserted into the header file*

You can now save this file in the usual way of saving a file because you have all you need for this header file. This is done by clicking the File option from the main menu bar and selecting Save from the flyout menu.

Including the Header File

Now that you have created this header file, let's go through how to include it in a program. However, before you can do that, you need to create the program file in which you will include it. This means you must have some idea of what your first program will be. It will be a program to drive a seven-segment display. The main concept for the program is that you will use a seven-segment display to count from 0 to 9 in intervals of 2 seconds. This will involve creating a source file for this program. I will not go through the details of the program until the next chapter; in this chapter, you are only concerned with creating and using header files.

Creating the Project Source File

To create the source file, you must first right-click the source files subdirectory in the project tree area. When you do this, the screen shown in Figure 1-16 will appear and you should select New and then main.c.

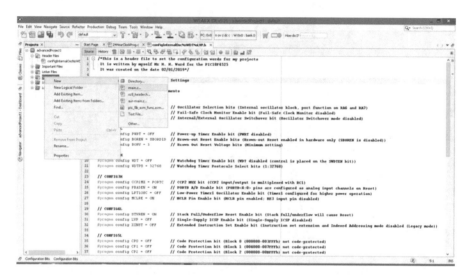

Figure 1-16. *Creating a new main.c program file*

Once you have selected the new main.c option, a new window will open, which is where you will create the name for the source file. You should name it sevenSegmentDisplay. The extension for the file name is c for the C language. The window should look like the one in Figure 1-17.

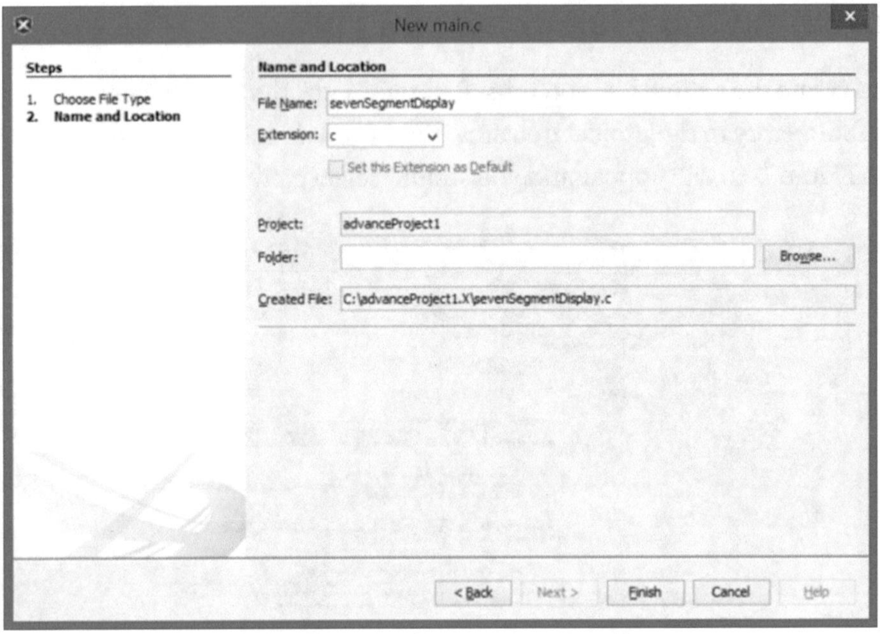

Figure 1-17. *Naming the source file*

Once you are happy with the file name, click Finish and the screen will now have a new window open in the editing screen. This will include a lot of text that Microchip automatically inserts. Again, you don't need it so delete all this text so that you have a clean editing window, as shown in Figure 1-18.

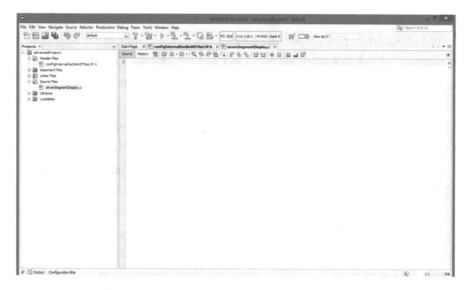

Figure 1-18. *The empty source file*

The next thing you should do is add some comments to show that you own this source file. Therefore, using the multiple line option for your comments, you should insert some comments along the following lines:

```
/*A program to control a seven segment display.
Written by Mr H. H. dated 02/01/2019
For the PIC 18F4525*/
```

You can amend the comments as you feel fit. The screen should now look similar to that shown in Figure 1-19.

Figure 1-19. *The comments added to the source file*

Now you need to tell the compiler to include the header file you just created. There are two ways you can add the header file. One is as a local header file, which is not much good really. If you have created a local header file, it will only be available to this local project. However, I will show you how to include the header file in this way first.

Make sure the cursor is waiting at the start of the next empty line in the source file you just created. Now start to write the phrase #include. You do need the # sign. Indeed, as you write the # sign, a pop-up menu will appear with some options for you to choose from. This is the IntelliSense part of the compiler software. It is like predictive text on your phone. The software tries to guess what you are doing, and the # sign has a specific meaning. You should see the word "include" at the bottom of the pop-up menu. You can either continue to write include or select the word from the pop-up menu. However, if the pop-up menu does not appear, simply write the word "include."

No matter which way you insert the word include, when you next press the space bar, after inserting the word include, to move the cursor away from the word include, you should see another pop-up menu appear, as shown in Figure 1-20.

Figure 1-20. *The include option*

You should see the name of the header file you just created in the pop-up menu. Select this file by clicking it to paste the file name into your source file. Again, if the pop-up menu does not appear, you can write "conFigInternal OscNoWDTNoLVP.h". Note that you must use the quotation marks. This is the name of the header file you want to include in your program.

It should then be present, as shown in Figure 1-21.

Figure 1-21. *The header file included in your program*

Creating a Global Header File

However, this is not the best way to use the header file because it is only available to this project since it is a local header file. You need to make it into a global header file, which means the header file will be available to be used in all of your projects. The way to do this is to save or copy the header file into the compiler software directory. This is slightly more involved because you need to find the `include` directory for Microchip on your computer. I found it on my laptop and the path for this directory is shown here:

```
C:\ProgramFiles(x86)\Microchip\xc8\v2.10\pic\include
```

You will have to find your directory. However, assuming you used the default installation, then the path should be the same as mine stated here. In earlier versions, it may be slightly different. You are looking for the `include` directory in your compiler software. You may need to use the file explorer to find the header file in the current project directory and copy the file to the `include` directory as stated above.

Assuming you have been able to copy this header file into the correct directory, this header file is now a global file and you can include it in any of your projects. It's a much better way to use the header file.

To include this global header file, delete the previous `include` line of your program. Now insert the `#` and `include` statements as before but

now when you hit the space bar to move the cursor away from the include
word, ignore the pop-up menu and type in the following symbol: <. The
IntelliSense will take over and insert the > symbol with the cursor flashing
inside the two symbols. Also, a pop-up menu will appear listing all of the
include files that are stored in the include directory of the xc8 compiler
software. If you now type the letter c in the space between the two < >
symbols, the fly-out menu will filter out all the files that don't start with
the letter c. You should see the header file you have just copied into the
include directory, as shown in Figure 1-22.

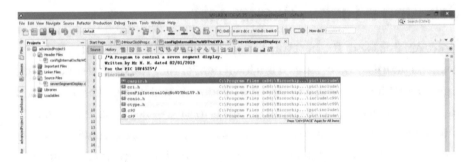

Figure 1-22. *The include pop-up menu*

If you click the header file you just copied, that file name should
appear between the < > symbols, as shown in Figure 1-23.

Figure 1-23. *The included conFigInternalNoWDTNoLVP header file*

If you have difficulty getting the pop-up menus to appear or work, you
can simply write the complete instruction as stated here:

```
#include <conFigInternaOscNoWDTNoLVP.h>
```

You do need the < > symbols. This approach can be used to include any global header file: simply write the name of the header file you want to include between the < > symbols.

Now you need to think about the very important header file that must be included in all of your projects. The header file you need is the xc.h file. To include it into your source file, you need to put the cursor onto the next line in the file (i.e. line 5) by pressing the Enter key on your keyboard. Now write the #include and press the space bar as before. Then, ignoring the pop-up window, type the first < and then the type x between the two symbols < > as before. The available header files will reduce to those shown in Figure 1-24.

Figure 1-24. *The pop-up window showing the filtered options*

Again you should see the name of the header file you are looking for in the pop-up window. Click the xc.h file to add it to the source file. The file should now look like that shown in Figure 1-25.

Figure 1-25. *The two include files*

You will look at the importance of this xc.h file later.

The PICSetUp.h Header File

Now that you have created and inserted your first global header file, you will create your second one.

This header file will set up the PIC to use the ports, the internal oscillator block, and the TMR0 timer as you intend to use them in all of your projects. Therefore, it's useful to list how you want to use these items now.

- PORTA: Set all 8 bits to be digital inputs.

- PORTB: Set all 8 bits to be digital outputs.

- PORTC: Set all 8 bits to be digital outputs.

- PORTD: Set all 8 bits to be digital inputs.

- PORTE: Set all 3 bits to be digital outputs.

- Turn the ADC off.

- The internal oscillator block will be set to produce an 8Mhz frequency that will be stable.

- Timer0, or TMR0, will be set to an 8-bit register that will apply the maximum divide rate so that it counts at a frequency of 7812.5Hz. This means that one tick takes 128µs.

Assuming you want all these exact same settings for all of your projects, you can create a header file for this setup. If you want something slightly different, you must write to the SFR (special function register) after this file has been used.

To create the header file, right-click the header files subdirectory in the project tree. Then select New from the flyout menu and XC8_header.h from the second flyout menu. Name the header file as PICSetUp and click Finish to create the header file.

This new file should be open in the editing window. Again, you should delete all the stuff that MPLABX automatically inserts in the file since you don't need it and I really want your screens to look the same as mine.

Assuming that you now have an empty screen, you can write the instructions for this header file. They are shown here as Listing 1-1. You do not have to write the line numbers as shown here. These numbers are there to enable me to refer to each instruction in my analysis of how the instructions work.

Listing 1-1. Instructions for the PICSetup.h Header File

```
1. void initialise ()
2. {
3. PORTA = 0;
4. PORTB = 0;
5. PORTC = 0;
6. PORTD = 0;
7. PORTE = 0;
8. TRISA = 0XFF;
9. TRISB = 0;
10. TRISC = 0;
11. TRISD = 0b11111111;
12. TRISE = 0;
13. ADCON0 = 0;
14. ADCON1 = 0b00001111;
15. OSCTUNE = 0;
16. OSCCON = 0b01110100;
17. T0CON = 0b11000111;
18. }
```

Analysis of Listing 1-1

line 1 void initialise ()

To understand this instruction, you should appreciate that all C programs run in a series of loops. There must be a main loop because this is where the micro must go to get the first instruction of the program.

There are then a series of what are sometimes referred to as functions or methods, but I prefer to call them subroutines, as they are small sections of programs that the main loop can call as many times as the main program needs to execute the instructions in the subroutine.

With this header file you are creating a subroutine. The subroutine will only be called once from the main program and it will set up the SFRs (special function registers) in the way you want to use them in the PIC.

All subroutines may or may not require the main program to pass parameters up to the subroutine. Also, the subroutine may or may not pass parameters back to the main program loop. All subroutines need a name that describes the purpose of the subroutine.

In this case, this subroutine will not be passing any parameters back to the main loop. This is signified by the use of the keyword void. Note as you type this keyword void into the text window inside the IDE, you will see it is case-sensitive and it must be in lowercase. As you finish writing the word, the font colour changes to blue. IntelliSense uses colours to recognize the significance of special words.

You must give the subroutine a name and in this case it is called initialise, as it does initialize the PIC. Then, as you enter the first normal opening bracket, IntelliSense automatically adds the normal closing bracket and inserts the cursor between the two brackets. Here you can define what type of variable the subroutine is expecting to be passed up to it when it is called from the main program. If the subroutine does not want a variable to be passed up to it, leave this space empty, as I have done here. Some programmers insert the word "void" here but its just personal preference.

Line 2 {

This is the opening curly bracket of the subroutine. As you type this opening curly bracket, and then press the Enter key, the software automatically adds a closing curly bracket. It then inserts the cursor between the two curly brackets but indented by one tab. The two curly brackets define the confines of the subroutine; indeed they will be connected by a line alongside the two brackets in the editing window.

The cursor is now waiting inside the confines of the subroutine for you to type in the instructions of the subroutine.

Line 3 PORTA = 0;

To fully appreciate this instruction, you should know that every PIC has ports, which get their name from naval ports that take goods into and out of the country. In the same way, the ports of the PIC take data into and out of the PIC. Inputs can be simple switches, sensors, or transducers, whereas outputs can be lamps, motors, or pumps.

What you are doing in the next five lines is making sure that anything that might be connected to the ports of the PIC is not switched on. Note a logic 0 means that the bits have 0v on them. The instruction PORTA = 0; means all 8 bits on PORTA are at logic 0 or 0V.

One more thing before I describe the next instruction is the semicolon symbol. It actually denotes the end of the current instruction. However, with lines 1 and 2 there is no need for the semicolon because they are statements for the compiler software, not instructions for the PIC.

Lines 4 to 7 simply turn off anything that might be connected to the other ports of the PIC.

Line 8 TRISA = 0XFF;

To understand this instruction, you must realize that with any port data can go into the PIC or out of the PIC. Indeed, with any bit of the port this can happen. With the PC18F4525 all ports have 8 bits, as this is an 8-bit PIC, except for PORTE, which has 3 bits. Note that the bits are numbered b7, b6, b5, b4, b3, b2, b1, and b0, going from left to right. Bit0 is the LSB (least significant bit) and bit7 is the MSB (most significant bit).

Well, you have to tell the PIC which way the data is to flow through the bits of each port, in or out. To facilitate this, each port has another SFR to set the direction of data through the bits of the port. This SFR is called a TRIS, so TRISA, TRISB, etc.

Each bit of the TRIS maps directly onto the same numbered bit of the port. If the bit in the TRIS is a logic 1, then the corresponding bit in the port will be an input. If the bit in the TRIS is a logic 0, then the corresponding bit in the port will be an output.

For example, if the data in TRISA is 00110101 then the bits in PORTA is

- B7 is an output.

- B6 is an output.

- B5 is an input.

- B4 is an input.

- B3 is an output.

- B2 is an input.

- B1 is an output.

- B0 is an input.

In line 8, the instruction is TRISA = 0XFF;. The 0X tells the compiler that the radix, or number system, for the number is hexadecimal. This converts to 11111111 in binary or 255 in decimal. Appendix tk explains how to convert numbers.

This instruction means that all the bits in TRISA are forced to go to a logic 1, which in turn makes all the bits in PORTA input. This is what you want.

Exercise 1.1   The answers to all exercises will be given at the end of each chapter.

In this exercise, write the data required to set the bits in PORTD as follows:

B7 is an output.

B6 is an output.

B5 is an input.

B4 is an input.

B3 is an input.

B2 is an input

B1 is an output.

B0 is an input.

State which SFR it must be written to.

Line 9 TRISB = 0;

Here, as you have not stated what radix, or number system, you are using, the compiler assumes it is the default radix, which is decimal. This means that this instruction is loading the TRISB with the value 0, which is 00000000 in binary. Therefore, all the bits in TRISB are forced to a logic 0, which in turn means that all the bits in PORTB are set as outputs.

Line 10 TRISC = 0;

This makes all bits in PORTC output.

Line 11 TRISD = 0b11111111;

The 0b in front of the number means the radix is binary and what follows is a binary number. This makes all the bits in TRISD logic 1 and so sets all bits in PORTD to inputs.

Line 12 TRISE = 0;

This simply sets all bits in PORTE to outputs.

Line 13 ADCON0 = 0;

To appreciate what you are doing here, you must realize that there can be two different types of inputs to the PIC. They are

- **Digital**: Simply off or on, open or closed, logic 0 or logic 1. They could be from simple switches or sensors.

- **Analog**: They are usually voltages that can range from 0v to 5v and are obtained from transducers that are used to measure physical parameters such as velocity, temperature, voltage, etc. These are presented to the PIC as analog signals and then the PIC converts them, using an ADC (analog-to-digital converter) to digital values to be used by the program.

The default setting is that all the inputs can be either digital or analog, and there are 13 such inputs in the PIC 18F4525, which are set as analog. This means you must do two things:

- Set all the inputs to digital inputs.

- Turn the ADC off since you are not using it.

To help understand how you get the correct number to write to the correct SFRs, here are two tables taken from the data sheet for the PIC18F4525. If you are using any device, be it a PIC, OPAMP, or any electronic device, you must be able to use the data sheets for that device. Tables 1-1 and 1-2 explain how to control the ADC.

Table 1-1. *The ADCON0 Register*

Bit7	Bit6	Bit5	Bit4	Bit3	Bit2	Bit1	Bit0
Not used	Not used	CHS3	CHS2	CHS1	CHS0	GO/DONE	ADON
Bit7		Not used, read as 0					
Bit6		Not used, read as 0					
		Bit5	Bit4	Bit3	Bit2	ADC channel selected	
		0	0	0	0	AN0	
		0	0	0	1	AN1	
		0	0	1	0	AN2	
		0	0	1	1	AN3	
		0	1	0	0	AN4	
		0	1	0	1	AN5	
		0	1	1	0	AN6	
		0	1	1	1	AN7	
		1	0	0	0	AN8	
		1	0	0	1	AN9	
		1	0	1	0	AN10	
		1	0	1	1	AN11	
		1	1	0	0	AN12	
		1	1	0	1	Not used	
		1	1	1	0	Not used	
		1	1	1	1	Not used	

(*continued*)

Table 1-1. (*continued*)

Bit7	Bit6	Bit5	Bit4	Bit3	Bit2	Bit1	Bit0
Bit1		1 means start a conversion and a conversion is taking place					
		0 means the conversion has finished					
Bit0		1 means enable the ADC					
		0 means disable the ADC					

The main purpose of this control register is to allow the programmer to choose which analog input, or channel, is connected to the ADC. I have stated that there are 13 possible analog inputs but that doesn't mean there are 13 ADC circuits. There is only one ADC circuit but it can be connected to any one of the 13 inputs that can take an analog signal in. This is a form of multiplexing where many inputs feed into one device one at a time. The choice of which input is connected to the ADC is controlled by the data in Bits 5, 4, 3, and 2 of the ADCON0 register. For example, if these four bits are set to 0011, going from b5 to b2 left to right, then it is the fourth input, AN3, that is connected to the ADC; see Table 1-1. Note that Bits 7 and 6 are not used so they are set to logic 0.

Bit0 is the bit that actually turns the ADC on or not. A logic 1 means the ADC is enabled whereas a logic 0 means it is disabled.

The last remaining bit, Bit1, is used to start the ADC conversion and tell the programmer when the conversion is finished or done. The programmer must set this bit to a logic 1 to start the ADC conversion. Then, when the conversion is finished, the microprocessor sets this bit back to a logic 0 automatically. This is a signal to tell the programmer that the ADC conversion has finished.

Table 1-2. *The ADCON1 Register*

Bit7	Bit6	Bit5	Bit4	Bit3	Bit2	Bit1	Bit0
Not used	Not used	VCFG1	VCFG0	PCFG3	PCFG2	PCFG1	PCFG0

Bit7	Not used, read as 0
Bit6	Not used, read as 0
Bit5	1 negative reference from AN2
	0 negative reference from VSS
Bit4	1 positive reference from AN3
	0 positive reference from VDD

Bit				Channel AN												
3	2	1	0	12	11	10	9	8	7	6	5	4	3	2	1	0
0	0	0	0	A	A	A	A	A	A	A	A	A	A	A	A	A
0	0	0	1	A	A	A	A	A	A	A	A	A	A	A	A	A
0	0	1	0	A	A	A	A	A	A	A	A	A	A	A	A	A
0	0	1	1	D	A	A	A	A	A	A	A	A	A	A	A	A
0	1	0	0	D	D	A	A	A	A	A	A	A	A	A	A	A
0	1	0	1	D	D	D	A	A	A	A	A	A	A	A	A	A
0	1	1	0	D	D	D	D	A	A	A	A	A	A	A	A	A
0	1	1	1	D	D	D	D	D	A	A	A	A	A	A	A	A
1	0	0	0	D	D	D	D	D	D	A	A	A	A	A	A	A
1	0	0	1	D	D	D	D	D	D	D	A	A	A	A	A	A
1	0	1	0	D	D	D	D	D	D	D	D	A	A	A	A	A
1	0	1	1	D	D	D	D	D	D	D	D	D	A	A	A	A
1	1	0	0	D	D	D	D	D	D	D	D	D	D	A	A	A

(continued)

35

Table 1-2. (*continued*)

Bit7		Bit6		Bit5	Bit4	Bit3	Bit2	Bit1		Bit0						
Bit				Channel AN												
3	2	1	0	12	11	10	9	8	7	6	5	4	3	2	1	0
1	1	0	1	D	D	D	D	D	D	D	D	D	D	D	A	A
1	1	1	0	D	D	D	D	D	D	D	D	D	D	D	D	A
1	1	1	1	D	D	D	D	D	D	D	D	D	D	D	D	D

This register mostly controls whether the 13 inputs are to be used as analog or digital. It is the first four bits (b0, b1, b2, and b3) that do this. Table 1-2 shows how this is achieved. If all four bits are a logic 0, then all 13 channels are set to analog inputs. However, if the four bits are 0011, going from B3 to B0 left to right, then the 13th channel, AN12, is set to digital and the rest are set to analog.

The ADC needs a reference voltage to help determine the level of the analog input. Bit4 controls where the PIC gets the positive reference. The default, and so normal setting, is to use the supply to the PIC (VCC or VDD).

Bit5 controls where the PIC gets the negative reference. The default, and so normal setting, is to use the supply to the PIC (VSS or ground).

Bits 6 and 7 are not used.

Armed with this knowledge, you can see that the instruction at line 13, ADCON0 = 0;, simply turns off the ADC. It also connects the first channel, or input, AN0, to the ADC but as the ADC is turned off this does not matter.

Line 14 ADCON1 = 0b00001111;

This sets the bits on the SFR ADCON1 to 00001111. This instruction uses Table 1-2. From it you can see that as the first four bits of the ADCON1 SRF are set to 1111, this makes all the inputs digital. This is what you want. When you eventually need some analog inputs, you will have to make some changes.

Line 15 OSCTUNE = 0;

These next two instructions control the oscillator. The operations of the PIC are all synchronized to a clock signal. All PICs give the programmer a wide range of where the clock can get its signal, from the external high-speed crystal or low-speed RC oscillator to a range of oscillators that are internal (i.e. inside the PIC itself).

When you wrote the configuration words you told the PIC you would use the internal oscillator block as the primary source for this clock signal. However, you didn't set the frequency of the oscillator you want to use. These next two instructions do that.

This first one is on line 15, OSCTUNE = 0;. This simply tells the PIC you are not worried about any drift in temperature that might alter the frequency of the oscillator. It is the next instruction that is the main one as far as the clock is concerned. To help understand the next instruction, Tables 1-3, 1-4, and 1-5 will be useful.

Table 1-3. *Use of the OSCCON Register*

Bit7	Bit6	Bit5	Bit4	Bit3	Bit2	Bit1	Bit0
IDLEN	IRCF2	IRCF1	IRCF0	IOSTS	IOFS	SCS1	SCS0

Bit7	1 Device enters sleep
	0 Device does not enter sleep
Bit6	See Table 1-4
Bit5	
Bit4	
Bit3	1 Time-out expired for oscillator start up
	0 Time-out running for oscillator start up

(continued)

Table 1-3. (*continued*)

Bit7	Bit6	Bit5	Bit4	Bit3	Bit2	Bit1	Bit0
Bit2		1 Internal oscillator stable					
		0 Internal oscillator not stable					
Bit1		See Table 1-5					
Bit0							

Table 1-4. *Bit6, Bit5, and Bit4 of the OSCCON Register Setting the Oscillator Frequency*

Bit6	Bit5	Bit4	Oscillator Frequency
ICRF2	ICRF1	ICRF0	
0	0	0	31kHz[1]
0	0	1	125kHz
0	1	0	250kHz
0	1	1	500kHz
1	0	0	1Mhz
1	0	1	2MHz
1	1	0	4MHz
1	1	1	8MHz

[1]*The 31kHz can be sourced from the main oscillator divided by 256 or directly from the internal RC oscillator*

Table 1-5. *Bit1 and Bit0 of the OSCCON Register Selecting the Source of the Oscillator Signal*

Bit1 SCS1	Bit0 SCS0	Oscillator Source
0	0	Primary oscillator as defined in configuration words
0	1	Secondary timer block
1	0	Internal oscillator block
1	1	Internal oscillator block

Line 16 OSCCON = 0b01110100;

The instruction is OSCCON = 0b01110100;. This sets Bit7 of the OSCCON to logic 0. It is Bits 6, 5, and 4 that are used to set the frequency of the oscillator to 8Mhz. Note you have a choice of 8 different frequencies as stated in Table 1-4.

Bit3 is set to 0, which is the default setting for this bit.

Bit2 is set to a logic 1, which means the frequency is stable.

Finally Bits 1 and 0 are both set to logic 0, which means the clock gets its source from the primary oscillator, which you set with the configuration words to be the internal oscillator block. Therefore, the clock uses this 8Mhz internal crystal as the source for the clock.

It is rather awkward that Microchip gives the programmer so many options for a wide range of parameters but as you gain more experience with embedded programming you will see why Microchip does this.

Line 17 T0CON = 0b11000111;

This final instruction is used to control a timer. The PIC18F4525 has four timer modules; TMR0 timer0, TMR1 timer1, TMR2 timer2, and TMR3 timer3. These timers are used to control some important operations that are timed controlled. Timer0 is a timer that simply counts clock pulses. It can be used to create a simply delay using the principle that if you count to a certain value, it will take a certain length of time to complete that count. The length of time taken depends upon two things: the value you want to count up to and the speed at which you will count.

The timer0 in the 18F4525 PIC can be set to be either an 8-bit register or a 16-bit register. As all the timers count in binary, the maximum value that timer0 can count up to is either 255 as an 8-bit register or 65535 as a 16-bit register. However, as the ECAD software we are using can only simulate 8-bit registers, let's set timer0 to be an 8-bit register.

As to how fast the timer will count, you have to realize that the clock always runs at a quarter of the oscillator. This means that since the oscillator you are using runs at 8MHz, the clock will run at 2MHz. This means that the time for one complete tick or count of the timer0 will take 500ns. Since the timer0 will take 256 ticks to count from 0 to 255, it will take 256 x 500ns = 128µs. This is far too quick for us humans. If you want to create a one-second delay with this counter counting at 2Mhz, there is a lot of work to do. It can be done with the timer counting at this frequency, but it would be easier if you could slow down the rate at which this timer counts. Well, Microchip gives us this option, and that is what you're doing here. Let's look at how each bit in the SFR T0CON, the control register for timer0, actually controls this timer. Table 1-6 shows what each bit controls.

Table 1-6. *T0CON Register (See Data Sheet)*

Bit7	Bit6	Bit5	Bit4	Bit3	Bit2	Bit1	Bit0
TMR00n	T08bit	TOCS	TOSE	PSA	T0PS2	T0PS1	T0PS0
Bit7		1 Enables Timer0					
		0 Disables Timer0					
Bit6		1 Timer0 is an 8-bit register					
		0 Timer0 is a 16-bit register					

(*continued*)

Table 1-6. (*continued*)

Bit7	Bit6	Bit5	Bit4	Bit3	Bit2	Bit1	Bit0
Bit5		1 Timer0 clock source is TOCK1 pin 0 Timer0 clock source is internal instruction cycle clock (CLKO)					
Bit4		1 Timer0 source edge bit on high-to-low TOCK1 pin 0 Timer0 source edge bit on low-to-high TOCK1 pin					
Bit3		1 Timer0 prescaler not assigned 0 Timer0 prescaler is assigned					
Bit2	Bit1	Bit0	Timer0 prescaler divide rate				
0	0	0	Divide by 2				
0	0	1	Divide by 4				
0	1	0	Divide by 8				
0	1	1	Divide by 16				
1	0	0	Divide by 32				
1	0	1	Divide by 64				
1	1	0	Divide by 128				
1	1	1	Divide by 256				

Bit7, which is set to a logic 1, enables the timer (i.e. turns it on).

Bit6, which is also set to a logic 1, means the timer is set as an 8-bit register (i.e. the maximum it can count up to is 255). If this bit was a logic 0, then timer0 would be set as a 16-bit register, which would be two 8-bit registers cascaded together, and the maximum number it could count to would be 65535. You set timer0 to an 8-bit register because the ECAD software you're using only works on 8-bit registers.

Bit5 is a logic 0. This makes the source for the timer as the internal clock.

Bit4 is a logic 0. This means the counter will increment on the low-to-high transition. This is known as positive edge triggering.

Bit3 is a logic 0. This means the prescalar is used and so you can divide the clock signal down to slow the rate at which timer0 counts.

The next three bits (Bit2, Bit1, and Bit0) set the divide rate to be the maximum. This divides the 2Mhz clock by 256, which means the timer now counts at a frequency of 7812.5Hz. This means every count takes 128µs; 256 times longer than before. This now means that the maximum length of delay is around 33ms (i.e. 128E-6 x 256 = 0.032768).

There is still some work to do to get this to a one-second delay but it is easier and you will do that in your program.

Line 18 }

This is simply the closing bracket of the `initialise` subroutine.

I hope the above analysis explains how these instructions work. I will use this approach with any new instructions that you go through in the programs in this book. I do feel you as a programmer should fully understand the code that you use in your programs. It is no good to simply use blocks of code that do what you want to do, but not understand how it works. If that is the approach to programming you use, then who is the real programmer? You or the guys who wrote the blocks of code? It should always be you.

Having inserted the instructions shown in Listing 1-1 into the `PICSetup.h` header file, you should save this header file using the File > Save option as normal. However, in this saved state, it is only a local header file, so you should now copy this header file into the `include` directory for your compiler as explained earlier with the `conFigInternaOscNoWDTNoLVP.h` header file.

You have now created two useful global header files that you will use in all of your programs from now on. I will leave the creation of the LCD header file until later in the book.

The last thing to do before you compile the project is to insert the include command to tell the compiler you want to include the new header file you just created. You should also create the main loop in the source file for the project. This is done by writing the following into the source file you created earlier :

```
# include <PICSetup.>
void main ()
{
initialise ();
}
```

Note that the only instruction in the main loop so far is the call to the subroutine you just created in the PICSetup.h header file. This is so that the first thing the main program does is run this subroutine to set up the PIC as you want.

Your IDE screen should look like that shown in Figure 1-26.

Figure 1-26. *The main loop in the source file*

One important aspect of these include files is that if an include file requires any information from another include file, then the other include file must be added to the program first. An example of this aspect is the PICSetUp.h header file. It uses labels for the SFRs such as PORTA, TRISA, ADCON0, etc. These are labels that have been created to allow the program to reference these SFRs. The compiler software really only wants to know the address, or number of the SFR in the PIC's memory. For example, the PORTA register is an 8-bit register that is located at address 0XF80. You could use this address in your programs when referring to PORTA. Indeed, this is what the compiler software needs to know. However, if you use this type of referencing, your program will be full of hexadecimal numbers, which is very hard to read. It's better if you use a meaningful label to reference any SFRs. This can be done by writing one of the following type statements:

```
#define PORTA 0XF80
PORTA EQU 0XF80
```

The first is done in the C programming language and the second is done in assembler.

Thankfully, someone has done this type of labelling for all of the SFRs and more you could use in all of your programs. These labels have been saved in the header file called xc.h. This is freely available to us and that is why it is in all of our projects. However, one thing you must remember is to use capital letters in your labelling because that is how they have been written in the xc.h header file. To check, write TRISA or any label in lowercase and you will find the compiler software throws an error.

If you understand the use of the xc.h header file, you should now appreciate why this header file is included in your program listing before you include the PICSetUp.h header file. The PICSetUp.h file uses the labels that are defined in the xc.h header file. If you include the PICSetUp.h file before the xc.h file, the compiler will throw an error. Try it and see what happens.

To compile the project, click the build icon in the main menu bar. This is the hammer symbol that has no brush with it, shown on the second menu bar. The project should now compile correctly, and this will be visible in the output window at the bottom of the IDE. If there are any errors, check the syntax of the project. Any errors will be indicated in blue in the output window. If you click the first error word in blue, the insertion icon should go to the relevant line in the program listing in the editing window. Note that the error maybe on that line or the line above that one.

If you now open the PICSetup.h header file by clicking the appropriate label in the menu bar, your screen should be similar to that shown in Figure 1-27.

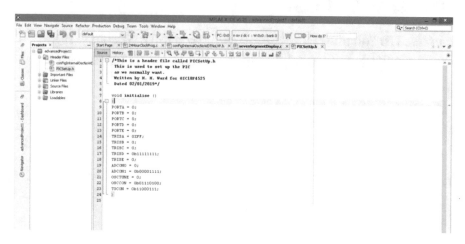

Figure 1-27. *The completed PICSetup.h header file*

Synopsis

This chapter explained the importance of header files and the difference between local and global header files. You should now be able to create your own header files for functions that you might use in exactly the same way in most of your programs. One such function, or subroutine, as I prefer to call them, is the variable delay. You will create a header file for that later in the book.

In the next chapter, you will look at how to use the PIC to control a seven-segment display, which is a useful device for displaying numbers.

Answer to Exercise

Exercise 1.1: You must write the following data to TRISD: 00111101 in binary or 3D in hexadecimal. The instruction for this is `TRISD = 0X3D;`.

CHAPTER 2

Controlling a Seven-Segment Display

In this chapter, you will look at using the PIC to control the display on a
seven-segment display. You will look at what the seven-segment display is
and the principle upon which it works.

You will then write a program to display a count going from 0 to 9. In
Chapter 3, you will extend this program to control a series of seven-segment
displays to run a 24-hour clock counting in minutes.

After reading this chapter, you will understand what a seven-segment
display is. You will know the difference between the common anode and
common cathode and how to use the PIC to control both types.

Controlling a Seven-Segment Display

A seven-segment display is a device that can be used to display numbers,
so it can be used to create a display for a digital clock. A typical seven
segment display is shown in Figure 2-1.

© Hubert Henry Ward 2020
H. H. Ward, *Intermediate C Programming for the PIC Microcontroller*,
https://doi.org/10.1007/978-1-4842-6068-5_2

Figure 2-1. *A typical seven-segment display*

The basic concept is that there are actually seven LEDs (light-emitting diodes), hence the name for the device. However, some displays have eight LEDs, with one extra for the decimal place, or dot. These LEDs are arranged as shown in Figure 2-4. They can be switched on in different arrangements to display the numbers 0 to 9 and, if required, the letters A, B, C, D, E, and F as in the hexadecimal number system.

They come in a range of colours: red, green, blue, yellow, and white. They can also come with extra bright LEDs.

The LED is an actual diode in that it has an anode terminal and a cathode terminal. These terminals are sometimes labelled A and K, since C can stand for capacitance or Coulomb. Current can only flow one way through the diode, and conventional current flows from the anode to cathode, hence the shape of the arrow in the symbol of the diode. To make the current flow through the LED, the anode voltage must be around 2.2V higher than the cathode. Note that for a normal diode, this voltage difference is around 0.7V but the LED needs a greater volt drop since it needs to emit light.

It is the method by which you apply this voltage difference that gives rise to the two types of seven-segment displays, which are common anode and common cathode.

Common Anode Seven-Segment Display

In a common anode seven-segment display, the anodes of all seven LEDs are connected together, hence they are common. They are usually connected to a +5V supply. Then, to turn each LED on, the cathode of each LED must be connected independently to ground or 0V. However, to limit the current that flows through the LEDs, and so prevent it from burning out, a resistor is inserted between the cathode and ground. This arrangement is shown in Figure 2-2.

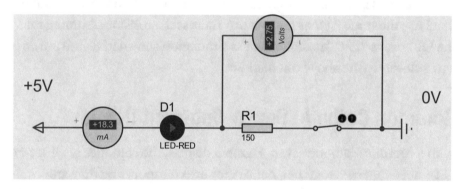

Figure 2-2. *The basic circuit to turn on an LED in a common anode*

In Figure 2-2, the LED is shown illuminated. The full 5V supply is divided between the LED and the resistor. Another reason why you need a resistor is to drop the extra 2.8V. The voltmeter is shown measuring 2.75V across the resistor R1. The remaining 2.25V must be dropped across the LED. The value of the resistor is chosen to limit the current flowing through the LED to its maximum. From the data sheet, this is around 25mA. However, a typical value is 20mA, which is good enough. Using this typical value and an expression for resistance (R), derived from Ohm's law, you have

$$I = \frac{V}{R}$$

$$\therefore R = \frac{V}{I}$$

$$\therefore R = \frac{2.8}{20E^{-3}} = 140\,\Omega$$

If you use the standard E12 series of resistors, there is no 140Ω resistor, so you must use a 150Ω, which is the next higher value. Note that you should always go higher so as to limit the current more, not less. Also note that I use the value 2.8V as the volt drop across the resistor assuming that the LED drops 2.2V. The meters in the simulation shown in Figure 2-2 do agree closely to the above calculations.

Common Cathode Seven-Segment Display

With a common cathode seven-segment display, the cathodes of all seven LEDs are connected together, hence they are common, and they are usually connected to a 0V supply. To turn each LED on, the anode of each LED can be connected independently to a +5V supply. However, to limit the current that flows through the LEDs, a resistor is inserted between the anode and the 5V supply. This arrangement is shown in Figure 2-3.

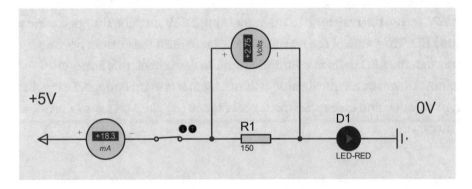

Figure 2-3. *The common cathode arrangement*

Some seven-segment displays come with their own driver circuit. This is a circuit that takes a 4-bit binary count and sets the required switching according to what number is to be displayed. However, you will use just the basic display because the PIC will do the work of this driver circuit. The seven-segment display you will use is a common anode type. You will connect the display to PORTB and use the output from PORTB to turn on and off the LEDs appropriately to display the current value between 0 and 9. Figure 2-4 shows how the seven LEDs are arranged on the display and Table 2-1 shows which cathode of the LEDs needs to be connected to the ground via the resistor to display the appropriate number.

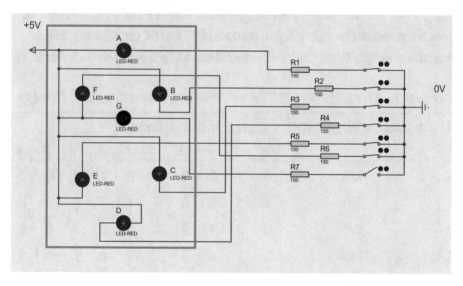

Figure 2-4. *The circuit of a common anode seven-segment display*

Figure 2-4 is an attempt to show you the circuitry of the common anode display. The seven LEDs are laid out to form a ring going from LED A to LED F in six LEDs. The seventh LED, LED G, lies central to the display. Figure 2-4 shows the six outer LEDs turned on by closing their respective switches to connect their respective cathodes to ground or 0V via the series resistor. This means those six LEDs are switched on and current flows through them. This forms the number zero.

Exercise 2.1

If the last switch is closed as well as all of the others, what number is displayed?

Controlling the Display with the PIC

When you use the PIC to control the display, there are no switches and you connect R1 to Bit0 of PORTB, R2 to Bit2, and so on, with R7 connected to Bit6. Then, to turn on the respective LED, you load a logic 0 or 0V onto the bit. To switch the respective LED off, you load a logic 1 or +5V onto the bit. In this way, the numbers 0 to 9 can be controlled from PORTB, as shown in Table 2-1.

Table 2-1. *The Logic at PORTB to Drive the Seven-Segment Display*

LED ID Letter	Bit of PORTB	Number to Be Displayed									
		0	1	2	3	4	5	6	7	8	9
A	Bit0	0	1	0	0	1	0	1	0	0	0
B	Bit1	0	0	0	0	0	1	1	0	0	0
C	Bit2	0	0	1	0	0	0	0	0	0	0
D	Bit3	0	1	0	0	1	0	0	1	0	1
E	Bit4	0	1	0	1	1	1	0	1	0	1
F	Bit5	0	1	1	1	0	0	0	1	0	0
G	Bit6	1	1	0	0	0	0	0	1	0	0
DOT	Bit7	0	0	0	0	0	0	0	0	0	0

Note it does not matter what logic is set to Bit7 as it is not connected to the display. I just left it at a logic 0. If the display has a decimal point, then Bit7 turns it on or off. The table shows how the PIC can control the display.

The Seven-Segment Display Program

All good programs start with an algorithm. An algorithm is basically a description in your own words of how you are going to get the PIC to carry out the requirements of the program. The goal of this program is to get a seven-segment display to count up from 0 to 9. The count will increment every two seconds.

The Algorithm

There is no defined format of how to construct the algorithmI like to create a bullet list as follows:

- You need to write a subroutine to create a delay. You make it a variable delay. The program increments the number on the display every two seconds from 0 to 9.

- The delay subroutine requires a global variable called n and a local variable called t.

- When the display gets to 9, the display will go back to 0 at the next increment.

- To initiate the start of the count, the program waits for a start button to be momentarily pressed to logic 1. The program will start the count with the display set at 0.

- There is a stop button that, if pressed, will halt the count at the current value on the display.

- The program includes the two header files that you have already created.

- You need two digital inputs for the two switches and, since you will be using header file PICSetUp, which you created earlier, you will use Bit0 of PORTA for the start button and Bit1 of PORTA for the stop button.

- There is no need for any analog inputs, therefore you don't need to turn the ADC on. Note that header file PICSetUp turns the ADC off.

- Since the seven-segment display requires seven outputs, you connect the display to PORTB, which is set to all outputs in your header file.

- You use the internal oscillator block for the source of the clock since this saves I/O and the cost of a crystal. Note that this is a requirement if you want to use the header file PICSetUp. This also means that you will be using the 8MHz internal crystal and TMR0 set to count at 7182.5Hz.

- There is no need for anything else, so really a basic 8-pin PIC will do the job. However, this book is based on the PIC18F4525 and the header file PICSetUp is written for the PIC18F4525, therefore you will use that PIC.

Note that I added the last item in the list to show that you can use the algorithm to decide which PIC you should use for your project. This could save money. You must remember that your project could go into production, and if you can save 10 pence by choosing a more basic PIC, then you should.

The Flowchart

It is always a good idea to construct a flowchart for your programs. However, since this book is really aimed at explaining how the C code works, I will only construct a flowchart for this first program. Note that I may add a small flowchart to show you how I solved a particular problem if the need arises.

The principle behind a flowchart is that it clearly identifies how the program should flow from one section to the next. Also, if written correctly, each block of the flowchart should link clearly to its corresponding set of instructions in the program listing.

The flowchart for this program is shown in flowchart 2-1.

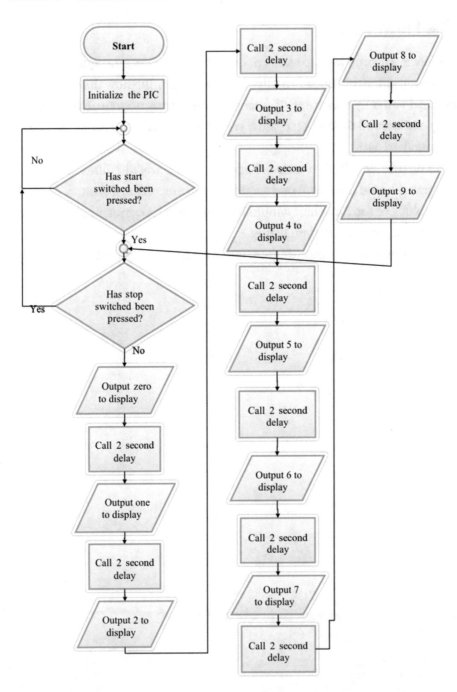

Flowchart 2-1. *The flowchart for Listing 2-1*

The Listing for the Seven-Segment Display Program

I will show the program listing here and then analyze the new instructions in the same way as I analyzed the instructions in Chapter 1. Note that I will only analyze any new instructions.

I will use two approaches to complete this project. The first will use only some basic methods while the second approach will involve the use of arrays and a pointer. The program for this basic approach is shown in Listing 2-1.

Listing 2-1. The sevenSegDisplay Program

```
1. //List any include files you want to use
2. #include <conFigInternalOscNoWDTNoLVP.h>
3. #include <xc.h>
4. #include <PICSetUp.h>
5. //declare any global variables
6. unsigned char n;
7. // declare any definitions
8. #define zero     0b01000000
9. #define one      0b01111001
10. #define two      0b00100100
11. #define three    0b00110000
12. #define four     0b00011001
13. #define five     0b00010010
14. #define six      0b00000011
15. #define seven    0b01111000
16. #define eight    0b00000000
17. #define nine     0b00011000
18. #define startButton PORTAbits.RA0
19. #define stopButton PORTAbits.RA1
```

```
20. //declare any subroutines
21. void delay (unsigned char t)
22. {
23. for (n = 0; n < t; n++)
24. {
25. TMR0 = 0;
26. while (TMR0 < 255);
27. }
28. }
29. void main ()
30. {
31. initialise ();
32. start: while (! startButton);
33. while (1)
34. {
35. if (stopButton) goto start;
36. PORTB = zero;
37. delay (61);
38. PORTB = one;
39. delay (61);
40. PORTB = two;
41. delay (61);
42. PORTB = three;
43. delay (61);
44. PORTB = four;
45. delay (61);
46. PORTB = five;
47. delay (61);
48. PORTB = six;
49. delay (61);
50. PORTB = seven;
```

```
51. delay (61);
52. PORTB = eight;
53. delay (61);
54. PORTB = nine;
55. }
56. }
```

Exercise 2.2

Before those of you with a good eagle eye say anything, there is an error in this program listing and the flowchart. There is nothing wrong with any of the instructions but there is something missing from the flowchart and the program listing. Can you see what it is and what its effect on the display will be? If you are struggling to see what the error is, run the program as stated above and you will see the effect. Can you see how to fix it?

The answer to this exercise is given at the end of the chapter. Good luck.

The Analysis of Listing 2-1

Line 1 //List any include files you want to use

Here I am just using comments to break up the program listing up into logical sections. The first section is where you tell the compiler program that you want to include some header files. Therefore, when the compiler program starts to compile your program instructions, it also finds the instructions in these header files and compiles them as well. Note that it is the linker program that finds these other files you want to include in your

project. In making this statement I am trying to make you aware that the
IDE, MPLABX, is a collection of a lot of programs that you use to write your
projects.

Line 2 #include <conFigInternalOscNoWDTNoLVP.h>

This is where you tell the compiler to include the first header file you
created to set the primary source of the clock to the internal oscillator
block and turn the WDT and LVP off.

Line 3 #include <xc.h>

This is a very important header file that was created by Microchip. It is
termed open source because it is freely available to us. It helps identify the
SFRs (special function registers) that you want to use in your programs. It
must be included in all of your projects if you want to use all of the labels
for the SFRs.

Line 4 #include <PICSetup.h>

This is the second header file you created to set up the PIC how
you want; see Chapter 1. Note that this file uses some of the labels that
are defined in the xc.h header file. Therefore it must be inserted in the
program after the xc.h header file has been included. Move it up to before
the #include xc.h line and see if the program will compile. It will not.

Line 5 // declare any global variables

This line splits the listing up for a section for global variables. Global
variables are simply memory locations created, with a suitable name to
refer to them, which can be used to store values. Since they are global, they
can be used by any section of the program.

The other type of variable is a local variable. The difference is that local
variables can only be used in the subroutine where they were created.

Line 6 unsigned char n;

This creates an 8-bit memory location with the name n. It is of type unsigned char. The char word means it is only 8 bits long. The word unsigned means that Bit7 is not used to tell us the "sign" of the variable, such as whether it is positive, Bit7 is a logic 0 or a negative, or Bit7 is a logic 1 number. With an unsigned char Bit7 is used to represent part of the number. This means you can store a value from 0 to 255 in this variable n. If you want to use Bit7 to represent the sign of the number, which is termed "signed number representation," then you would simply write "char" instead of "unsigned char." The variable n will then store a value from -127 to 127. This is an important difference, the difference between char and unsigned char.

Note the same applies to int and unsigned int. However, an int uses 16 bits. Int stands for integer.

Line 7 // declare any definitions;

In this section, you are telling the compiler that wherever it sees the symbolic name written after the keyword #define, you actually mean what is written after that symbolic name. You should make the symbolic name as sensible as possible in terms of what it is going to represent. The actual meaning of the symbolic name can be almost anything, such as

- an instruction, like PORTB = 0

- a reference to a bit, such as PORTAbits.RA0

- a numeric value, such as 0b00001111

Line 8 #define zero 0b01000000

With respect to line 8 you tell the compiler that whenever it sees the symbolic name "zero," it should read this as the binary number 0b01000000. When this value is loaded into PORTB, which is connected to the seven-segment display, all seven LEDs, except the last one named G in Figure 2-4, are lit. Note that the display is a common anode and so sending out a logic 0 to all the cathodes except the G cathode forces the cathodes to ground, or 0V, and so turns those LEDs on. The fact that the G cathode is connected to a logic 1 or 5V outputted from the PIC means that the G LED is turned off.

This means that the seven-segment display will actually display the number 0. This is why the symbolic name is "zero."

The next lines, 7 to 17, do exactly the same except that they define the binary number to make the display show the numbers 1, 2, 3, 4, 5, 6, 7, 8, and 9. Figure 2-4 should help you understand this.

Line 18 #define startButton PORTAbits.RA0

This is the same type of instruction except that it tells the compiler software that where it sees the symbolic name startButton, it knows that you mean the reference PORTAbits.RA0, or bit0 of PORTA.

Line 19 #define stopButton PORTAbits.RA1

This tells the compiler that where it sees the label stopButton, you mean the reference PORTAbits.RA1, or bit1 of PORTA.

Note with all these definitions there is no semicolon (;) at the end. That is because these are not instructions for the PIC. They are commands to the compiler software.

Line 20 //declare any subroutines

Here you are splitting the program up and creating a section of subroutines. Subroutines are small sections of a program that are written outside the main program loop.

You should use a subroutine if your program uses a section of instructions in EXACTLY the same way more than once in your program. With the subroutine you only write the instructions once instead of writing them many times. Note that even twice is deemed to be many times. This concept saves your program memory, and believe you me, memory is the villain for all programmers.

To run a subroutine, the main section of program has to call the subroutine. The micro then jumps out of its normal sequential operation and goes through the instructions of the subroutine. When it completes the subroutine, the micro jumps back to the main program at the point where it called the subroutine.

Line 21 void delay (unsigned char t)

This actually creates the subroutine. It starts off with the keyword void, which is blue in the C editor. This word means that the subroutine will not be passing any values back to the main loop.

The next word, delay, is the name for the subroutine; note that it is in black and bold in the editor. You should give the subroutine a suitable name to reflect its purpose.

Next, you set up a set of normal brackets. Here you can instruct the main program that you want it to pass a value up to the subroutine when the main program calls it. You use the statement inside the bracket to define what type of data you want the main program to send up to it. The statement unsigned char t means this subroutine wants an 8-bit unsigned number to be sent up to it when it is called from the main program, or from other subroutines as with nested subroutines. The subroutine will then copy this value into the variable t. Note in this instance the variable t is a local variable that can only be used in this subroutine.

I feel I should point out that a subroutine can use any global variable you have previously defined. Indeed, this subroutine is using the variable n which, because it is a global variable, the subroutine can use.

If the subroutine did not want the main program to pass a variable up to it when called, then you would leave the space between the two normal brackets empty.

Line 22 {

This is the opening curly bracket that defines the start of the loop within which all the instructions of the subroutine are written. Note that there must be a closing curly bracket for this loop. Indeed, as you type the first opening curly bracket, IntelliSense takes over and puts in the closing curly bracket and inserts the cursor between the two curly brackets.

Line 23 for (n = 0; n < t; n++)

This is a very powerful "for do loop" type instruction. It is really four instructions in one.

First, it loads the variable n with the value 0 using n = 0; and then compares the value of n, which is now 0, with the value that the main program passed up and the subroutine assigned to the local variable t, using n < t;. For this analysis, assume the value of t is 2.

The comparison asks the question, is n less than t? In this case, it is because n has just been loaded with 0. Therefore, the result of the test is said to be true, so the micro will carry out the instructions inside the following loop. When the micro has carried out all the instructions inside the loop, it will automatically increase the value of n by one, using the n++ shown in the normal bracket.

Now the micro carries out the comparison again, n < t;. Well, n is still less than t since n is now 1 and t is 2, so the micro must carry out the instructions in the loop a second time. Again, at the end, the micro will increment the value of n.

Now the micro again carries out the comparison but this time n is equal to t as both have the value of 2. Therefore the comparison is not true, as n is not less than t. So the micro does not carry out the instructions in the loop. It simply breaks away from the "for do loop" and carries on with the rest of the program.

The semicolons after n = 0; and n < t; need to be there because these are single-line instructions. The n++ is not a single-line instruction. It is the last instruction in a series of multiple-line instructions stated inside the curly brackets.

I hope this explains how the "for do loop" works. It is a very powerful way of making the micro carry out a set of instructions a controlled number of times.

Line 24 {

This is the opening curly bracket of the "for do loop." You need the curly brackets because there is more than just one instruction inside the "for do loop."

Line 25 TMR0 = 0;

This is the first instruction in the "for do loop." It loads the SFR TMR0 with the value 0. This is the register that is associated with timer0. Timer0 is a counting piece of firmware that increments its own register, TMR0, at a frequency you set using the control register for timer0, which is the T0CON register. Note that you set this register using the PICSetup.h header file to increment at a frequency of 7812.5Hz. This means it will increment every 128μs. Note that you also set the timer0 to be an 8-bit register, which means the maximum value it can count up to is 255.

Line 26 while (TMR0 < 255);

This is another very powerful C instruction. The principle on which it works is *while (the test I specify inside these bracket is true) do what I tell you to do here.*

I have written the instruction in the above manner to explain how it works. The while sets up a test. The test is written inside the normal brackets; in line 26, the test is, is the value in the TMR0 less than 255, TMR0 < 255? If the value is less than 255, the test is true and so the micro must carry out the instructions specified here outside the normal bracket.

To fully understand this particular instruction, you must appreciate that the semicolon signifies the end of the current instruction. You can see that there are no instructions between the closing normal bracket and the semicolon. This is because you want the micro to do **nothing** while the test is true. This is because you are creating a delay that lasts until the micro increments the value of the TMR0 register to 255. Note that the PIC automatically increments the TMR0 register. When the TMR0 reaches 255, the test will become untrue since TMR0 is no longer less than 255. Therefore, since the test is untrue, the micro can break away from doing nothing and carry on with the rest of the program.

The while (TMR0 < 255); creates a 255 x 128µs delay, which is approximately a 32.77ms delay. I say approximately because to be accurate you need to add the time it takes to carry out the instructions. How timer0 is set up to count at one every 128µs was explained in Chapter 1.

I hope this has helped you to understand how this *while (test is true) do what I say here* type of instruction works. The doing section may be just a single-line instruction, as with line 26. However, it could be a number of instructions. If this is the case, the set of instruction will be written inside a set of opening and closing curly brackets.

Line27 }

This is simply the closing curly bracket for the "for do loop" started on line 23.

Line 28 }

This is the closing bracket for the delay subroutine.

Line 29 void main ()

This is the most important loop. To appreciate how this works, it is important to appreciate that all C programs work within a collection of loops. In this way, once the program has started, it should run in a series of loops continuously. This main loop is the only loop all C programs must have. All other loops are functions, or methods or subroutines, as I like to call them, which are called from this main loop. The micro goes to the main loop to get the very first instruction of the program. From the main loop the instructions control how the micro carries out all of the instructions of the program.

The `main` loop must be of type void since it cannot pass any value back to itself. The name must be `main` and the brackets will normally be empty as no values are normally passed to it.

Line 30 {

This is simply the opening curly bracket for the `main` loop. IntelliSense will add the closing curly bracket and put the cursor between the two brackets for you.

Note that the confines of the two curly brackets are linked by a straight line, at the top of which is a small square. Inside the square is a minus (-) sign. This is so that you can close down any block of curly brackets if you are happy you have finished writing the instructions in them. If you do close the block down, the minus becomes a plus (+). You can use this plus sign to reopen the section of code. This option is to save screen space if you so wish.

Line 31 initialise ();

This is the first instruction inside the `main` loop and so it is the first instruction the micro carries out.

The instruction is actually a call to a subroutine. However, this subroutine has not been written in this current source code. It is a routine you wrote in the header file `PICSetUp.h`. However, as you have told the compiler to include this header file in line 4, there is no problem. The micro will break away and find the instructions in that subroutine and carry them out. In this way, the PIC is set up in the manner you want. This was described in Chapter 1.

Line 32 start: while (! startButton);

This introduces to you the goto label type instruction. The word `start:` is set up as label. It is the colon (:) that tells the compiler program that the word `start` is a label. The compiler assigns an address in the PIC's memory for this label. Later in the program, at line 35, there will be an instruction that tells the micro to go to this address assigned to the label start.

The next part of the instruction sets up another *while (test is true) do what I say here* type instruction. The test is (! startButton). The ! signifies the logic NOT. It is really saying that while the startButton is a logic 0 (i.e. not at a logic 1), the test is true. This is the same as using the instruction of while (startButton == 0); but it is somewhat more succinct.

You should remember that in line 18 you defined the phrase startButton to mean PORTAbits.RA0. This then means that the test is, is the logic on bit0 of PORTA a logic 0? If it is a logic 0, the test is true. If it goes to a logic 1, the test will become untrue. While the test is true, the micro must carry out the instruction you write between the closing bracket of the test and the semicolon. Again, there are no instructions here, so you are getting the micro to do nothing while the test is true (i.e. while there is a logic 0 at the input of Bit0 of PORTA).

Connect the start switch to the input of Bit0 on PORTA. If you don't press the start switch, the logic on Bit0 will be logic 0. Only when you press the start button will the logic change to a logic 1, while you press the button and change back to a logic 0 when you let go. However, this momentary change to a logic 1 will cause the test on line 32 to become untrue and so release the micro from the test. The micro will then be free to carry on with the rest of the program.

I know this is a wordy description of how you simply get the micro to wait until you press the start button, but I hope when you read through it you can understand how the instruction works.

Line 33 while (1)

Yet another *while (test is true) do what I say here* type instruction. Well, they are very useful. This test is rather special in that is just the number (1). What you have to appreciate is that the micro can only see logic 1 or logic 0 (really, 5V or 0V). Also, when a test results in a true, the logic the micro sees is a logic 1. When the test is untrue, it sees a logic 0. Well, with this while instruction the micro will only ever see a logic 1. This means the test will always be true. In this way, you force the micro to carry out the instructions listed between the curly brackets forever. That is why this is called the forever loop.

The instructions associated with the while (test) take up more than one line, so the instructions are placed between a set of opening and closing curly brackets.

Line 34 {

This is the opening curly bracket for the forever loop.

Line 35 if (stopButton) goto start;

This introduces the *if (this test is true) then do what I tell you to do* type of instruction. The instruction is in the form of a test, and if the test is true, then you must do what you are told to do "else" you do something else.

In line 35, the test is, is the logic on the stop button a logic 1? Note that you are not using the ! NOT label. If the test is true, the micro must carry out the instruction or instructions that are written here. This is a simple one-line instruction that tells the micro to go to the label start. Note that you defined the label start on line 32.

This instruction is asking the question, has someone pressed the stop button? If they have, then the micro must go back to the start label where you get it to wait until someone presses the start button. If no one has pressed the stop button, then the micro simply carries on with the rest of the program.

This shows the difference between the while and the if type instructions. The while traps the micro in that instruction while the test is true, whereas the if only asks, is my test true? If it is true, do what I tell you to do. If it's not true, carry on with the rest of the program; the micro is not trapped.

Line 36 PORTB = zero;

This line forces the data stored in the PORTB register to take on the value indicated by the phrase zero. Note you defined the phrase zero to mean the binary number 0b01000000 in line 8. This then means that the seven-segment display shows the figure zero.

Line 37 delay (61);

This calls the subroutine delay and passes up the value 61 to the subroutine. The subroutine then loads the local variable t with the number 61. This makes the "for do loop" in that subroutine to be carried out 61 times. Each time there is a delay of around 33ms, therefore the total delay is 61x33ms = 2.013s, an approximately 2-second delay.

Line 38 PORTB = one;

This overwrites the data in PORTB with the data to display the figure one on the seven-segment display.

Line 39 delay (61);

This calls another 2-second delay.

Lines 40 to 54 repeats this procedure so that the seven-segment display shows the numbers two through to nine with a 2-second delay between them.

Line 55 }

This is the closing curly bracket for the forever loop started on line 33.

Line 56 }

This is the closing curly bracket of the main loop started on line 29.

I hope the above analysis explains how the instructions work.

Improving the Seven-Segment Display Program

There is an issue with this program in how it works. This is not the error asked about in exercise 2.2; that error is still there in Listing 2-1. I am assuming you have repaired that error. If you haven't, then see the answer for exercise 2.2 at the end of this chapter, implement the repair, and come back here.

If you run the program, you may determine what the new issue is. Try running the new program and see if you recognize the problem.

Not to worry; I will explain what the problem is and go through a program that avoids it or at least is an improvement for it in this section of the chapter.

The Problem with the Program

I hope that after running the program a few times you have realized that you have to hold the stop button for at least 2 seconds, if not 20 seconds, before the program stops the display incrementing and the display always stops with the display showing the number 9.

The reason why this happens is because the instruction that looks as the stop button is on line 35. If you are not pressing the stop button when the micro carries out that instruction on this line, then the micro will not notice you have pressed the stop button. Also, it won't look at this instruction again until it has gone through all the other lines. Then, after reaching line 55, it loops back to line 35 via lines 33 and 34. The micro will then see that you have pressed the stop button, assuming you are still pressing it, and go to the label start:. Not very good programming.

One way around this issue is to insert this instruction, if (stopButton) goto start;, after each of the calls to the delay subroutine. This method is called software polling, where you continually keep asking the question. This approach is not the most efficient since it wastes a lot of time checking the stop switch, in this case, even if it hasn't been pressed. It also wastes a lot of memory in writing the same instruction many times.

One solution involves new instructions using arrays and pointers. This will save memory and speed up the response of the program.

Arrays

An array is a method by which you can create a list of variables and store them in locations one after the other and then use them sequentially one at a time or randomly. It is very much like a look-up table. It is very important to appreciate that the memory locations are set up one after the other in order. The array can store a variable using all the common data types such as unsigned char, integer, float, etc.

To create an array, you simply declare it using the data type you want to use and then give it a sensible name followed by the square bracket. Inside the square bracket you state how many memory locations you want to place in your array, such as [6]. When the compiler program compiles the program, it will place the start of the array in a memory location and then create the total number of memory locations immediately after the start location, one after the other. Each location will have its own reference number, with the first location having the reference 0. If, as in this example, the array has 6 memory locations, they are referenced as 0, 1, 2, 3, 4, and 5.

Using Pointers

Pointers can be used to point to locations inside an array. To create a pointer, it is best to create an array and then create the pointer with the same name and type as the array. This is best explained by going through the example instructions shown below.

```
1. unsigned char dataStore [10];
2. unsigned char *dataPointer;
3. dataPointer = dataStore;
```

```
4. data0 = *dataPointer;
5. dataPointer++;
6. data1 = *dataPointer;
7. dataPointer++;
```

Analysis of The Pointer Example

Line 1 unsigned char dataStore [10];

This creates an array of 10 locations one after the other, each being an 8-bit memory location since you are using the data type unsigned char.

Line 2 unsigned char *dataPointer;

This creates a memory location that can be loaded with the particular address of a location in the dataStore array. Note that the * is to tell the compiler that this is not a simple variable; it is a pointer that will point to an address in an array.

Line 3 dataPointer = dataStore;

This tells the compiler to load the pointer dataPointer with the address of the first location in the array dataStore.

Line 4 data0 = *dataPointer;

Earlier in the listing you declared the variable data0 as an unsigned char. With this instruction, the micro will load a copy of what is stored in the first location of the dataStore array into data0. This is because in the previous instruction you made the pointer point to that memory location in the array.

Line 5 dataPointer ++;

This increments the value in this dataPointer by one. This means that as the information in the dataPointer is the address of the first location in the dataStore array, then by incrementing it, the pointer dataPointer is now pointing to the next memory location in the dataStore array.

Line 6 data1 = *dataPointer;

Earlier in the listing you declared the variable data1 as an unsigned char. With this instruction, the micro will load a copy of what is stored in the second location of the dataStore array into data1.

I hope this goes some way to explaining what an array is. The following program is an example of how to set up and use an array.

The Improved Program

In this section of text, you will see how, by using arrays, you can program the counting sequence from before in a more efficient manner. See Listing 2-2.

Listing 2-2. The sevenSegImproved.c File

```
1. /* An improved program to display a count
2. from 0 to 9 on a seven segment display
3. Written by H. H. Ward Dated 29/10/19
4. For the PIC18F4525*/
5. //List any include files you want to use
6. #include <conFigInternalOscNoWDTNoLVP.h >
7. #include <xc.h>
8. #include <PICSetUp.h>
9. //declare any global variables
10. unsigned char n, m;
11. // declare any definitions
12. #define zero     0b01000000
```

```
13. #define one       0b01111001
14. #define two       0b00100100
15. #define three     0b00110000
16. #define four      0b00011001
17. #define five      0b00010010
18. #define six       0b00000011
19. #define seven     0b01111000
20. #define eight     0b00000000
21. #define nine      0b00011000
22. #define startButton PORTAbits.RA0
23. #define stopButton PORTAbits.RA1
24. unsigned char sevenDisplay [10] =
25. {
26. zero,
27. one,
28. two,
29. three,
30. four,
31. five,
32. six,
33. seven,
34. eight,
35. nine,
36. };
37. unsigned char *displayPointer;
38. //declare any subroutines
39. void delay (unsigned char t)
40. {
41. for (n = 0; n < t; n++)
42. {
43. TMR0 = 0;
```

```
44. while (TMRO < 255);
45. }
46. }
47. void main ()
48. {
49. initialise ();
50. start: while (! startButton);
51. while (1)
52. {
53. displayPointer = sevenDisplay;
54. for (m = 0; m <10; m ++ )
55. {
56. if (stopButton) goto start;
57. PORTB = *displayPointer;
58. displayPointer ++;
59. delay (61);
60. }
61. }
62. }
```

I hope you can appreciate that the only new instruction starts at line 24 which is

Line 24 unsigned char sevenDisplay [10] =

This sets up an array called sevenDisplay that has 10 memory locations. However, the equal sign (=) means that the following lines dictate what is initially loaded into those 10 memory locations.

The values to be used are listed between the following two curly brackets. However, to make them more readable, you use the phrases defined in lines 12 to 21 before.

In line 26, you place a copy in the first location in the array of the 8-bit binary number to display zero on the seven-segment display.

The remaining values are stored in the following lines.

One more thing you should note is that line 36 is

```
};
```

where the semicolon is added to indicate that this is the end of the instruction since this is a list of values to be stored in the array. That is also why there is a comma after each of the phrases.

Line 37 unsigned char *displayPointer;

This is where you create the pointer that you will use to point to individual memory locations in the array. Note that you don't have to use the phrase Pointer as part of the name; it is just my preference.

Lines 30 to 46 create your variable delay, which you created previously.

Lines 47 to 52 were discussed in Listing 2-1.

Line 53 displayPointer = sevenDisplay;

This loads the displayPointer with the address of the first memory location in the sevenDisplay array. This gets the displayPointer ready for the instruction on line 57.

Line 54 for (m = 0; m <10; m ++)

This sets up the "for do loop" that controls what data is sent to the display connected to PORTB. Note you must use a different variable than n because n is used in the delay subroutine that this "for do loop" calls within it. In line 10 you declared the variable m as an unsigned char.

Line 55 {

The opening curly bracket of the "for do loop".

Line 56 if (stopButton) goto start;

Here you are checking to see if the stop button has been pressed. If it has been pressed, the program will jump back to the start label on line 50 where the program then waits for the start button to be pressed. If the stop button has not been pressed, the program moves onto the next line.

Line 57 PORTB = *displayPointer;

This loads a copy in PORTB of the data in the memory location in the array sevenDisplay that the pointer, displayPointer, is pointing to. As this is the first run through the "for do loop," the data will be the 8-bit binary value for zero (see lines 26 to 35) and so the display will show the number 0. As it runs through the "for do loop" until n = 10, it will display the numbers 0 to 9 on the seven-segment display.

Line 58 displayPointer ++;

This increments the value in the displayPointer by 1. This means that the pointer will now be pointing to the next memory location in the array sevenDisplay. This then gets the data for "one" to be displayed next.

Line 59 delay (61);

This calls the delay subroutine with the value 61 to be copied into the local variable t in the subroutine. This creates a 2-second delay.

Line 60 }

This is the closing bracket of the "for do loop."

You should create a new project named sevenSegImproved with a source file also named sevenSegImproved.c. Then write the instructions listed in Listing 2-2. You should see an improvement the first time you run it. Note that you can stop the display on any number.

I hope you can see that you are actually checking the stop button after each time you display a number on the seven-segment display. This is the software polling mentioned earlier. This is not the most efficient method of doing this. It would be more efficient if you used interrupts. You will use interrupts in Chapter 7.

Exercise 2.3

I want you to speed up the change of display so that it takes around 33ms for the numbers to change. Also, restrict the count to go from 1 to 6. Then run the new program. Having done this, can you suggest what this new program may be used for? A possible use for the new program is given at the end of the chapter.

Synopsis

In this chapter, you learned about the seven-segment display and how you can use a PIC to control one. You have also become more familiar with the while and if instructions. You also learned how to use definitions to make the program more readable.

You also looked at using arrays and the "for do loop" to reduce the number of instructions in a program.

In the next chapter, you will extend this program to control a 24-hour digital clock that counts up in minutes and hours using four seven-segment displays.

Answers to the Exercises

Exercise 2.1: If last switch was closed, the center LED, LED G, would be turned on as well, so this would represent the number 8.

Exercise 2.2: There is a call to the 2-second delay subroutine missing between sending the number 9 to the seven-segment display and then sending the number 0 to the display. This means that the display will not show the number 9 because as soon as it displays 9, the program will swap it with the number 0. You need to add the following instruction after line 54:

```
delay (61);
```

The program will then display the number 9 and wait 2 seconds before displaying the number 0.

Exercise 2.3: The possible use of the faster program could be an electronic dice.

CHAPTER 3

The 24-Hour Clock

In this chapter, you will create a project that runs a 24-hour clock. Initially the clock will be displayed on an arrangement of seven-segment displays. Then the clock will be displayed on a liquid crystal display (LCD).

The seven-segment display will show minutes and hours but the LCD will show seconds, minutes, hours, and days of the week.

To begin, you will look at how to solve the logistics of incrementing the displays at different instances. This is because there are 60 second in one minute and 60 minutes in one hour but 24 hours in one day.

To solve this problem, and indeed any problem you want to solve, you must break it down into identifiable steps. Then you create a sequence of instructions that will allow you to bring these events together and produce a solution to the task.

After reading this chapter, you will have an understanding of the following:

- How to break down a task into small steps

- What an LCD is

- How to control an LCD using C programming

- The problem of switch bounce and how it can be overcome

- How to use the #define function to create a macro for a series of instructions

- How to use the switch and case statements

© Hubert Henry Ward 2020
H. H. Ward, *Intermediate C Programming for the PIC Microcontroller*,
https://doi.org/10.1007/978-1-4842-6068-5_3

The Seven-Segment Display

Since this example will only show minutes and hours, you will only need four seven-segment display. Note that there will be units and tens for both minutes and hours. To help refer to these different displays, you will create four variables with the names

- `minUnits`
- `minTens`
- `hourUnits`
- `hourTens`

The Algorithm for the 24-Hour Clock Using Seven-Segment Displays

The following steps are my interpretation of how to go about solving the tasks. There may be other methods but I think this is a logical approach that can be used to solve the task. You should identify what the system has to do and then go about designing a solution to enable the system to fulfill those steps.

You have already identified that you will need four seven-segment displays, one for each digit to be displayed.

Both `minUnits` and `hourUnits` will display a value from 0 to 9. `minTens` will display a value from 0 to 6 and `hourTens` will display a value from 0 to 2. However, you need to appreciate that when `hourTens` goes from 0 to 1, `hourUnits` will also go from 0 to 9. However, when `hourTens` displays the number 2, `hourUnits` will only go from 0 to 3. This is because when the clock displays 23 59, at the next increment of the minute units the whole display will go back to 00 00.

1. **Identifying how the displays will change**

   a. Since the system is a clock, the displays will change in steps of minutes (i.e. every minute the display will change). This means you will require a one-minute delay.

2. **Setting the clock**

   a. You will need a method by which you can set the clock to the correct time and then get the clock to increment from this time onwards. This can be done using three buttons. To identify the buttons, give them the following names:

      i. incButton

      ii. decButton

      iii. setButton

3. Their names should suggest their functions but, just to be clear, the functions are

   a. The incButton will increment the current digit by one each time the button is momentarily pressed.

   b. The decButton will decrement the current digit by one each time the button is momentarily pressed.

   c. The setButton will set the current digit to the value it has been changed to and move onto the next digit to be set or end the setting of the time.

4. Once the display has been set, it will increment once a minute and it will change in this fashion:

   a. minUnits will increment from 0 to 9 and on the next change the units will return to 0 and minTens will increment.

   b. minUnits will continue to change in the same way.

   c. minTens will increment accordingly until the point when minTens has a value of 5 and minUnits has a value of 9 (i.e. 59).

      i. Upon the next increment, minUnits and minTens will return to 0 and hourUnits will increment.

      ii. Now, since minUnits and minTens continue to increment, then on the change from minTens = 5 and minUnits = 9 they will both go back to 0 and hourUnits will increment again. This will continue until hourUnits displays 9. On the next increment of hourUnits, it will return to 0 and hourTens will increment from 0 to 1.

5. This sequence will continue until hourTens displays 2. Then, on the next increment of hourUnits from 3 to what would be 4, the whole display will go back to 0.

6. To control the sequence the program, you will need a timer that will increment in minutes.

7. The system will need the following inputs, outputs, and timers:

   a. Three momentarily switches as inputs

   b. Four 8-bit ports to control the display of the four seven-segment displays

c. One timer to count in minutes

d. The four output ports will be

    i. PORTA

    ii. PORTB

    iii. PORTC

    iv. PORTD

e. The one input PORT will be PORTE.

f. There will be no analog inputs, therefore the ADC can be switched off.

8. You will use the internal oscillator block to generate the primary oscillator. This is because you can't use PORTA for the crystal.

9. The first section of the program, after you have initialized the PIC as you need it, will be to set the hours and minutes and so set the time for the clock. Note that the clock should initially display zero on all four seven-segment displays.

10. The final section will be to increment the display accordingly every minute.

11. Now you have the algorithm so you can start designing the program. This step would normally involve constructing a flowchart. However, flowcharts take up a lot of room and I am more interested in showing you how to program the PIC in C.

The Initialization of the PIC

As you are using the internal oscillator block and switching off both the WDT and the LVP, you can use the header file conFigInternalOscNoWDTNoLVP.h you created earlier. You can also use the other header file, PICSetUp.h, but you may need to change some of the settings, as stated here:

- TRISA = 0X00; to change PORTA from input to output

- TRISD = 0x00; to change PORTD from input to output

- TRISE = 0xFF; to change PORTE from output to input

As always, it is useful to create some definitions that will make the reading of the program easier. In Chapter 2, you created some definitions for the binary numbers to display the numbers 0 to 9 on the seven-segment display. They are

```
#define zero     0b01000000
#define one      0b01111001
#define two      0b00100100
#define three    0b00110000
#define four     0b00011001
#define five     0b00010010
#define six      0b00000011
#define seven    0b01111000
#define eight    0b00000000
#define nine     0b00011000
```

You will also use the following definitions for the three buttons:

```
#define incButton PORTEbits.RE0
#define decButton PORTEbits.RE1
#define setButton PORTEbits.RE2
```

Since the program will respond to the activation of these buttons, it will make use of the if statement (as in *if (incButton), then increment the display*). Also, every minute it will change the display in a way that depends upon the current value on the display. This will also involve the use of the if statement.

The complete listing for the program is shown in Listing 3-1.

Listing 3-1. The 24-Hour Clock on Seven-Segment Displays

```
1. /*A program to control a 24Hr clock
2. Displayed on 4 seven-segment display
3. Written for the PIC18f4525 by Mr H. H. Ward
4. dated 15/01/2019 */
5. #include <conFigInternalOscNoWDTNoLVP.h>
6. #include <xc.h>
7. #include <PICSetUp.h>
8. //Some definitions
9. #define zero     0b01000000
10. #define one      0b01111001
11. #define two      0b00100100
12. #define three    0b00110000
13. #define four     0b00011001
14. #define five     0b00010010
15. #define six      0b00000011
16. #define seven    0b01111000
17. #define eight    0b00000000
18. #define nine     0b00011000
19. #define incButton PORTEbits.RE0
20. #define decButton PORTEbits.RE1
21. #define setButton PORTEbits.RE2
22. //some variables
23. unsigned char n, m;
```

```
24. unsigned char minUnits = 0, minTens = 0, hourUnits = 0,
    hourTens = 0;
25. //some subroutines
26. void debounce ()
27. {
28. TMR0 = 0;
29. while (TMR0 < 101);
30. }
31. //some arrays
32. unsigned char displaynumber [10] =
33. {
34. zero,
35. one,
36. two,
37. three,
38. four,
39. five,
40. six,
41. seven,
42. eight,
43. nine,
44. };
45. void main ()
46. {
47. initialise ();
48. TRISA = 0;
49. TRISD = 0;
50. TRISE = 0xFF;
51. //set minutes
52. minunitsset:
53. PORTA = displaynumber [minUnits];
```

```
54. if (incButton)debounce ();
55. if (incButton)
56. {
57. minUnits ++;
58. while (incButton);
59. PORTA = displaynumber [minUnits];
60. }
61. if (decButton )debounce ();
62. if (decButton)
63. {
64. if (minUnits > 0) minUnits --;
65. else minUnits = 0;
66. while (decButton);
67. PORTA = displaynumber [minUnits];
68. }
69. if (setButton) debounce ();
70. if (setButton) goto mintensset;
71. goto minunitsset;
72. //*************************************************
73. mintensset:while (setButton);
74. PORTB = displaynumber [minTens];
75. if (incButton)debounce ();
76. if (incButton)
77. {
78. if (minTens < 6)
79. minTens ++;
80. else minTens = 6;
81. while (incButton);
82. PORTB = displaynumber [minTens];
83. }
```

```
84. if (decButton)debounce ();
85. if (decButton)
86. {
87. if (minTens > 0)
88. minTens --;
89. else minTens = 0;
90. while (decButton);
91. PORTB = displaynumber [minTens];
92. }
93. if (setButton) debounce ();
94. if (setButton) goto hoursunitsset;
95. goto mintensset;
96. //sethours
97. hoursunitsset: while (setButton);
98. PORTC = displaynumber [hourUnits];
99. if (incButton)debounce ();
100. if (incButton)
101. {
102. hourUnits ++;
103. while (incButton);
104. PORTC = displaynumber [hourUnits];
105. }
106. if (decButton)debounce ();
107. if (decButton)
108. {
109. if (hourUnits > 0)
110. hourUnits --;
111. else hourUnits = 0;
112. while (decButton);
113. PORTC = displaynumber [hourUnits];
114. }
115. if (setButton) debounce ();
```

```
116. if (setButton) goto hourstensset;
117. goto hoursunitsset;
118. //***********************************************
119. hourstensset: while (setButton);
120. PORTD = displaynumber [hourTens];
121. if (incButton)debounce ();
122. if (incButton)
123. {
124. if (hourTens < 2)
125. hourTens ++;
126. else hourTens = 2;
127. while (incButton);
128. PORTD = displaynumber [hourTens];
129. }
130. if (decButton)debounce ();
131. if (decButton)
132. {
133. if (hourTens > 0)
134. hourTens --;
135. else hourTens = 0;
136. while (decButton);
137. PORTD = displaynumber [hourTens];
138. }
139. if (setButton) debounce ();
140. if (setButton) goto clock;
141. goto hourstensset;
142. //***********************************************
143. clock: while (1)
144. {
145. for (m = 0; m <60; m++)
146. {
```

```
147. for (n = 0; n <29; n++)
148. {
149. TMR0 = 0;
150. while (TMR0 < 255);
151. }
152. }
153. minUnits ++;
154. if (minUnits == 10)
155. {
156. minUnits = 0;
157. minTens ++;
158. if (minTens == 6)
159. {
160. minTens = 0;
161. hourUnits ++;
162. if (hourTens < 2)
163. {
164. if (hourUnits == 10)
165. {
166. hourUnits = 0;
167. hourTens ++;
168. }
169. }
170. else if (hourTens == 2)
171. {
172. if (hourUnits == 4)
173. {
174. hourUnits = 0;
175. hourTens =0;
176. }
177. }
178. }
```

```
179. }
180. PORTA = displaynumber [minUnits];
181. PORTB = displaynumber [minTens];
182. PORTC = displaynumber [hourUnits];
183. PORTD = displaynumber [hourTens];
184. }
185. }
```

Analysis of Listing 3-1

I hope that the instructions in lines 1 to 25 don't seem new, since you have used them before. I will start at line 26.

Line 26: void debounce ()

This is a subroutine, and I covered how to set up and use a subroutine in Chapter 2. However, the function that this subroutine fulfils needs some explanation.

This subroutine creates a software solution to the problem caused by switch bounce. This is when a switch physically bounces between open and closed when you attempt to close the switch and when you attempt to open the switch. This bouncing action, which is caused by the switch obeying Newton's Law of Motion (every action has an equal and opposite reaction) causes the voltage at the input connected to the switch to physically bounce, as shown in Figure 3-1.

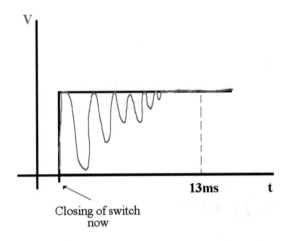

Figure 3-1. *The bouncing voltage from a switch at any input*

The black line is the ideal voltage response when the switch closes. The red line is the practical voltage response. The diagram is only to give the impression of what the voltage, across the switch, does when you close the switch.

The logic levels upon which a micro responds have the following ranges of voltage:

- Logic 0 is 0V to 0.8V at the input.

- Logic 1 is 2V to 5V at the input.

- Logic 0 is 0v to 0.4V at the output.

- Logic 1 is 2.7V to 5V at the output.

So the micro would actually think that the logic at the input had gone to a logic 1 many times during this bounce time. However, the programmer expects the logic to go to logic 1 once only because they only presses the button once.

There are a few ways engineers can try to overcome this problem. Some switches have springs inside them to try to prevent this bouncing action. Other systems use debounce circuits, which can be made from two NAND or NOR gates interconnected or cross coupled to solve this problem. However, you are a programmer and you will actually use a software approach whereby you add some program instructions to overcome this issue.

The principle behind this approach is to recognize that someone has pressed the switch, as the input will go to a logic 1. The PIC will then wait a small amount of time and check the input again to see if it has really gone to a logic 1 before responding to the action. The small amount of time is to allow this bouncing action to die down, as shown in Figure 3-1, and so ensure that the PIC doesn't see the many times the logic bounces between logic 0 and logic 1. A reasonable time to allow this bouncing action to die down is approximately 13ms. This is what your program will do. Every time the input from the switch goes high, it will wait around 13ms and then check to see if the input is really at a logic 1 before it does anything about it. In this way, the program sees that the input goes high only once, instead of thinking it has gone high three or four times, as shown in Figure 3-1.

Note that this debounce subroutine can be used to overcome noise on a switch. Noise on a switch is where an input picks up a voltage spike that makes the micro think the input has gone to a logic 1. However, in reality the input has not gone high.

Lines 27, 28, 29, and 30 create a 13ms delay. This is because you make the PIC do nothing until the value in the TMR0 SFR has reached 101; see line 29. Since the TMR0 takes 128µs to count 1, it will take 101 X 128µs = 12.928ms.

Line 31 is just a way of splitting up the program listing.

Line 32: unsigned char displaynumber [10] =

This sets up an array of 10 memory locations and loads each location with the data listed between lines 33 and 44. Therefore the array stores the binary numbers for displaying the value 0 to 9 on the seven-segment displays.

Line 45: void main ()

This is the main loop of the C program, which must be in all C programs. Line 46 is the opening curly bracket for this loop.

Line 47: initialise ();

This calls the subroutine `initialise`, which is written in header file `PICSetup.h`. This is a subroutine to set up the PIC as you want. You change the use of PORTA, PORTD, and PORTE in lines 48, 49, and 50.

The first section of the program is to allow the user to set the current time on the seven-segment display. This is why line 51 is

Line 51: // set minutes

I am using comments to split up the program listing in the IDE. You don't have to do this but I think it is useful.

Line 52: minunitsset:

This is a label I created because I will be using the goto instruction, which requires a label to go to. Note that you don't have to put a label on its own separate line. The following instruction could have been written on line 52, but after the label:

Line 53: PORTA = displaynumber [minUnits];

This loads the 8 bits on PORTA with a copy of the data that is stored in the array `displaynumber` [ ]. The actual memory location within the array, whose 8 bits are copied into PORTA, is controlled by the variable `minUnits`. In line 24, this variable, along with three others, was created and loaded with the value of 0. Therefore, this loads the 8 bits in PORTA with the data that is stored in the first (i.e. location 0) of the array `displaynumber`.

You could replace this instruction with PORTA = displaynumber [0]; as the value of 0 is currently stored in the variable `minUnits`. However, using a variable as with `minUnits` makes it easier to increment the value, so it is more efficient.

If you look at the array that is created within lines 32 to 44, you will see that the data that is stored in the first location of this array is the 8 bits named "zero."

Line 9 defines these 8 bits as 0b01000000. This is the 8 bits to display the number 0 on the first seven-segment display. This is the units for the minutes display. So in this instance you are making the display connected to PORTA display the number 0.

Line 54: if (incButton) debounce ();

This asks the question, has the incButton been pressed? If it has, it calls the debounce subroutine where you wait for the bouncing action to die down.

If the incbutton has not been pressed, the micro will go to the next instruction on line 55. The incbutton will not have been pressed so the micro will go to the instruction on line 61 where you ask if the decbutton has been pressed. If the decbutton has not been pressed, the micro will go to line 69 where you ask if the setbutton has been pressed. If the setbutton has not been pressed, the micro will go to line 71 where it will be forced to go to the label minunitsset label on line 52.

This is a wordy description but it, hopefully, shows you how you can use the if statement to control what the micro does.

Line 55: if (incButton)

Here you again ask the question, has the incButton been pressed? The difference now is that the bouncing of the switch has died down. If it has and the incbutton has been pressed, then the PIC must carry out the instructions that are listed between the next opening and closing curly brackets. So these two lines deal with the bouncing action of the input switch.

Line 56 is the opening bracket of the if statement.

Line 57:   minUnits ++;

This increments the value in the variable minUnits. This is getting the value in minUnits ready for the instruction on line 59; however, now the value in minUnits is now 1, not 0.

Line 58: while (incButton);

This gets the PIC to do nothing while the logic at the input, which is connected to the incButton, is at a logic 1. This is to make sure the PIC waits until the user has let go of the incButton. Really, it would be useful to call the debounce subroutine here again as the switch would bounce just the same when going from high to low as it does when it goes from low to high. However, the transition to logic 0 is not as important as the transition to logic 1. There may be some programs where it is just as important, so you should consider switch bounce in those cases also.

Line 59: PORTA = displaynumber [minUnits];

This is a repeat of the instruction on line 53 but this time the value in minUnits has been incremented, to 1 in this instance, and so it is the data stored in the second memory location in the array that is copied into PORTA. This means that the number 1 is displayed on the first seven-segment display. This is why you didn't write the instruction PORTA = displaynumber[0] on line 53.

Line 60: }

This is the closing brackets of the if statement.

Line 64: if (minUnits > 0) minUnits --;

This is here to make sure the PIC only decrements the value in the variable minUnits if the current value is greater than 0. This is a one-line if test so you don't need the opening and closing curly brackets.

Line 65: else minUnits = 0;

This states what the micro must do if the test stated in line 64 is not true and minUnits is not greater than 0. This prevents the program from making minUnits go negative. Note if the micro carries out the instruction on line 64, the micro will skip this instruction on line 65. The if and the else are linked together in C. The micro will only carry out the instruction with the else statements if the previous if test was untrue.

Line 66: while (decButton);

This makes sure the micro waits until the decrement button has been released and the logic at that input has gone back to logic 0.

Line 67: PORTA = displaynumber [minUnits];

Now the micro loads the seven-segment display connected to PORTA, which is the units for the minutes, with the current value from the array displaynumber.

Line 68 is the closing curly bracket of the if loop.

Line 69: if (setButton) debounce ();

This checks if the setButton has been pressed. If it has, the program calls the debounce subroutine.

Line 70: if (setButton) goto mintensset;

This asks if the setButton has really been pressed. If it has, it tells the PIC to go to the label mintensset, which is on line 73.

Line 71: goto minunitsset;

This is where the PIC should go if the setButton has not been pressed. This is back to line 52 where the listing asks if the incButton has been pressed.

In this way, the PIC will continually change the minUnits of the seven-segment display until the setButton has been pressed.

Line 72: //***********

This is just to split up the listing in the IDE.

Line 73: mintensset: while(setButton);

This is the label where the PIC must go to if the setButton is pressed and the user has finished setting the minUnits. Note the use of the colon. This tells the compiler that this is a label and it must assign it a location in the PIC's program memory when the program is downloaded to the PIC. The while(setButton); is there to make sure the micro waits for the logic at the setButton input to go back to logic 0 before it does anything else. If you don't, then there is the chance that the micro will see a logic 1 at the set input and it will skip some or all the next steps.

Line 74: PORTB = displaynumber [minTens];

This loads the second seven-segment display with the current number in the displaynumber array identified by the value in the variable minTens. This will initially be the number 0.

Lines 75 to 95 allow the user to increment and decrement the value in the minTens variable and so set the tens value for the minutes in the seven-segment display connected to PORTB.

Lines 96 to 141 do the same but for the hours units and minutes seven-segment displays.

Line 142: //*************

This defines the end of the setting the correct time on the seven-segment display.

Line 143: clock: while (1)

This is the label for the goto in line 140. The PIC goes to this label when the user has finished setting the correct time on the clock. The while (1) sets up a forever loop so that the program doesn't go through the instructions to set the clock again.

Line 144: {

This is simply the opening curly bracket of the forever loop.

```
Line 145      for (m = 0; m <60; m++)
Line 146          {
Line 147              for (n = 0; n <29; n++)
Line 148                  {
Line 149                      TMRO = 0;
Line 150                      while (TMRO < 255);
Line 151                  }
Line 152          }
```

Lines 145 to 152 create a one-minute delay. This uses two nested
for do loops. Lines 149 and 150 create a 33ms delay (i.e. 256 x 128µs =
32.77ms). Then line 147 sets up the inner for do loop, which makes the
PIC carry out this 32ms delay 29 times, which creates the one-second
delay. Line 145 sets up the outer for do loop, which makes the PIC carry
out the one-second delay a further 60 times. This approximately creates
a one-minute delay. The delay can't be extremely accurate since you
can't work out how long it will take the PIC to carry out the rest of the
instructions in the loops. The only way you can be very accurate is to
physically time how long it takes to count the minutes and then adjust the
values in the for do loops until you get an accurate one-minute change in
the display. However, I used the listing here to switch a lamp on and off at
one-second intervals. Then I physically scoped the output and it does look
very accurate.

Line 153: minUnits ++;

After the PIC has waited the one-minute delay, the PIC increments the
value stored in the variable minUnits.

Line 154: if (minUnits == 10)

This checks to see if the value stored in minUnits has reached 10. If it has, the PIC must carry out the instructions on lines 156 and 157. Here the PIC will reset minUnits back to zero and add one to the value stored in the variable minTens.

Line 158: if (minTens == 6)

Since minTens has been incremented in line 157, the program must now check if the value in minTens has reached 6 or not. If it has, then the program must reset minTens back to 0; this is done on line 160. The program must also add one to hoursUnits; this is done on line 161.

However, incrementing the hoursUnits variable will eventually affect the hoursTens variable. The value at which the incrementing of the hoursUnits variable affects the hoursTens variable depends upon the current value of the hoursTens variable. This is because the hours display follows the sequence described below:

00, 01, 02, 03, 04, 05, 06, 07, 08, 09, 10, 11, 12, 13, 14, 15, 16, 17, 18, 19, 20, 21, 22, 23.

Then, when the full display in hours and minutes reaches 23:59. the next increment in the minutes causes the display to return to 00:00.

This shows that there are two times when the hoursUnits variable can count up to 9 and they are

- First, when the hoursTens variable is at 0

- Second, when the hoursTens variable is at 1

Note that when the hoursTens variable is at 2, the hourUnits variable can only count up as follows:

0, 1, 2, 3.

At the next increment, which is when the hourUnits variable tries to change from 3 to 4, both the hourUnits and hourTens variable return to 0. So do the minute variables.

This action is accommodated in lines 162 to 178.

```
Line 162            if (hourTens < 2)
Line 163                {
Line 164                    if (hourUnits == 10)
Line 165                        {
Line 166                            hourUnits = 0;
Line 167                            hourTens ++;
Line 178                        }
Line 169                    }
Line 170                else if (hourTens == 2)
Line 171                    {
Line 172                        if (hourUnits == 4)
Line 173                            {
Line 174                            hourUnits = 0;
Line 175                            hourTens =0;
Line 176                            }
Line 177                        }
Line 178                }
```

I hope you have learned enough from the previous analysis to understand how the nested if statements perform the required actions.

Line 179: }

This is the closing curly bracket for the if statement at line 158.

Lines 180, 181, 182, and 183 force the seven-segment displays on each of the four output PORTS to display the current values in their respective variables.

Line 184 and 185 are the closing curly brackets of the program.

I hope this analysis does go some way towards explaining how this program works. The complete circuit for the project and simulation is shown in Figure 3-2.

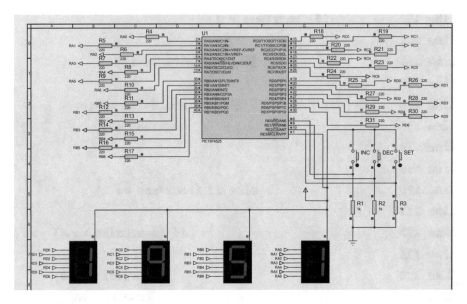

Figure 3-2. *Simulation of the seven-segment 24-hour clock*

Note the use of input and output nodes to save cluttering the simulation with too many wires. Also note there are 220Ω resistors inline with all of the outputs. This is to limit the current being sent to each of the LEDs in the seven-segment displays.

A 24-Hour Clock with the LCD Display

The previous project used the seven-segment displays to show the current time. While the seven-segments are not too expensive, they are limited to what they can display. A more interesting display can be achieved using a simple 16-character two-line LCD. There are a variety of LCDs but this one is very popular and it can be used to display text as well as numbers.

The following section will detail how you can program this LCD to display a 24-hour clock. I always like to give a full analysis of the programs in my books but there is a full description of how the LCD works (i.e. how you send instructions and data to the LCD and how it can be set up to run in 4-bit or 8-bit operation) in my first book on the PIC18F4525, *C Programming for the PIC Microcontroller*. Therefore I will restrict my analysis to how the instructions control the setting up of the clock and the running of the clock.

The program listing for the 24-hour clock is shown in Listing 3-2.

Listing 3-2. The Complete Program for the 24-Hour Clock on the LCD

```
1. /*This is a basic program to control the LCD using the
   PIC 18F4525
2. Written by H H Ward dated 31/01/15
3. Extended 03/01/19 to include the day of the week display*/
4. #include <xc.h>
5. #include <conFigInternalOscNoWDTNoLVP.h>
6. #include <PICSetUp.h>
7. //some definitions
8. #define firstbyte      0b00110011
9. #define secondbyte     0b00110011
10. #define fourBitOp      0b00110010
11. #define twoLines       0b00101100
12. #define incPosition    0b00000110
13. #define cursorNoBlink  0b00001100
14. #define clearScreen    0b00000001
15. #define returnHome     0b00000010
16. #define lineTwo        0b11000000
17. #define doBlink        0b00001111
18. #define shiftLeft      0b00010000
19. #define shiftRight     0b00010100
20. #define shdisright     0b00011100
21. #define lcdPort        PORTB
22. #define eBit           PORTBbits.RB5
23. #define incbutton      PORTAbits.RA0
```

```
24. #define decbutton        PORTAbits.RA1
25. #define setbutton        PORTAbits.RA2
26. #define Mon              lcdData = 0x4D; lcdOut ();
         lcdData = 0x6F; lcdOut (); lcdData = 0x6E; lcdOut ();
27. #define Tue              lcdData = 0x54; lcdOut
(); 	 lcdData = 0x75; lcdOut (); lcdData = 0x65; lcdOut ();
28. #define Wed              lcdData = 0x57; lcdOut ();
         lcdData = 0x65; lcdOut (); lcdData = 0x64; lcdOut ();
29. #define Thur             lcdData = 0x54; lcdOut ();
         lcdData = 0x68; lcdOut (); lcdData = 0x72; lcdOut ();
30. #define Fri              lcdData = 0x46; lcdOut ();
         lcdData = 0x72; lcdOut (); lcdData = 0x69; lcdOut ();
31. #define Sat              lcdData = 0x53; lcdOut ();
         lcdData = 0x61; lcdOut (); lcdData = 0x74; lcdOut ();
32. #define Sun              lcdData = 0x53; lcdOut ();
         lcdData = 0x75; lcdOut (); lcdData = 0x6E; lcdOut ();
33. //some variables
34. unsigned char n, lcdData, lcdTempData, rsLine, daynumber
    = 1, setbutcounts = 0;
35. char str[80];
36. char lcdInitialise [8] =
37. {
38. firstbyte,
39. secondbyte,
40. fourBitOp,
41. twoLines,
42. incPosition,
43. cursorNoBlink,
44. clearScreen,
45. returnHome,
46. };
```

```
47. //the subroutines
48. void sendData ()
49. {
50. lcdTempData = (lcdTempData << 4 | lcdTempData >>4);
51. lcdData = lcdTempData & 0x0F;
52. lcdData = lcdData | rsLine;
53. lcdPort = lcdData;
54. eBit = 1;
55. eBit = 0;
56. TMR0 = 0; while (TMR0 < 20);
57. }
58. void lcdOut ()
59. {
60. lcdTempData = lcdData;
61. sendData ();
62. sendData ();
63. }
64. void setUpTheLCD ()
65. {
66. TMR0 = 0; while (TMR0 <255);
67. n = 0;
68. rsLine = 0X00;
69. while (n < 8)
70. {
71. lcdData = lcdInitialise [n];
72. lcdOut ();
73. n ++;
74. }
75. rsLine = 0x10;
76. }
```

```
77. void line2 ()
78. {
79. rsLine = 0X00;
80. lcdData = lineTwo;
81. lcdOut ();
82. rsLine = 0x10;
83. }
84. void clearTheScreen ()
85. {
86. rsLine = 0X00;
87. lcdData = clearScreen;
88. lcdOut ();
89. //lcdData = returnHome;
90. //lcdOut ();
91. rsLine = 0x10;
92. }
93. void sendcursorhome ()
94. {
95. rsLine = 0X00;
96. //lcdData = clearScreen;
97. //lcdOut ();
98. lcdData = returnHome;
99. lcdOut ();
100. rsLine = 0x10;
101. }
102. void shiftcurleft (unsigned char l)
103. {
104. for (n = 0; n < l; n ++)
105. {
106. rsLine = 0X00;
107. lcdData = shiftLeft;
```

```
108. lcdOut ();
109. rsLine = 0x10;
110. }
111. }
112. void shiftcurright (unsigned char r)
113. {
114. for (n = 0; n < r; n ++)
115. {
116. rsLine = 0X00;
117. lcdData = shdisright;
118. lcdOut ();
119. rsLine = 0x10;
120. }
121. }
122. unsigned char n, secunits = 0X30, sectens = 0X30, minunits
     = 0X30, mintens = 0X30, hourunits = 0X30, hourtens = 0X30;
123. void writeString (const char *words)
124. {
125. while (*words)
126. {
127. lcdData = *words;
128. lcdOut ();
129. *words ++;
130. }
131. }
132. void debounce ()
133. {
134. TMR0 = 0;
135. while (TMR0 < 101);
136. }
```

```
137. //The main program
138. void main ()
139. {
140. initialise ();
141. setUpTheLCD ();
142. clearTheScreen ();
143. while (1)
144. {
145. writeString ("Set The Day");
146. line2 ();
147. while (!setbutton)
148. {
149. if (incbutton) debounce ();
150. if (incbutton) daynumber ++;
151. while (incbutton);
152. if (decbutton) debounce ();
153. if (decbutton) daynumber --;
154. while (decbutton);
155. if (daynumber == 1)
156. {
157. Mon;
158. line2 ();
159. }
160. if (daynumber == 2)
161. {
162. Tue;
163. line2 ();
164. }
165. if (daynumber == 3)
166. {
167. Wed;
```

```
168. line2 ();
169. }
170. if (daynumber == 4)
171. {
172. Thur;
173. line2 ();
174. }
175. if (daynumber == 5)
176. {
177. Fri;
178. line2 ();
179. }
180. if (daynumber == 6)
181. {
182. Sat;
183. line2 ();
184. }
185. if (daynumber == 7)
186. {
187. Sun;
188. line2 ();
189. }
190. if (daynumber == 8) daynumber = 1;
191. if (daynumber == 0) daynumber = 1;
192. }
193. debounce ();
194. while (setbutton);
195. clearTheScreen ();
196. writeString ("Set The Clock");
197. while (!setbutton)
198. {
```

```
199. line2 ();
200. writeString ("Hours");
201. lcdData = 0x3A;
202. lcdOut ();
203. lcdData = hourtens;
204. lcdOut ();
205. lcdData = hourunits;
206. lcdOut ();
207. shiftcurleft (1);
208. if (incbutton) debounce ();
209. if (incbutton) hourunits ++;
210. while (incbutton);
211. if(hourunits == 0X3A)
212. {
213. hourunits = 0X30;
214. hourtens ++;
215. }
216. if (hourtens == 0X32 & hourunits == 0X34 )
217. {
218. hourtens = 0x30;
219. hourunits = 0x30;
220. }
221. if (decbutton) debounce ();
222. if (decbutton)
223. {
224. if (hourunits == 0x30)
225. {
226. hourunits = 0x39;
227. hourtens --;
228. }
229. else hourunits --;
230. }
```

```
231. while (decbutton);
232. if (setbutton) debounce ();
233. if (setbutton) goto minset;
234. }
235. minset:    line2 ();
236. writeString ("Minutes");
237. lcdData = 0x3A;
238. lcdOut ();
239. for (n = 0; n < 15; n ++)
240. {
241. TMR0 = 0;
242. while (TMR0 < 255);
243. }
244. setmins:  lcdData = mintens;
245. lcdOut ();
246. lcdData = minunits;
247. lcdOut ();
248. shiftcurleft (2);
249. if (incbutton) debounce ();
250. if (incbutton) minunits ++;
251. while (incbutton)
252. ;
253. if(minunits == 0X3A)
254. {
255. minunits = 0X30;
256. mintens ++;
257. }
258. if (decbutton) debounce ();
259. if (decbutton)
260. {
261. if (minunits == 0x30)
262. {
```

```
263. minunits = 0x39;
264. mintens --;
265. }
266. else minunits --;
267. }
268. while (decbutton);
269. if (!setbutton) goto setmins;
270. clearTheScreen ();
271. writeString ("The Time/Day is");
272. lcdData = 0xA0;
273. lcdOut ();
274. while (1)
275. {
276. if (daynumber == 1)
277. {
278. Mon;
279. line2 ();
280. }
281. if (daynumber == 2)
282. {
283. Tue;
284. line2 ();
285. }
286. if (daynumber == 3)
287. {
288. Wed;
289. line2 ();
290. }
291. if (daynumber == 4)
292. {
293. Thur;
```

```
294. line2 ();
295. }
296. if (daynumber == 5)
297. {
298. Fri;
299. line2 ();
300. }
301. if (daynumber == 6)
302. {
303. Sat;
304. line2 ();
305. }
306. if (daynumber == 7)
307. {
308. Sun;
309. line2 ();
310. }
311. for (n = 0; n < 29; n ++)
312. {
313. TMRO = 0;
314. while (TMRO < 255);
315. }
316. secunits ++;
317. if (secunits == 0X3A)
318. {
319. secunits = 0X30;
320. sectens ++;
321. if ( sectens == 0X36)
322. {
323. sectens = 0X30;
324. minunits ++;
```

```
325. if (minunits == 0X3A)
326. {
327. minunits = 0X30;
328. mintens ++;
329. if (mintens == 0X36)
330. {
331. mintens = 0X30;
332. hourunits ++;
333. if(hourunits == 0X3A)
334. {
335. hourunits = 0X30;
336. hourtens ++;
337. }
338. }
339. }
340. }
341. if (hourtens == 0X32 & hourunits == 0X34 )
342. {
343. hourtens = 0x30;
344. hourunits= 0x30;
345. daynumber ++;
346. if (daynumber == 8) daynumber = 1;
347. }
348. }
349. line2 ();
350. lcdData = hourtens;
351. lcdOut ();
352. lcdData = hourunits;
353. lcdOut ();
354. lcdData = 0x3A;
355. lcdOut ();
356. lcdData = mintens;
```

```
357. lcdOut ();
358. lcdData = minunits;
359. lcdOut ();
360. lcdData = 0x3A;
361. lcdOut ();
362. lcdData = sectens;
363. lcdOut ();
364. lcdData = secunits;
365. lcdOut ();
366. lcdData = 0xA0;
367. lcdOut ();
368. }
369. }
370. }
```

Lines 7 to 121 can be removed and used to create a header file for the 4-bit LCD on PORTB. However, lines 23 to 32 would have to be excluded since they define which input the three buttons are connected to and the macros for the days of the week. This means the following instructions can be used to create a header file named 4bitLCDPortb.h that can be made global so that it can be used on all projects that use the same type of LCD connected to PORTB. Note that it must be used in a 4-bit operation and with the RS pin connected to RB4 and the E pin connected to RB5.

The header file is shown in Listing 3-3.

Listing 3-3. The LCD Header File

```
1. /*This is a header file to set up the LCD
2. It will use just 4 bits and be connected to PORTB
3. The RS pin is connected to RB4
4. The E pin is connected to RB5
5. Written by Mr H. H. Ward dated 02/01/2019*/
```

```
 6. //some definitions
 7. #define firstbyte      0b00110011
 8. #define secondbyte     0b00110011
 9. #define fourBitOp     0b00110010
10. #define twoLines      0b00101100
11. #define incPosition    0b00000110
12. #define cursorNoBlink  0b00001100
13. #define clearScreen    0b00000001
14. #define returnHome     0b00000010
15. #define lineTwo        0b11000000
16. #define doBlink        0b00001111
17. #define shiftLeft      0b00010000
18. #define shiftRight     0b00010100
19. #define shdisright     0b00011100
20. #define lcdPort        PORTB
21. #define eBit           PORTBbits.RB5
22. #define RSpin          PORTBbits.RB4
23. //some variables
24. unsigned char n, lcdData, lcdTempData, rsLine;
25. char str[80];
26. char lcdInitialise [8] =
27. {
28. firstbyte,
29. secondbyte,
30. fourBitOp,
31. twoLines,
32. incPosition,
33. cursorNoBlink,
34. clearScreen,
35. returnHome,
36. };
```

```
37. //some subroutines
38. void sendData ()
39. {
40. lcdTempData = (lcdTempData << 4 | lcdTempData >>4);
41. lcdData = lcdTempData & 0x0F;
42. lcdData = lcdData | rsLine;
43. lcdPort = lcdData;
44. eBit = 1;
45. eBit = 0;
46. TMRO = 0; while (TMRO < 20);
47. }
48. void lcdOut ()
49. {
50. lcdTempData = lcdData;
51. sendData ();
52. sendData ();
53. }
54. void setUpTheLCD ()
55. {
56. TMRO = 0; while (TMRO <255);
57. n = 0;
58. rsLine = 0X00;
59. while (n < 8)
60. {
61. lcdData = lcdInitialise [n];
62. lcdOut ();
63. n ++;
64. }
65. rsLine = 0x10;
66. }
```

```
67. void line2 ()
68. {
69. rsLine = 0X00;
70. lcdData = lineTwo;
71. lcdOut ();
72. rsLine = 0x10;
73. }
74. void clearTheScreen ()
75. {
76. rsLine = 0X00;
77. lcdData = clearScreen;
78. lcdOut ();
79. rsLine = 0x10;
80. }
81. void sendcursorhome ()
82. {
83. rsLine = 0X00;
84. lcdData = returnHome;
85. lcdOut ();
86. rsLine = 0x10;
87. }
88. void shiftcurleft ( unsigned char l)
89. {
90. for (n = 0; n < l; n ++)
91. {
92. rsLine = 0X00;
93. lcdData = shiftLeft;
94. lcdOut ();
95. rsLine = 0x10;
96. }
97. }
```

```
98. void shiftcurright (unsigned char r)
99. {
100. for (n = 0; n < r; n ++)
101. {
102. rsLine = 0X00;
103. lcdData = shdisright;
104. lcdOut ();
105. rsLine = 0x10;
106. }
107. }
```

Analysis of the Header File for the LCD

There two types of information that can be sent to the LCD:

- The ASCII (American Standard Code for Information Interchange) code for all of the characters that can be displayed on the LCD; call this data.

- The instructions that set up the display on the LCD

Lines 6 to 19 create some meaningful phrases to represent the 8-bit binary numbers that are the respective instructions for controlling the LCD. For example, the 8-bit binary number for the instruction to send the cursor to the start of the second line on the display is 0b11000000.

This is defined as lineTwo on line 15 of the program listing. Note the 0b at the beginning is to show it is a binary number.

Line 20: #define lcdPort PORTB

This shows that the LCD is connected to PORTB. The way it works is that whenever the compiler sees lcdPort in the program, it knows to read this as being PORTB.

One advantage of creating these definitions is it is easy to accommodate physically connecting the LCD to another port such as PORTD. You need only make the change in the program at this definition (i.e. #define lcdPort PORTD).

Line 21: eBit PORTBbits.RB5

This does the same but with the phrase eBit. Where you write eBit in the program the compiler knows you mean bit5 of PORTB.

The eBit is a pin on the LCD that must be sent high then low, with no delay in between, every time some information, be it data to be displayed or an instruction, is sent to the LCD. This is to make the firmware inside the LCD aware that new information has been sent to the LCD and it should deal with the new information.

Line 22: #define RSpin PORTBbits.RB4

This does the same for RSpin. It is the logic on this pin that the firmware, inside the LCD, uses to distinguish if the new information is an instruction or data. If this RSpin is set to a logic 0, then the new information is an instruction. If RSpin is set to a logic 1, then the new information is simply data to be displayed on the LCD.

Line 23: // some variables

This is just a useful way of splitting the listing up.

Line 24: unsigned char n, lcdData, lcdTempData, rsLine,.

Here you are setting up some memory locations and giving them a useful names. They are 8-bit memory locations as defined by the type char, and all 8 bits are used to represent their value as defined by the term unsigned. This means that they can hold a value from 0 to 255.

You are using the term unsigned as with all microprocessor-based systems you use signed number representation. This is a method by which you use the MSB (most significant bit), Bit7 in this case, to show whether the number is positive or negative. For positive numbers, the MSB will be a logic 0; for negative numbers, the MSB will be a logic 1. If you are using signed number representation, it means the MSB can't be used to make up the value stored in the variable. This means a signed char, which is simply referred to as a char, can hold a value from -127 to +127 and not go to 255. So if you want to be able to store a value up to 255, you must use an unsigned char, as you are doing here.

Line 25: char str[80];

Here you are creating an array that has 80 memory locations. This will be used with the writeString subroutine.

Line 26: char lcdInitialise [8] =

This creates a second array that has 8 memory locations. However, you use the = sign since the following lines will state what is stored in each of the memory locations. This array is used in setting up the LCD (i.e. it is used by the setUpTheLCD subroutine).

Line 27: {

This is the opening curly bracket of the confines of this program instruction to fill the array.

Line 28: firstbyte,

This is the phrase for the 8-bit number 0b00110011. It is the first instruction that has to be sent to the LCD.

Line 29: secondbyte,

This is a repeat of the firstbyte and it has to be sent to the LCD next.

Line 30: fourBitOp,

This phrase represents the binary number 0b00110010. It is used to put the LCD into 4-bit mode, not 8-bit mode. It means the information is sent to the LCD in two 4-bit chunks. Four bits is normally referred to as a nibble.

Line 31: twoLines,

This represent the binary number 0b00101100. It sets the LCD up to use two lines of characters.

Line 32: incPosition,

This represent the binary number 0b00000110. It sets the LCD up to increment the position of the cursor (i.e. move it one place to the right) after each character has been sent to the LCD.

Line 33: cursorNoBlink,

This represent the binary number 0b00001100. It sets the LCD up to not display the cursor as a blinking black rectangle.

Line 34: clearScreen,

This represent the binary number 0b00000001. It ensure the screen is cleared of all characters.

Line 35: returnHome,

This represent the binary number 0b00000010. It ensures the cursor is sent to the start of the first line on the LCD.

Line 36: };

This is the closing bracket of this array. Note there is a semicolon after the bracket. This is because this is an instruction. Note also the phrases inside the curly brackets have a comma after them. This is because they make up a list and they are not individual instructions.

Line 37: // some subroutines

This is simply to split the listing up.

Line 38: void sendData ()

This is subroutine to send information, be it data or instructions, to the LCD.

Line 39: {

The opening curly bracket of the subroutine.

Line 40: lcdTempData = (lcdTempData << 4 | lcdTempData >>4);

To understand this instruction, you need to appreciate that 8 bits is termed a byte. Also, the 8 bits can be split into two 4-bit parts, which are termed a nibble. The first 4 bits, or nibble, are Bits 0, 1, 2, and 3 and they are termed the low nibble and the other four bits are termed the high nibble. What this instruction will do is swap over the two nibbles stored in the variable lcdTempData. This is because you are using the LCD in 4-bit mode and you want to send the high nibble first. However, it is Bits 0, 1, 2, and 3, the low nibble of PORTB, that are connected to the LCD data in lines.

This means the 8 bits of information you want to send to the LCD must be sent in two nibbles. The high nibble must be sent first, followed by the low nibble. In this instruction, you make the high nibble move into Bits 0, 1, 2, and 3 ready to send this first to the LCD. Note that the low nibble will have moved to Bits 4, 5, 6, and 7.

Line 41: lcdData = lcdTempData & 0x0F;

This instruction is performing a bit logical AND with the data in lcdTempData and the number 0X0F. 0X0F in binary is 00001111. The logical AND will result in a logic 1 if the two bits being ANDed are both logic 1. For example, if the 8 bits in lcdTempData are 11001010, then the instruction will do the following:

125

$$\begin{array}{rl} \text{lcdTempData} & 11001010 \\ \text{AND with 0X0F} & \underline{00001111} \\ \text{Result} & 00001010 \end{array}$$

This is because only Bits 1 and 3 are logic 1 in both binary numbers.

What this instruction does is make sure only the first four bits of lcdTempData are copied into lcdData; the high nibble in lcdData will all be at a logic 0. This gets the variable lcdData ready to be sent to the LCD.

This type of operation is termed bit masking since you can "mask out" bits you are not interested in.

Line 42:   lcdData = lcdData | rsLine;

This is a very complicated instruction. To explain how it achieves its purpose. let's consider the situation whereby the data in the variable lcdData is the result detailed in the previous instruction. In other words, the data in lcdData is

00001010

The first four bits, the 1010, are the information that will go to the data pins of the LCD. However, Bit4 of the 8 bits in lcdData will also be sent, via PORTB, to the RS pin on the LCD. This is done in line 43.

Remember that you defined the RSpin to be PORTBbits.RB4 on line 22. The logic on this pin is used to tell the LCD what type of information this is: instruction or data. If the logic on Bit4 is a logic 0, then the information will be an instruction to control the LCD. If the logic on Bit4 is a logic 1, then the information will be data to be displayed on the LCD screen.

This then means you will have to now modify Bit4 of the variable lcdData, which at present is a logic 0, accordingly. The way you do this is perform a logic OR on each bit of lcdData with the 8 bits in the variable rsline. However, before you perform the bit OR, you would have changed

Bit4 of the rsline accordingly (i.e. making it a logic 0 if the information is an instruction, or a logic 1 if the information is simply data). The remaining bits in the variable rsline will be kept at logic 0.

In this way, Bit4 of the rsline variable will be used to tell the LCD if the current information being sent to the LCD is an instruction or data. The problem is that it is Bit4 of PORTB that is connected to the RS pin of the LCD, not Bit4 of the variable rsline. The problem is therefore how do you get Bit4 of PORTB to mimic what is on Bit4 of the variable rsline?

One solution is to perform a logical OR with the two bits. You should appreciate that after the logical AND operation done on line 41, Bit4 of the lcdData will always be a logic 0. If you now perform the logic OR operation with Bit4 of lcdData with Bit4 of the rsline variable, as you do in line 42, then Bit4 of lcdData will become a copy of Bit4 of rsline. The examples shown in Table 3-1 should help explain this.

Table 3-1. *The Logical OR Operation on Bit4 of lcdData and rsline*

Example 1	
Bit4 lcdDat	0
Bit4 Rsline	0
OR Result	**0**
Example 2	
Bit4 lcdDat	0
Bit4 Rsline	1
OR Result	**1**

Note the result of the logical OR operation is what Bit4 of the variable lcdData will be. This should show that the logic in Bit4 of the lcdData after the logical OR instruction of line 42 will be a copy of what Bit4 of the variable rsline is.

In this way, you can set Bit4 of the lcdData by previously setting Bit4 of the rsline variable. You will see that in line 58 you load the variable rsline with 0X00. This will make bit4 a logic 0 ready to send out instructions to the LCD.

Note that the symbol | in C represents the logical bit OR operation.

Line 43: lcdPort = lcdData;

This simply makes a copy of what is in lcdData in lcdPort. However, lcdPort is simply PORTB. The LCD is connected to PORTB and so this instruction sends the information to the LCD. This means the correct nibble will be sent to the LCD and also the appropriate logic on the RS pin.

Line 44: eBit = 1;

This sends eBit, which is Bit5 of PORTB to a logic 1.

Line 45: eBit = 0;

This sets eBit to a logic 0. This means eBit on the LCD goes high, then low. This is to tell the LCD that the information at its input has changed and it should deal with it.

Line 46: TMR0 = 0; while (TMR0 < 20);

There are two instructions here. The first, TMR0 = 0;, simply loads the TMR0 with the value 0. The TMR0 is a register that stores the current value Timer0 has counted to. This is to make sure you start counting from 0. The second instruction, while (TMR0 < 20);, makes the micro do nothing until the value in the TMR0 register becomes greater than 20. This simply creates a delay of $20 \times 128\mu s = 2.56ms$.

This is needed to allow the LCD time to deal with the information that has just been sent to it.

Line 47: }

This is the closing curly bracket of the sendData subroutine.

Line 48: void lcdOut ()

This is a subroutine to get the information ready to send to the LCD and then call the sendData subroutine.

Line 49: {

The opening curly bracket of the lcdOut subroutine.

Line 50: lcdTempData = lcdData;

This loads a copy of what is in the variable lcdData into the variable lcdTempData. This is to get this ready to have its nibbles swapped in the sendData subroutine.

Note if a subroutine is going to use another subroutine, in what's termed nested subroutines, the subroutine the current subroutine will use must be listed before (i.e. above) this one in your program listing.

Line 51: sendData ();

This calls the subroutine sendData for the first time. It sends the high nibble of what's in lcdTempData. Note that the 8 bits will be swapped in this subroutine in line 40.

Line 52: sendData ();

This calls the subroutine sendData for the second time. This sends the low nibble of what's in lcdTempData. Note that the 8 bits will be swapped in this subroutine in line 40.

Line 53: }

This is the closing bracket of the lcdOut subroutine.

Line 54:   void setUpTheLCD ()

This is the subroutine to set up the LCD. This will send the instructions to configure the LCD as you want to use it.

Line 55: {

This is the opening curly bracket of the setUpTheLCD subroutine.

Line 56: TMR0 = 0; while (TMR0 <255);

This is two instructions and they create a 32ms delay. It is important to wait this minimum time before sending any information to the LCD to allow the internal circuitry of the LCD to settle down.

Line 57: n = 0;

This loads the value of 0 into the variable n ready for the while loop on line 59.

Line 58: rsline = 0X00;

This loads 0 into the variable rsline. This makes sure that Bit4 of rsline is at logic 0. This is getting the variable rsline ready for the logical OR operation described on line 42. Note that a logic 0 means the information going to the LCD is an instruction.

Line 59: while (n < 8)

This sets up a while test type loop. While the value in n is less than 8, the result of the test is true. Remember you loaded the value 0 into n in line 57.

While the result of the test is true, the micro will carry out the instructions inside the following curly brackets.

Line 60: {

The opening curly bracket of the while loop.

Line 61: lcdData = lcdInitialise [n];

This loads the variable lcdData with the data stored in the location of the lcdInitialise array identified by the variable [n] inside the square bracket. The current value of the variable n is 0. This means that the contents of the first location in the array will be copied into the variable lcdData. This means that the data of the firstByte will be loaded into the variable lcdData. This is now ready to be sent to the LCD.

Line 62: lcdOut ();

This calls the subroutine lcdOut to send the information to the LCD.

Line 63: n ++;

This increments the value stored in the variable n. This gets it ready for the micro to carry out the while test on line 59.

Lines 59 to 64 are used to send the first eight instructions that are stored in the array lcdInitialise to the LCD.

Line 64: }

This is the closing curly bracket of the while loop on line 59.

Line 65: rsline = 0X10;

This loads the following binary number into the variable rsline: 00010000. This ensures that Bit4, which will eventually be sent to the RS pin on the LCD, is a logic 1. This is to tell the LCD that the next information to be sent to the LCD is data to be displayed.

As you send data to be displayed to the LCD more often than you send instructions, it is common sense to make Bit4 of the variable rsline a logic 1 as its default setting.

Line 66: }

This is the closing curly bracket of the lcdOut subroutine on line 48.

Line 67: void line2 ()

This is a subroutine that will send to the LCD the instruction to send the cursor to the start of line two on the display.

Line 68: {

This is the opening bracket of the subroutine.

Line 69: rsLine = 0X00;

This makes Bit4 of the rsline a logic 0. This is because the program will be sending an instruction to the LCD next.

Line 70: lcdData = lineTwo;

This loads the instruction, to get the LCD to move the cursor to the start of line two on the LCD, into the variable lcdData ready to be sent out to the LCD.

Line 71: lcdOut ();

This calls the subroutine to start the process of sending the instruction to the LCD.

Line 72: rsline = 0X10;

This sets Bit4 of the rsline back to a logic 1 since the next information to be sent to the LCD will most likely be data to be displayed.

Line 73: }

This is the closing curly bracket of the line2 subroutine from line 67.

Lines 74 to 80 do the same but for the instruction clearTheScreen, which will clear the LCD screen of all data and send the cursor to the start of the LCD screen.

Lines 81 to 87 do the same but with the instruction to returnhome. This will simply send the cursor back to the start of the LCD screen but without clearing any of the data from the screen.

Lines 88 to 97 send the instruction to shift the cursor a number of places to the left. The number of places the cursor moves is controlled by the local variable l sent up to the subroutine when the subroutine is called from the main program.

Lines 98 to 107 do the same but shift the cursor a specified number of places to the right. Note in both shifting subroutines any data that the cursor passes over is left on the display.

The above analysis hopefully explains what the instructions do. This header file can now be used in all projects that use the LCD connected to PORTB and in 4-bit mode.

There is a more detailed description of how the LCD is controlled and how it works in my first book, *C Programming for the PIC Microcontroller*.

The Analysis of Listing 3-2

I will now return to the full listing for the 24-hour clock and day program for the LCD. This is shown in Listing 3-2.

Lines 26 to 32 define how you display the days of the week.

Line 26: #define Mon   lcdData = 0x4D; lcdOut (); lcdData = 0x6F; lcdOut (); lcdData = 0x6E; lcdOut ();

This is a very powerful use of the #define operation of the MPLABX compiler. The phrase that is being defined here is Mon (for Monday). The information that follows is really three sets of two instructions, one set for each character in the phrase "Mon." To help explain what you are doing here, you should appreciate that the LCD will display the time in hours, minutes, and seconds but it will also display the current day of the week in terms of Mon, Tue, Wed, etc. Each day of the week will be displayed with three characters.

Mon is made up of three characters as follows:

- M, which has the ASCII code of 4D

- O, which has the ASCII code of 6F

- N, which has the ASCII code of 6E

See the ASCII table in Appendix 5.

To send these characters to the LCD, you must load the variable lcdData with the ASCII for the character. Then you must call the subroutine lcdOut ();. Therefore to send the character M, you must do

lcdData = 0x4D; lcdOut ();

The other two characters must follow.

This means you are using the #define to tell the compiler that whenever you have written the phrase Mon, it knows you are actually writing the three sets of two instructions. This is sometimes referred to as a macro and it is a very good way of giving meaning to a series of instructions and inserting them into you program in a succinct and appropriate manner.

Lines 27 to 32 repeat the same process for the remaining days of the weeks.

The lines from 1 to 121 have been analyzed already since they make up the header file we just went through. Therefore I will move on to line 122.

Line 122: unsigned char n, secunits = 0X30, sectens = 0X30, minunits = 0X30, mintens = 0X30, hourunits = 0X30, hourtens = 0X30;

These are variables used to store important values. Note that all the variables except n have been loaded with the initial value of 0X30. This is the ASCII for the character 0. See the ASCII table in Appendix 5.

Line 123: void writeString (const char *words)

This is the start of the `writeString` subroutine. It allows you to send a string of characters that must be included in the call to the subroutine every time it is called, to the LCD. The mechanics of this subroutine were written by someone else; I just added my variable labels such as `lcdData` and the subroutine call `lcdOut ()`. It's what is termed open source and thus freely available for programmers to use in their programs.

The basic concept is that an array of 80 memory locations has been set aside to store the characters. A variable number of the array's memory locations are filled when the subroutine is called and each data in those locations is sent to the LCD one at a time.

The array that is used is the one declared on line 35 of Listing 3-2. The array is `char str[80]` (i.e. of type char and having 80 memory locations created one after the other).

The instruction uses the local pointer *word created in the instruction on line 123. The asterix (*) declares the variable `word` to be a special pointer in that the contents of the variable will actually be the address of a location in the array.

Line 124: {

This is simply the opening curly bracket of the subroutine.

Line 125: while (*words)

This is a very special test. Here is my interpretation of how this `while` works. I am fairly confident it is correct as it makes sense to me. I say this just in case someone can correct me.

This test will be true as long as the contents of the address the pointer *words is pointing to is not the "null" character. Note this "null" character is the last character to be sent up to the subroutine when the main program calls it. While the test is true, the micro must carry out the instructions detailed between the following curly brackets.

Line 126: {

The opening curly bracket.

Line 127:   lcdData = *words;

This loads the variable lcdData with the information in the address that the pointer *words is pointing to. This would be, at this time in the loop, the first location in the array str [80] that was filled when the subroutine was called.

Line 128: lcdOut ();

This calls the subroutine to start the process of sending the data in lcdData to the LCD.

Line 129: *words ++;

This increments the contents of the word pointer. This means it will be pointing to the next memory location in the array.

Line 130: }

This is the closing bracket of the while loop.

Line 131: }

This is the closing bracket of the subroutine. This subroutine will cycle through the instructions until the data in the memory location pointed to by the pointer *words (i.e. the location in that array is the null character). At that point, the micro has completed sending the characters to the screen identified when the subroutine was called. The micro can then return back to the main loop of the program.

Line 132: void debounce ()

This is the start of a subroutine to deal with the bouncing of a switch. This was analyzed in Chapter 2.

Line 137:   // The main program

This is just to split the listing up.

Line 138: void main ()

This is the start of the main loop.

Line 139:   {

This is the opening curly bracket of the main loop.

Line 140: initialise ();

This calls the subroutine that is in the header file PICSetUp.h. This simply sets the PIC up as you want. This is detailed in the PICSetUp.h header file in Chapter 1.

Line 141: setUpTheLCD ();

This calls the subroutine to set up the LCD.

Line 142: clearTheScreen ();

This calls the subroutine to clear the LCD and send the cursor to the start of the first line.

Line 143: while (1)

This sets up the forever loop so that the micro does not carry out the instructions in lines 140, 141, and 142 again.

Line 144: {

This is the opening curly bracket of the forever loop.

Line 145: writeSring ("Set The Day");

This calls the subroutine to send the string of characters written between the " " (quotation marks) inside the bracket. Note this will actually store the ASCII code for the characters in the array char str[80].

Line 146: line2 ();

This calls the subroutine to send the cursor to the start of line two on the LCD.

Line 147: while (!setbutton)

This test to see if the logic on setbutton, which is on bit0 of PORTA, is at logic 0. If it is, the test is true and the micro must carry out the instructions listed between the following curly brackets.

If the logic on bit0 of PORTA is logic 1, then the test is untrue and the micro must go to the next instruction on line 193.

Line 148: {

This the opening curly bracket of the while loop.

Line 149: if (incbutton) debounce ();

If the incbutton goes high, this call the debounce subroutine to wait the 13ms to allow the voltage at the input to settle down.

Line 150: if (incbutton) daynumber ++;

If the logic on the input is still high, this increments the value of the variable daynumber.

This should be true because in normal use it would take a person longer then 13ms to release the button.

Line 151: while (incbutton);

This makes the micro wait until the logic at the input returns to logic 0 (i.e. the user lets go of the button). In more critical situations, you may have to consider the bounce of the switch as you let go of the button.

Line 152 to 154 do the same as above except with the decrement button and you decrement the value stored in daynumber.

Line 155: if (daynumber == 1)

This test is asking if the value in the variable daynumber is equal to 1. If so, the test is true and the micro must carry out the instruction listed between the following curly brackets.

Line 156: {

The opening curly bracket for this test.

Line 157: Mon;

This is using the definition of the phrase Mon, which is on line 26. This makes the micro send the three characters for Mon to the LCD.

Line 158: Line2 ();

This calls the subroutine to move the cursor to the start of line two on the LCD.

Line 159:   }

This is the closing bracket of the if statement for displaying Mon.

Lines 160 to 189 perform the same functions but for the remaining days of the week. In this way, the user can select which day of the week the clock can start counting from.

Line 190:   if (daynumber == 8) daynumber = 1;

This is to correct the situation that will happen if you increment daynumber from 7 to 8. There are only 7 days in the week. If you try to increment daynumber to 8, this test will become true and the instruction will force daynumber to be loaded with 1.

Line 191: if (daynumber == 0) daynumber = 1;

This does the same if you try to decrement daynumber from 1 to 0.

Line 192: }

This is the closing bracket of the while (!setbutton) loop started on line 147.

Line 193: debounce ();

This calls the debounce subroutine. You need this because if the micro is at this instruction of the program, someone has pressed the setbutton and the voltage at that pin will be bouncing.

Line 194: while (setbutton);

This makes the micro wait until the logic at the setbutton input has gone low. This makes the micro wait until the user has released the setbutton.

As an exercise, try commenting out lines 194 and 195 and see what happens.

Then comment out just line 194.

By comment out, I mean you should simply insert two forward slashes (//) in front of each line.

Lines 195 to 200 get the display ready to allow the user to set the hours on the display.

Line 201: lcdData = 0X3A;

This loads the variable with the ASCII for the character the colon (:).

Line 202: lcdOut ();

This calls the subroutine lcdOut to start the process of displaying the semicolon on the LCD.

Lines 203 to 206 display the two variables for hourTens and hourUnits, which currently both have the value 0X30, which is the ASCII for 0.

Line 207: shiftcurleft (1);

This calls the subroutine to shift the cursor one place to the left. This will place the cursor under the 0 for the hourUnits display.

Lines 208 to 210 deal with the increment button being pressed.

Line 211: if (hourtens == 0X3A)

This tests to see if the variable hourtens has gone to 0X3A. This will happen if the variable has been incremented from 0X39 (i.e. the ASCII for 9). See the ASCII table in Appendix 5. Note that 0X3A is the hex for the colon and it means you have incremented too far. Really the hourtens value should not go above 2 in a normal setting.

Line 212: {

This is the opening curly brackets of the instructions that must be carried out if the above test is true.

Line 213: hourunits = 0X30;

This loads the variable hourunits with 0X30, which is the ASCII for 0.

Line 214: hourtens ++;

This simply increments the variable hourtens.

Line 215: }

This is the closing bracket of the if on line 211.

Line 216: if (hourtentens == 0X32 & hourunits == 0X34)

This tests to see if the current increment has resulted in the hours getting ready to display 24. This should not happen since this is midnight and the time should change to 00:00:00.

Line 217: {

This is the opening curly bracket of this if statement.

Line 218: hourtens = 0X30;

This loads the variable hourtens with 0X30, the ASCII for 0.

Line 219: hourunits = 0X30;

This loads the variable hourunits with 0X30, the ASCII for 0.

Line 220: }

This is the closing curly bracket for the if statement on line 216.

Line 221: if (decbutton) debounce ();

This tests to see if the decbutton has been pressed. If it has, the program calls the debounce subroutine.

Line 222: if (decbutton)

This tests to see if it really was pressed.

Line 223: {

This is the opening curly bracket to enclose the instructions the program must do if the decbutton was pressed.

Line 224: if (hourunits == 0X30)

This tests to see of the variable hourunits is already at 0.

Line 225: {

This is the opening curly bracket of what to do if the above test is true.

Line 226: hourunits = 0X39;

This loads hourunits with the value 0X39, which is the ASCII for 9.

Line 227: hourtens --;

This decrements the contents of the variable hourtens.

Line 228: }

This is the closing curly bracket of the if statement on line 224.

Line 229: else hourunits --;

This is what to do if hourunits did not have the data 0X30 in it at the time of decrementing.

Line 230: }

This is the closing curly bracket of the if statement on line 222.

Line 231: while (decbutton);

This waits until the logic on the input of the decbutton has gone low.

Line 232: if (setbutton) debounce ();

This tests to see if the setbutton has been pressed and, if it has, calls the debounce subroutine.

Line 233: if (setbutton) goto minset;

This tests to see if setbutton was really pressed, and if it was, makes the micro jump to the label minset. This is at line 235.

Line 234:   }

This is the closing bracket of Lines 235 to 269. They perform the same increments and decrements but this deals with mintens and minunits.

Line 270: clearTheScreen ();

This clears all data from the LCD and sends the cursor to the start of the first line ready to display the time and day.

Line 271 writeSring ("The Time/Day is ");

This calls the subroutine writeString to start the process of displaying the characters between the two quotation marks (" ").

Line 272: lcdData 0XA0;

This loads the data 0XA0, which is the ASCII for a space, into the variable lcdData ready to be sent to the LCD.

Line 273: lcdOut ();

This calls the subroutine lcdOut to start the process of sending the data to the LCD.

Line 274: while (1)

This is the forever loop.

Line 275: {

This is the opening curly bracket of the forever loop.

Lines 276 to 310 test to determine what value is in the daynumber so that the program can display the correct characters for the current day of the week that has been set in the preceding section of the program.

Lines 311 to 315 create a one-second delay.

Lines 316 to 348 increment the secunits and all the other variables depending upon their current values. This is much the same as the operation described in the increments due to the incbutton being pressed.

Line 349 to the end of the listing sends the correct characters to the LCD to display the current time.

Figure 3-3 show the 24-hour clock running on a practical LCD display.

Figure 3-3. *The 24-hour clock on the LCD display*

Improvements for the 24-Hour Clock LCD Program

There are two sections of Listing 3-2 that are repeated in exactly the same way. They are the sections of program that include lines 154 to 189 and lines 276 to 310. These 36 lines of programming are carried out in exactly the same way, so you should create a subroutine that has the 36 lines written just once. The program should call the subroutines at the two relevant points in the main program.

I have created the subroutine named `displayday` using the following instructions:

```
void displayday ()
{
  if (daynumber == 1)
{
```

```
Mon;
line2 ();
}
if (daynumber == 2)
{
Tue;
line2 ();
}
if (daynumber == 3)
{
Wed;
line2 ();
}
if (daynumber == 4)
{
Thur;
line2 ();
}
if (daynumber == 5)
{
Fri;
line2 ();
}
if (daynumber == 6)
{
Sat;
line2 ();
}
if (daynumber == 7)
{
Sun;
```

```
line2 ();
}
}
```

The main program will call this subroutine at the appropriate point using the following instruction:

```
displayday ();
```

The first call will be at line 154 and the second call will be at what was line 276, so after

```
while (1)
{
```

but before

```
for (n = 0, n <29; n ++)
```

I hope you can appreciate and make the change as I want to move onto the second improvement. It is not essential that you do this, but I want to show you how you can be more efficient with your programs if you use subroutines. Remember that memory is the thief of all programmers and every instruction takes up memory.

Using Switch and Case Keywords

I am not fully convinced that this next change is an improvement but it is an alternative method for performing this kind of action and I want to show you how this switch and case function works.

When you are using multiple if statements, as you are in this new subroutine, an alternative method of achieving the same results is to use the switch and case keywords.

The simplest way to explain how this works is to list the instructions and then analyze them. In this example, you will replace the multiple if statements in the subroutine displayday with the switch and case statements. Listing 3-4 shows the new subroutine using these new keywords.

Listing 3-4. Using the Switch and Case Statements

```
1. void displayday ()
2. {
3. switch (daynumber)
              1. {
                     a. case 1 :
                     b. {
                     c. Mon;
                     d. line2 ();
                     e. }
                     f. break;
                     g. case 2:
                     h. {
                     i. Tue;
                     j. line2 ();
                     k. }
                     l. break;
                     m. case 3:
                     n. {
                     o. Wed;
                     p. line2 ();
                     q. }
                     r. break;
                     s. case 4:
                     t. {
                     u. Thur;
```

```
      v. line2 ();
      w. }
      x. break;
      y. case 5:
      z. {
     aa. Fri;
     bb. line2 ();
     cc. }
     dd. break;
     ee. case 6:
     ff. {
     gg. Sat;
     hh. line2 ();
     ii. }
     jj. break;
     kk. case 7:
     ll. {
     mm. Sun;
     nn. line2 ();
     oo. }
     pp. break;
  2. }
3. }
```

Analysis of the New Subroutine

Lines 1 and 2 are the normal way of creating a subroutine.

Line 3: switch (daynumber)

This is the start of the switch instruction. It is basically forcing the micro to switch or choose between some different options defined using the case keyword.

It works similar to a subroutine in that the switch is expected the main program to pass a value identifying which case the micro should switch to.

In this example, the number will be what is in the variable daynumber. Note the value in this variable is set in the main program using the inc and dec buttons.

The Indented Line 1: {

This is the opening curly bracket of the switch statement.

Line a: case 1:

This is the first choice the switch asks the micro to consider. If the value in the variable daynumber is 1, then the micro will carry out the instructions for this case.

Line b: {

This is the opening curly brackets of case 1.

Line c: Mon;

This tells the micro to carry out the three instructions defined by the definition for Mon earlier in the program.

This sends the three characters M, o, and n to the LCD.

Line d: line2 ();

This calls the subroutine to send the cursor to the start of the second line on the LCD.

Line e: }

This is the closing curly bracket of the case 1 routine.

Line f: break;

This is a keyword that forces the micro to break away from the subroutine at this point in the instructions.

The micro will now return to the main program at the instruction one after the point at which it called the subroutine.

The lines g to pp detail the instructions for the other case values.

In this way, the micro can be made to choose what instructions it must carry out depending on a value that is submitted to the switch statement. The switch statements do not have to be put into a subroutine as shown here. They can be inserted in the section of program where the switch needs to be carried out. They are only put into a subroutine here because the instructions for the switch are exactly the same at the two sections they would have gone into in the main program.

Note that the subroutine has to be written in the IDE before the main loop since it is from within the main loop that the subroutine is called.

Synopsis

In this chapter, you learned about the seven-segment display and the LCD. You studied how to use the displays to create a 24-hour clock. You learned about the following C programming techniques:

- Arrays and pointers

- Using the #define statement to create a macro

- Switch and case statements

In the next chapter, you will look at why you might want to create a square wave and then look at using the CCP module to create a square wave.

CHAPTER 4

Creating a Square Wave

In this chapter, you are going to look at creating a square wave on one of the CCP outputs.

After reading this chapter, you should understand what the CCP module is. You should also appreciate why you would want to create a square wave output and how to use the PWM aspect of the CCP module to create a square wave.

In Chapter 6, you will look at an alternative approach to creating a square wave. The approach will involve using the compare aspect of the CCP module and using interrupts.

Why Create a Square Wave?

To answer this question, you are going to look at the two uses of a square wave. The first is in producing musical notes and the second is in setting the speed of a DC motor.

© Hubert Henry Ward 2020
H. H. Ward, *Intermediate C Programming for the PIC Microcontroller*,
https://doi.org/10.1007/978-1-4842-6068-5_4

Musical Notes

To appreciate what this has to do with creating a square wave, you have to understand how we humans distinguish musical notes from each other. Indeed, it is really how we distinguish all of the different sounds around us. Each note, or sound, has its own particular frequency or combination of frequencies. Table 4-1 lists the frequency of some of the more important musical notes. A more complete list of the frequency of the musical notes is given in Appendix 8.

Table 4-1. *The Frequency of the More Common Musical Notes*

Note	Frequency (Hz)	Wavelength (cm)
G_3	196.00	176.02
$G^\#_3/A^b_3$	207.65	166.14
A_3	220.00	156.82
$A^\#_3/B^b_3$	233.08	148.02
B_3	246.94	139.71
C_4	261.63	131.87
$C^\#_4/D^b_4$	277.18	124.47
D_4	293.66	117.48
$D^\#_4/E^b_4$	311.13	110.89
E_4	329.63	104.66
F_4	349.23	98.79
$F^\#_4/G^b_4$	369.99	93.24
G_4	392.00	88.01

C4 is the note that is more commonly known as middle C.

Note that the velocity at which sound travels through the air is 343m/s and the wavelength (λ) is related to frequency and velocity using the standard expression shown in Equation 4-1:

$$\lambda = \frac{v}{f} \qquad \textbf{(Equation 4-1)}$$

The term wavelength relates to the distance the sound travels to complete one full cycle of the signal or sound.

Knowing that the note G3 has a frequency of 196Hz, (i.e. 196 cycles in one second), then the wavelength of note G3 is shown in Equation 4-2:

$$\lambda = \frac{343}{196} = 1.75m \text{ or } 175cm \qquad \textbf{(Equation 4-2)}$$

Exercise 4.1

The answers to the exercises are at the end of the chapter. In this exercise, you should calculate the wavelength of the following frequencies, knowing that the velocity at which they travel is the velocity of sound:

Frequency = 48.999Hz

Frequency = 1046.502Hz

Frequency = 2,200Hz

If you could produce a signal at any of the frequencies in Table 4-1, then you could produce the respective musical note. The signal does not have to be a perfect sinusoidal waveform, but it would be better if it was.

In this way then, if you could get the PIC to produce a square wave at the correct frequencies, you could produce a series of musical notes. This is what you will do in the next chapter: you will produce a simple musical keyboard with eight notes.

The Speed of the Simple DC Motor

With respect to the control of a DC motor we are talking about setting the speed of the motor. This does not mean you will be controlling the speed because the load varies. You will simply be setting the speed of the motor. Controlling the speed (i.e. ensuring the speed stays the same irrespective of the load applied to the motor) is a whole different ballgame. Speed control is a book by itself.

The speed of the motor depends upon the voltage that is applied to that motor. Therefore, if you can vary the voltage applied to the motor, you can vary the speed of the motor.

Pulse Width Modulation

Pulse width modulation (PWM) is a very useful method of varying a DC voltage supply. To appreciate what PWM is, and what pulse width you are modulating, it's useful to look at a typical DC square wave. This is shown in Figure 4-1.

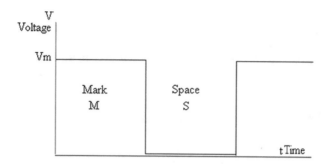

Figure 4-1. *A typical square wave*

The wave form, shown in Figure 4-1, is DC as the voltage never changes polarity. In this case, it is always positive. The wave form has what is termed a 50/50 duty cycle since the up time, or on time, named "mark" time, is the same as the down time, or off time, named "space" time. The mark time (M), or up time, is the pulse that is referred to in PWM. The width is the length of time that the mark, or pulse, extends for. The modulation in PWM refers to the fact that you vary the length of time that the mark extends for (i.e. PWM). Note that since the total time (i.e. the mark time plus the space time, known as the periodic time, T) does not vary, then as you increase the mark time you must decrease the space time and visa-versa.

If the waveform was that of a voltage being applied to a DC motor, then the motor would respond to the average of the voltage. For any DC square wave, the average voltage can be calculated using the expression in Equation 4-3:

$$Vavge = \frac{VmM}{T} \, or = \frac{VmM}{M+S} \qquad \textbf{(Equation 4-3)}$$

Note that Vavge is the average voltage, Vm is the voltage maximum, M is the mark time, T is the periodic time for the wave form (i.e. the time to complete one full cycle), and S is the space time.

157

Note that $\dfrac{M}{M+S}$ is termed the duty cycle. When the M time is equal to the space time, then the duty cycle is termed 50/50 and the average voltage is $\dfrac{Vm}{2}$.

I hope the above paragraphs explain the importance of creating a square.

Creating a Square Wave with the PWM Mode

One way you can create a square wave is to use the PWM mode of the CCP module of the PIC. This is the Capture Compare and Pulse Width Modulation module of the PIC. This module is a mixture of hardware, in that the actual circuitry is inside the PIC, and firmware, preprogrammed operations that are in the PIC. In this chapter, you will look at using the CCP in PWM mode to create the square wave.

What the programmer has to do is create the timing for the period T and the mark time, M. This is done using the timer2 inside the PIC, which just counts clock pulses. The procedure for doing this is as follows.

First, you must set the CCP module to PWM mode. This is done by writing to the control register CCPXCON. However, the 18F4525 has two CCP modules, which then means it has two CCPX outputs, hence the X, which should be replaced with 1 or 2 depending upon which CCP module and output you are using. Table 4-2 shows the use of the bits in the CCPXCON control register. Note that there will be two such control registers and the X is replaced with 1 and 2.

Table 4-2. *The Bits of the CCPXCON Register*

Bit7	Bit6	Bit5	Bit4	Bit3	Bit2	Bit1	Bit0
-	-	DCxB1	DCxB0	CCPxM3	CCPxM2	CCPxM1	CCPxM0
Bits 7 and 6		These are not used and should be read as 0.					
Bits 5 and 4		These are used to store the two LSBs of the 10-bit number for the duty cycle.					
Bits 3, 2, 1, and 0		These are used to set the use of the CCP module according to the setting shown in Table 4-3.					

Table 4-3 shows how Bits 3, 2, 1, and 0 set up the CCP into its respective mode of operation.

Table 4-3. *The Four Bits That Configure the CCP Modules*

Bit3	Bit2	Bit1	Bit0	Setting
0	0	0	0	Capture/Compare/PWM disabled
0	0	0	1	Reserved
0	0	1	0	Compare mode, toggle output on match
0	0	1	1	Reserved
0	1	0	0	Capture mode every falling edge
0	1	0	1	Capture mode every rising edge
0	1	1	0	Capture mode every fourth rising edge
0	1	1	1	Capture mode every sixteenth rising edge
1	0	0	0	Compare mode, initialize CCPx pin low
1	0	0	1	Compare mode, initialize CCPx pin high

(*continued*)

Table 4-3. *(continued)*

Bit3	Bit2	Bit1	Bit0	Setting
1	0	1	0	Compare mode, generate software interrupt
1	0	1	1	Compare mode, trigger special event
1	1	0	0	PWM mode P1A, P1C active high P1B P1D active high
1	1	0	1	PWM mode P1A, P1C active high P1B P1D active low
1	1	1	0	PWM mode P1A, P1C active low P1B P1D active high
1	1	1	1	PWM mode P1A, P1C active low P1B P1D active low

It should be noted that the last four settings in Table 4-3 show the mode for the PWM when the PIC is used in the extended mode. In this mode, the programmer has the ability to produce a H drive output. However, if all you want is a simple square wave output, then these four bits can be set to 1100, b3 and b2 can be a logic 1, and b1 and b0 can be set to a logic 0.

If you want to produce two square wave outputs, you must write to both CCP1CON and CCP2CON registers as well as load both CCPR1L and CCPR2L with the correct value. This will produce two square waves of the same frequency set by the value in the PR2 register. A program that produces two square waves is shown in Listing 4-2.

The following is an explanation of the bits in the CCPXCON register.

- Bits 7 and 6 of the CCP1CON register are not used, so leave them at logic 0.

- Bits 5 and 4 are where you store the two least significant bits of the binary number that is used to control the width of the mark pulse. You will look at this later in the chapter.

- It is the least significant four bits (b3, b2, b1, and b0 of both CCPXCON registers) that control what mode the CCP module is in. Since you are trying to create a square wave with PWM, you want to set this module to PWM mode. This is done by setting these four bits as follows:

  - b3 = 1

  - b2 = 1

  - b1 = x

  - b0 = x

    - The x means it does not matter what logic level they are.

The data sheet does indicate that b1 and b0 can be set to any logic level; see section 15 in the datasheet. However, this is true only if you are dealing with just one CCP and creating one square wave output. The PIC18F4525 has two CCP modules, which means you can create two square wave outputs. When you do this, the phase relationship between the two square waves can be affected. This concept will be discussed later in this chapter.

One last thing before you start creating your square wave. You need to know on what pin the two square waves will be outputted by the PIC. The two outputs are CCP1 and CCP2. CCP1 is fixed on PORTC Bit2 (i.e. PORTCbits.RC2). However, CCP2 has two possible output locations. It can be sent out on PORTBbits.RB3 or PORTCbits.RC1. To decide which of these two bits the CCP2 is on, you must use one of the CONFIG words when you first set the CONFIG words up. The default setting is PORTCbits. RC1. I normally leave it at this so that I can use my configuration header file in all my projects.

The process of creating a square wave is based around letting timer2 count up until a time equal to the periodic time T of the desired square wave has been reached. Timer2, like all timers, simply counts clock pulses and so a count of one will equal a specific time according to the clock frequency used by timer2. Therefore, you need to know the number of pulses the timer has to count to reach the periodic time of the frequency of the square wave. This number is loaded into a special function register called PR2. When the value in timer2 matches the value in this PR2 register, then the square wave starts a new cycle.

To determine the specific value to load into PR2, Microchip provides an equation shown as equation 15.1 in section 15.4 of the datasheet. However, it is not the easiest equation to use, so I have rearranged it to produce an equation for PR2, which is what you want to work out. You simply want to know what value you need to load into the PR2 to set the frequency of the square wave. See Equation 4-4:

$$PR2 = \frac{OscFreq}{Frequency \times 4 \times TMR2Preset} - 1 \qquad \textbf{(Equation 4-4)}$$

Creating a 500Hz Square Wave

The best way to explain the process is to go through a simple example. In the following example, you will create a 500Hz square wave with an 8Mhz internal oscillator and a TMR2Preset value of 16. I will explain what the timer preset value does later.

Putting all the values into equation 4-4 you get Equation 4-5:

$$PR2 = \frac{8E^6}{500 \times 4 \times 16} - 1 = 249 \qquad \textbf{(Equation 4-5)}$$

This means that to get a square wave with a frequency of 500Hz using an 8MHz oscillator, you simply have to load the PR2 with the value of 249, which is 0b11111001 or 0XF9, and then set the mark-to-space ratio.

I feel I should point out that timer2 counts clock pulses and the clock runs at a quarter of the frequency of the oscillator; note that is why there is a number 4 in Equation 4-4. This means that, with an oscillator frequency of 8Mhz, the clock runs at a 2Mhz. However, you have the ability to slow timer2 even more by dividing this 2Mhz frequency further. To control how much more you divide this frequency by, and so slow it down, use the timer2 preset value. There are three possible values this preset can be set to: 1, 4, and 16. You are using the value 16 for this timer preset, hence the 16 in Equation 4-5. This means that timer2 is counting at a rate of 2Mhz divided by 16, so at a frequency of 125kHz. The periodic time for this frequency is $T = \frac{1}{f} = \frac{1}{125E^3} = 8E^{-6}$ therefore $= 8\mu s$. This means it takes $8\mu s$ for timer2 to count one tick. This means that it will take $250 \times 8\mu s$ for timer2 to count from 0 to 249. Therefore, it will take 2ms for the timer to count from 0 to 249, which is the periodic time for the 500Hz square wave you are trying to produce.

I hope this explains how Equation 4-4 works and how the PIC uses timer2 to create a square wave. As I stated earlier, you want to know the number the timer2 must count up to create a time equal to the periodic time of the frequency of the square wave you are creating.

The Mark Time or Duty Cycle

So far, you have loaded the PR2 register with the correct number to create a 500Hz square wave but there must be a mark time and a space time or a duty cycle. You can't leave this calculation out because the registers involved will have data in them already but it will most likely be an unusable value. You need to make sure the value in the register used to control the mark-to-space ratio is the one you want.

You will start by creating a 50/50 duty cycle, which means the mark and space time are both equal to $\frac{T}{2} = \frac{2ms}{2} = 1ms = 1E^{-3}$.

Again Microchip give us an equation to help with this. However, you really want to know the number that you can store in the appropriate register, which the PIC will use to control the duty cycle of the square wave. I have rearranged the expression from Microchip to give an expression for that number; it is shown in Equation 4-6.

$$Number = \frac{MarkTime \times OscFreq}{TMR2Preset} \quad \textbf{(Equation 4-6)}$$

This is taken from equation 15.2 in section 15.4 of the datasheet for the PIC18F4525.

Knowing that for a 50/50 duty cycle, the mark time must be $1E^{-3}$ for your 500Hz square wave so you can calculate the number as shown in Equation 4-7:

$$Number = \frac{MarkTime \times OscFreq}{TMR2Preset}$$

$$\therefore Number = \frac{1E^{-3} \times 8E^{6}}{16} \quad \textbf{(Equation 4-7)}$$

$$\therefore Number = 500$$

So you have calculated two numbers that, when used properly, will give you a 500Hz square wave with a 50/50 duty cycle. There are two issues to consider when it comes to storing these numbers.

First, you set the TMR2 Preset value using the T2CON register. There are three possible values for the TMR2 preset: 1, 4, and 16. Why did I choose 16? Well, if I had chosen 4, the PR2 number would have worked out at 996, and if I had chosen 1, the PR2 number would be 3984. So what is wrong with that? The answer is that this PIC is an 8-bit PIC and unless you can change them, as you can with some SFRs, all registers are 8 bits and an 8-bit register can only hold a value up to 255. So that is why a preset value of 16 was chosen: to reduce the value to below 255. You have the other possible values for the TIMER 2 Preset because you may want different frequencies for the square wave, and you could use different oscillator settings.

Now, as the registers are only 8 bits long, how can you store the number for the duty cycle since the value of 500 uses nine binary numbers? Microchip have given us a solution for this problem similar to the way you store the 10-bit results of the ADC conversion**. You can store the most significant 8 bits in a special register called CCPRXL. Note that there are two, one for each CCP module, so the X will be either 1 or 2.

The two least significant bits go into b5 and b4 of the CCPXCON registers; again, X is 1 or 2. The number you calculated using Equation 4-7 was 500 or 0b111110100. This means b5 and b4 of the CCPXCON registers are set to logic 0 and the 0b01111101 (note that the extra 0 at Bit7 is there to complete the 8-bit number) is loaded into the appropriate CCPRXL registers. You will use CCPR1L since you will be using the CCP1 output and thus the CCP1CON register to create the square wave.

** Please refer to my first book, *C Programming for PIC Microcontrollers*, for a complete explanation of the ADC.

This will then make a 500Hz square wave appear on the CCP1 of the PIC with a 50/50 duty cycle, assuming you have set the CCP1 pin to output.

The program is shown in Listing 4-1.

Listing 4-1. The Program for the 500Hz Square Wave

```
1. #include <xc.h>
2. #include <conFigInternalOscNoWDTNoLVP.h>
3. #include <PICSetup.h>
4. void main ()
5. {
6. initialise ();
7. T2CON = 0x06;
8. PR2 = 249;
9. CCP1CON = 0b00001100;
10. CCPR1L = 0X7D;
11. while (1);
12. }
```

Analysis of Listing 4-1

The new instructions for the program are analyzed here.

Line 7 T2CON = 0X06;

This instruction simply loads the control register T2CON with the following 8-bit number: 0b00000110.

To understand what this instruction is doing, it's useful to look at the usage of the T2CON register. This is shown in Table 4-4.

Table 4-4. *The T2CON Register for Controlling Timer2*

Bit7	Bit6	Bit5	Bit4	Bit3	Bit2	Bit1	Bit0
-	T2OUTPS3	T2OUTPS2	T2OUTPS1	T2OUPS0	TMR2ON	T2CKPS1	T2CKPS0
Bit7		Not used					
Bit6		These are used to enable Post scales for timer2					
		0000 = 1:1					
Bit5		0001 = 1:2					
		"					
		"					
Bit4		"					
		1111 = 1:16					
Bit3							
Bit2		TIMR2ON	Logic 0 means off, Logic 1 means on				
Bits 1 - 0		TMR2 Preset	00 = 1		01 = 4	1x = 16	

The following is an explanation of what loading the T2CON register with 0b00000110 does.

This sets Bit2 to a logic 1, which simply turns the timer2 on.

This instruction also sets Bit1 to a logic 1 and Bit0 to a logic 0. This sets the timer2 preset to a value of 16.

Note also that Bits 6, 5, 4, and 3 are set to logic 0, which sets the Post Scalar to 0000. The use of the Post Scalar will be explained in Chapter 6.

Note that Bit7 is not used, so it is set to a logic 0.

In essence, then, this instruction turns Timer2 on and sets the preset value to 16.

Line 8 PR2 = 249;

This loads the PR2 register with the number 249, which is the value you calculated using Equation 4-5 to achieve a frequency of 500Hz. Note that you are using the default radix, which is the decimal number system.

Line 9 CCP1CON = 0b00001100;

This simply loads the CCP1CON, the control register for the CCP1 module with the value 0b00001100. A description of the usage of this control register is given in Tables 4-2 and 4-3. The particular use of the bits is given here.

Bit 7 and 6 of the CCP1CON register are not used, so leave them at logic 0.

Bits 5 and 4 are set to a logic 0 as this is what the two least significant bits of the binary conversion of 500 are as calculated using Equation 4-7.

The remaining fours bits (3, 2, 1, and 0) are set to 1100, respectively, to put the CCP module into the PWM mode of operation.

In essence, loading the CCP1CON register with 0b00001100 sets the CCP module to PWM mode.

Line 10 CCPR1L = 0X7D;

This loads the CCPR1L 8-bit register with the MSB bits of the 500 value created with Equation 4-7 (i.e. it loads 0b01111101 or 0X7D as shown).

In essence, it is the value in the CCPR1L register that sets the width of the up or mark time of the square wave.

Line 11 while (1);

This is using the while (test) type instruction. If the result of the test is true, the program must do what the instruction tells it to do. With the test being the simple (1), then the test result is always true since a logic 1 means true. This means that the micro must always do what the instruction tells it to do.

As there is nothing between the (1) and the semicolon, which signifies the end of the instruction, this while (1) test means the micro will do nothing forever. In this way, you are halting the micro at this point in the program.

This is all you need to do, so there will now be a 500Hz square wave outputted by the PIC on the CCP1 output. This is on bit2 of PORTC.

To test the program, it was simulated using the ECAD software PROTEUS. The circuit and the simulation are shown in Figure 4-2.

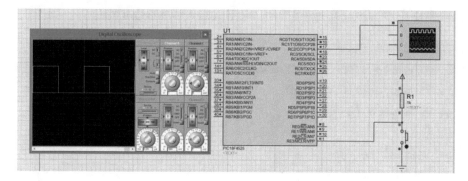

Figure 4-2. *The simulation of the 500Hz square wave*

The oscilloscope shows a square wave with mark and space time equal to each other. Also, as the time for each square division of the screen is 0.2ms and there are 10 squares in one complete cycle, the periodic time T for the waveform is 10 x 0.2m = 2ms. This is the correct periodic time for the 500Hz square wave.

Creating Two Square Wave Outputs

This section of the text will just look at creating two square waves. It will also look at controlling the phase relationship between the two square waves.

The first difference is that you must load the CCP1CON and the CCPR1L registers but also the CCP2CON and the CCPR2L registers. To keep the two square waves at the same frequency and the same duty cycle, you must load the registers with the same values. The only variance is that the CCP1CON register is used to control the phase relationship of the two square waves. This is achieved by changing the logic in Bit1 and Bit0 of the CCP1CON register; the CCP2CON register does not affect the phase relationship between the outputs. The program is shown in Listing 4-2.

Listing 4-2. The Program for Two Square Wave Outputs

```
1.  #include <xc.h>
2.  #include <conFigInternalOscNoWDTNoLVP.h>
3.  #include <PICSetup.h>
4.  void main ()
5.  {
6.  initialise ();
7.  T2CON = 0x06;
8.  PR2 = 249;
9.  CCP1CON = 0b00001100;
10. CCPR1L = 0X7D;
11. CCP2CON = 0b00001100;
12. CCPR2L = 0X7D;
13. while (1);
14. }
```

The circuit for the simulation is shown in Figure 4-3 and the oscilloscope screen showing the two square waves is shown in Figure 4-3.

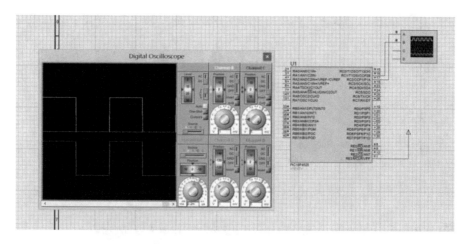

Figure 4-3. *The circuit simulation*

Channel A, the yellow waveform, displays the CCP1 output and channel B, the blue waveform, displays the CCP2 output. It's quite clear they are both 50/50 duty cycle and they are at 500Hz.

One thing that I should point out is that they are in phase with each other. This is because I have set Bit1 and Bit0 of the CCP1CON register to logic 0.

If you now set Bit1 and Bit0 of the CCP1CON register to logic 1, which is still allowed, the two square waves will be out of phase by 180°. Try it and see what happens.

Note that if you set Bit0 of the CCP1CON register to a logic 0 while keeping bit 1 at a logic 1, the two waveforms will still be 180° out of phase. The oscilloscope display for b1 is a logic 1 and b0 is a logic 0, as shown in Figure 4-4.

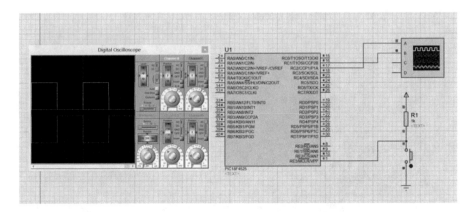

Figure 4-4. *Here b1 is set to logic 1 and b0 is set to logic 0.*

The two wave forms are out of phase by 180° because when the channel A trace is positive, the channel B trace is at 0V. When the channel B trace is positive, the channel A trace is at 0V. This means the two wave forms are said to be in "anti-phase" with each other.

Setting the Speed of a DC Motor

Now that you have learned how to create one or two square wave outputs, let's make use of them. Setting the speed of a DC motor is just one of the many useful applications of PIC programming and yet it is probably one of the easiest. Indeed, all you have to do is vary the duty cycle of the square wave since the DC motor will respond to the average voltage. For example, when the duty cycle is 50/50, then you should have half-speed. If it is 75/25, you have 3/4 speed, and when it is 25/75 you have 1/4 speed. However, you should bear in mind that this is with an ideal motor. All real motors have friction and inertia to deal with but the speed can, in essence, be set in this way.

Therefore, to vary the speed you need only change the number stored in the CCPRXL and the other two bits. Note that I am saying *setting*, not *controlling*, because if you want to control the speed of the motor you need to measure the actual speed and use it in some sort of closed loop control. This can be done using a PIC micro but this is more than I intend to do in this book.

To help explain setting the speed of the motor, let's change the duty cycle of the CCP1 output in Listing 4-1 to 75/25 and see what happens to the voltage output on the oscilloscope.

First, calculate the mark time, which is done in Equation 4-8:

$$MarkTime = T \times \frac{M}{M+S} = 2E^{-3} \times \frac{75}{75+25} = 1.5E^{-3} = 1.5mS \quad \textbf{(Equation 4-8)}$$

Now use this mark time to calculate the number for CCPR1L as shown in Equation 4-9:

$$Number = \frac{MarkTime \times OscFreq}{TMR2\text{Preset}}$$
$$\therefore Number = \frac{1.5E^{-3} \times 8E^{6}}{16} \quad \textbf{(Equation 4-9)}$$
$$\therefore Number = 750$$

This number converts to 0b1011101110, which means b5 in CCP1CON is set to logic 1 and b4 is set to logic 0. Then 0b10111011 or 0XBB is loaded into the CCPR1L.

The changes to create the 75/25 square wave output are shown in Listing 4-3.

Listing 4-3. The Changes to Produce a 75/25 Square Wave Output

```
1.  #include <xc.h>
2.  #include <conFigInternalOscNoWDTNoLVP.h>
3.  #include <PICSetup.h>
4.  void main ()
5.  {
6.  initialise ();
7.  T2CON = 0x06;
8.  PR2 = 249;
9.  CCP1CON = 0b00101100;
10. CCPR1L = 0XBB;
11. while (1);
12. }
```

The simulation to show that the mark is 75% and the space is 25% is shown in Figure 4-5.

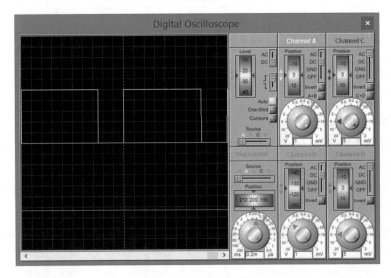

Figure 4-5. *The square wave output with 75% mark and 25% space*

Exercise 4-2

Determine the minimum value of the numbers to be stored in the PR2, CCP1CON, and CCPR1L registers if you want a 20/80 duty cycle with a 2kHz square wave, using the 8MHz internal oscillator.

Driving the Motor

You now have to think about how you can drive the DC motor. Unless you are using very small 5V DC motors, you cannot drive them directly from the PIC. Even with 5V motors, the current the motor could take would have to be fairly small, in the order of 100mA maximum. This is because most outputs of the PIC can only source, or sink, a small amount of current.

This being the case, you will most likely need to use a driver chip. There are many that are suitable, such as the ULN2004A and the ULN2803A. They are Darlington transistors arrays. The ULN2004A is a 16-pin device with seven Darlington transistors; the ULN2803A is an 18-pin device with eight Darlington transistors. Each of the Darlington transistors can sink up to 500mA. They can be connected in parallel if required to accommodate a device that sinks more current. They can be supplied by a VCC up to 30V.

If that current capability is not enough, you can use a single Darlington transistor, and the TIP122 is one such transistor. It can sink up to 5Amps of current.

The ULN Drivers and the TIP122 actually switch the ground onto the load, so they sink the current of the load through them. Since most loads are inductive, and the switching off of inductive loads can lead to high voltage spikes across the Darlington transistor, or other switching device, these drivers all have flywheel diodes to protect them. One final point to appreciate about these driver ICs is that they can be driven from TTL voltages.

All these parameters make them ideal for interfacing the PIC to real-word circuits.

Creating a Three-Speed DC Motor Program

This will extend the basic square wave program to firstly drive the motor at half speed and then, when one of three buttons is momentarily pressed, the speed of the motorc will be changed as follows:

- If no button is pressed, the motor runs at half speed.

- If the button connected to RA0 is pressed, the motor speed increases to 3/4 speed.

- If the button connected to RA1 is pressed, the motor speed increases even further.

- If the button connected to RA2 is pressed, the motor speed reduces to 1/4 speed.

- If the button connected to RA3 is pressed, the motor speed returns to 1/2 speed.

The code is shown in Listing 4-4.

Listing 4-4. The Three-Speed Control of a DC Motor

```
1. #include <xc.h>
2. #include <conFigInternalOscNoWDTNoLVP.h>
3. #include <PICSetup.h>
4. void main ()
5. {
6. initialise ();
7. T2CON = 0x06;
8. PR2 = 249;
```

```
 9. CCP1CON = 0b00001100;
10. CCPR1L = 0X7D;
11. while (1)
12. {
13. if(PORTAbits.RA0) CCPR1L = 0xBB;
14. if(PORTAbits.RA1) CCPR1L = 0xDB;
15. if(PORTAbits.RA2) CCPR1L = 0x3E;
16. if(PORTAbits.RA3) CCPR1L = 0x7D;
17. }
18. }
```

The only new instructions are those on lines 13, 14, and 15. They are all of the type *if (the test is true) then do what I say here.*

Line 13 if(PORTAbits.RA0) CCPR1l = 0XBB;

The test asks if the logic on Bit0 of PORTA is a logic 1. This will only come about if someone has pressed the switch connected to Bit0 of PORTA. If someone has pressed the switch, then the test will be true and the PIC will carry out the instruction CCPR1L = 0XBB;, which simply loads the CCPR1L with the value 0XBB. This is the value needed to increase the speed to 75%, as calculated in Equation 4-6.

Lines 14 and 15 change the speed of the motor in a similar way.

This program is not using the debounce subroutine that was used in Chapter 3. This because you are not concerned with how many times the switch is pressed. However, in a practical situation, it would be useful to use the debounce subroutine if only to prevent any stray noise on the switches changing the speed of the motor unintentionally.

The Proteus schematic for the simulation is shown in Figure 4-6.

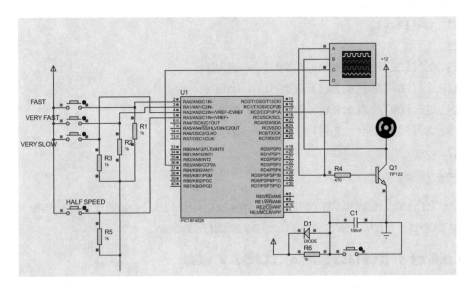

Figure 4-6.   *The schematic for the three-speed motor*

Note that I am using the TIP122 Darlington transistor to switch the motor to ground and so sink the current from the motor. R4 is needed to prevent the transistor pulling the output of the PIC down to around 1.4V. It also sets the current being fed into the base of the TIP122.

The resistors R1, R2, R3, and R5 are there to limit the current flowing through the switches to around 5mA, thus protecting the switches. I refer to this arrangement for the switching as a pull up, as pressing the switch pulls the voltage at the input up to VCC. Others may refer to the arrangement as pull down resistors since the resistors are in the path down to 0V.

Using a Variable Input Voltage to Change the Speed of a DC Motor

This will involve using an analog input; you will use PORTA Bit0 and the ADC to convert the analog voltage to a binary value. Then you'll use this value to vary the mark time of the square wave feeding the transistor that turns the motors on. This concept is shown in the circuit in Figure 4-7.

The algorithm: The PIC will constantly read the input voltage at the analog input on Bit0 of PORTA. You use that result of the ADC to vary the mark time of the square wave feeding the Darlington transistor.

The program is shown in Listing 4-5.

Listing 4-5. The Variable Speed DC Motors

```
1. #include <xc.h>
2. #include <conFigInternalOscNoWDTNoLVP.h>
3. #include <PICSetup.h>
4. #include <math.h>
5. void changeSpeed ()
6. {
7. ADCONobits.GODONE = 1;
8. while (ADCONobits.GODONE);
9. CCPR1L = round(ADRESH * 0.95);
10. }
11. void main ()
12. {
13. initialise ();
14. TRISA = 0X0F;
15. ADCON0 = 0X01;
16. ADCON1 = 0X0E;
17. ADCON2 = 0b00010001;
18. T2CON = 0x05;
```

```
19. PR2 = 249;
20. CCP1CON = 0b00001100;
21. CCPR1L = 0X7D;
22. while (1)
23. {
24. changeSpeed ();
25. }
26. }
```

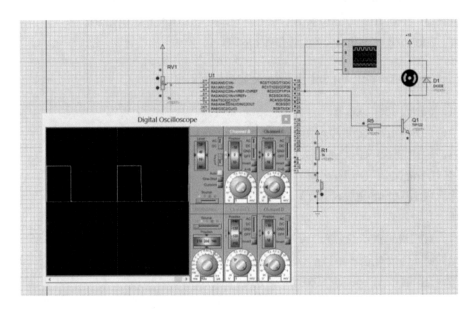

Figure 4-7. *Setting the speed of a DC motor with a variable resistor*

Analysis of Listing 4-5

The new instructions are as follows:

Line 4 #include <math.h>

This tells the compiler to include the header file `math.h`. This is an open source header file and it includes a whole range of math functions. You need it since you are using the "round" function, which is used to round up a decimal number to an integer.

Line 5 void changeSpeed ()

This is where you create a subroutine to change the speed of the motor. It reads the voltage at the analog input and then coverts it to a binary value that can be loaded into the CCPR1L register to control the PWM of the square wave feeding the DC motor.

Line 6 {

This is the standard opening curly bracket for the subroutine.

Line 7 ADCONobits.GODONE = 1;

This tells the PIC to start the ADC (analog-to-digital conversion) process.**

Line 8 while (ADCONobits.GODONE);

This tells the PIC to wait until the ADC has finished. Note the use of *while (the test is true) do nothing in this case.*

Line 9 CCPR1L = round(ADRESH * 0.95);

This loads the CCPR1L with the 8-bit number stored in the ADRESH. Note that the ADRESH is where the PIC stores the high byte of the result of the ADC conversion. However, the 8-bit number is multiplied by 0.95 first before it is loaded into the CCPR1L register. However, multiplying an integer by 0.95 could result in a decimal value as the result. A decimal number cannot be loaded into the CCPR1L, so the value must be rounded up first before it is stored in the CCPR1L. This is why you need to use the round function that is listed in the `maths.h` header file included in line 4.

Another problem is that the value stored in the CCPR1L register cannot be allowed to produce a mark time that is equal to or greater than the period of the square wave. If this was allowed to happen, the square wave would collapse. Since the period time is set by the value in the PR2 register, which in this case is 249, the value for the mark time cannot be allowed to be the same or greater than the value in the PR2 register (i.e. it cannot be the same or greater than 249 in this case). Therefore, if you set the maximum value that can be loaded into the CCPR1L register at 242, a value that is less than 249, then you can determine the multiplying factor that you need to use here.

To do so, you must be aware that the 8-bit value in the ADRESH can go up to a maximum of 255, as it is an 8-bit register. Then using Equation 4-10, you have

$$Factor = \frac{\max Value}{255} = \frac{242}{255} = 0.95 \quad \textbf{(Equation 4-10)}$$

This is how the value of 0.95 is calculated.

Line 10 }

This is simply the closing curly bracket for the subroutine.

Line 11 void main ()

This is setting up the main loop as before.

Line 12 {

This is the opening bracket of the main loop.

Line 13   initialise ();

This is the call to go through all the instructions of the `initialise` subroutine. Note that this subroutine is written in the `PICSetUp.h` header file.

Line 14 TRISA = 0X0F;

This is required because in the `PICSetup.h` header file you made all the bits on PORTA inputs by writing 0XFF to TRISA. However, as an example of what you have to do if you want something different from what is set in that header file, you are changing the use of the bits on PORTA. Bits 7, 6, 5, and 4 are all set to outputs and Bits 3, 2, 1, and 0 are set to inputs. So you insert an instruction here that overwrites the data in TRISA that you wrote in within the header file, and replaces it with data that you specify here.

Line 15   ADCON1 = 0X01;

This line and the next two lines all write to registers that control the ADC module inside the PIC. For a thorough analysis of how this module works and how these registers allow you as a programmer, to control it, you should read my first book, *C Programming for PIC Microcontrollers*. However, I will briefly explain what these three instructions do.

This one, on line 15, simply turns the ADC module on and connects it to channel 0, which is on Bit 0 of PORTA.

Line 16   ADCON1 = 0X0E;

This sets all 13 channels, except channel 0, to digital. Channel 0 has to be set to analog as this is the input, Bit0 of PORTA, to which the variable voltage, which will be used to control the speed of the DC motor, will be connected to. That is why it must be set as an analog input and this instruction does that.

Line 17 ADCON2 = 0b00010001;

This controls how long the PIC waits for the whole acquisition and conversion of the analog input to complete. If it does not wait long enough, the result may be inaccurate. If the PIC waits too long, it could be wasting time. Therefore, you must get this setting correct.

In this way, these three instructions control how the ADC conversion operates.

Line 18 T2CON = 0X05;

Table 4-2 describes what each of the 8 bits in this control register does. Loading 0X05 into the register actually loads 0b00000101 in binary into the register. From that, you can see that Bit2 is a logic 1, which simply turns timer2 on.

Also, Bit1 is a logic 0 and Bit0 is a logic 1. This sets the timer2 preset value to 4.

To appreciate what this does, you need to consider the next instruction in the listing.

Line 19 PR2 = 249;

This loads the PR2 register with the value of 249 in decimal. If you now look at Equation 4-11, which can be used to calculate the periodic time of the square wave you can generate, you get the following result:

$$PERIOD = \frac{(PR2+1)\left[4 \times \text{Timer2PreSet}\right]}{OSCFequency} \quad \textbf{(Equation 4-11)}$$

Putting your values in gets you Equation 4-12:

$$PERIOD = \frac{(249+1)\left[4 \times 4\right]}{8E^6} \quad \textbf{(Equation 4-12)}$$

$$\therefore PERIOD = \frac{400}{8E^6} = 500E^{-6} = 500 \mu s$$

Knowing that the PERIOD is given the symbol T and that the frequency can be calculated using Equation 4-13:

$$f = \frac{1}{T}$$

(Equation 4-13)

$$\therefore f = \frac{1}{500E^{-6}} = 2kHz$$

This shows that it is the combination of the value loaded into the PR2 register and the Timer2 Preset value that sets the frequency of the square wave created, in this program, to 2kHz.

Line   20 CCP1CON = 0b00001100;

This simply sets the CCP1 module into PWM mode so that you can create a square wave on the CCP1 output, which is on Bit2 of PORTC.

Line 21 CCPR1L =   0X7D;

This sets the square wave up with a 50/50 duty cycle. This number, 0X7D, was calculated using Equation 4-2.

Line 22 while (1)

This sets up a forever loop that makes the micro carry out the instructions listed between the following set of curly brackets forever.

Line 23 {

The opening curly bracket for the forever loop.

Line 24   changeSpeed ();

This is the only instruction inside the curly brackets. All it does is call the subroutine changeSpeed. In this subroutine, the micro reads the input on bit0 of PORTA. It then converts the value from analog to digital in the ADC module. It then loads the CCPR1L register with the modified result.

Note that it is the CCPR1L register that alters the mark time of the square wave. Therefore, all the program does forever is alter the pulse width of the voltage applied to the motor and thus it alters the speed of the motor.

Note that since there is only one instruction inside the curly brackets, this instruction could have been written as

```
while (1) changeSpeed ();
```

This would have saved two lines in the program (i.e. lines 23 and 25).

Line 25 }

This is the closing bracket of the forever loop.

Line 26 }

This is the closing bracket for the main loop.

I hope this explains how the program uses the PWM to set the speed of a simple DC motor by using a variable input.

Creating a Musical Note

As stated earlier, all sounds have their own individual frequency, or combination of frequencies, that allows us humans to separate them from other sounds. Some sounds have a combination of frequencies but a pure note will have just one frequency. The note middle C has a frequency of 261.63Hz with a wavelength of 1.3187 m. See the table in Appendix 7. Ideally the signal should be a perfect sinusoidal waveform. However, a square at 261.63Hz will be good enough for most uses. If you want a more perfect wave, you can pass the square wave through a low-pass filter. However, a simple passive filter will attenuate the signal, therefore an active filter may be better. This is not covered in this book.

Creating the Middle C Note

Creating the middle C note will require creating a square wave at the frequency of 261.63Hz. Applying what you have learned thus far means you will need to determine what value needs to be inputted to the PR2 register and what number to store in the CCPR1L register. As this note is middle C, which would normally be the middle of the range of notes, the value in the PR2 register should be ideally 124 (i.e. the middle value that can be stored in the 8-bit register, the PR2). This is to allow you to increase or decrease the frequency produced equally either side of middle C. Therefore, you know that the PR2 value should be 124 and the period of the 261.63Hz square wave is 3.822ms, so see Equation 4-14.

$$T = \frac{1}{f} = \frac{1}{261.63} = 3.822ms \qquad \textbf{(Equation 4-14)}$$

Using the expression for the period shown in Equation 4-11, you can calculate a suitable oscillator frequency as follows in Equation 4-15:

$$PERIOD = [PR2+1]\left(\frac{4 \times TMR2Preset}{OSCFreq} \right) \qquad \textbf{(Equation 4-15)}$$

$$\therefore OSCFreq = [PR2+1]\left(\frac{4 \times TMR2Preset}{PERIOD} \right)$$

$$OSCFreq = [124+1]\left(\frac{4 \times 16}{3.822E^{-3}} \right) = 2.093145\,MHz$$

This is using a TMR2Prset value of 16. You could have used a value of 4 or a value of 1. This means there could be three possible oscillator frequencies you could have used to produce a PR2 value of 124 that would produce a square wave of 261.63 Hz. They are listed in Table 4-5.

Table 4-5. *The Three Possible Oscillator Frequencies to Produce the Note Middle C*

TMR2Preset Value	Oscillator Frequency
1	130.822kHz
4	523.286kHz
16	2.093145MHz

Since you are using the internal oscillator block, then using the data sheet you can see that any of the available oscillator frequencies would give the same percentage error of around 4.4%. Therefore, it is up to you which oscillator frequency you should use. I chose the 2Mhz oscillator frequency that uses a TMR2Preset value of 16.

So, using these values, you can now calculate the actual PR2 value you must use to produce a square wave with a frequency of 261.63Hz. This is done as follows shown in Equation 4-16:

$$PR2 = \frac{OCSFreq}{Frequency \times 4 \times TMR2Preset} - 1 \quad \textbf{(Equation 4-16)}$$

$$PR2 = \frac{2E^6}{261.63 \times 4 \times 16} - 1 = 118.4375$$

As the PR2 register can only store whole integers, let the PR2 value = 118.

The square wave should have a 50/50 duty cycle so the pulse width should equal half the period. Therefore, the pulse time should be 1.911ms. Using this value, the number that must be stored in the CCPR1L register can be calculated as follows in Equation 4-17:

$$NUMBER = \frac{MarkTine \times OscFreq}{TMR\,2\,Preset} \quad \textbf{(Equation 4-17)}$$

$$NUMBER = \frac{1.911E^{-3} \times 2E^6}{16} = 238.875$$

Again, this must be an integer, so let the number be 239. This converts to a 10-bit binary as 0011101111. The two LSB are 1, 1 and they must be stored in Bit5 and Bit4 of the CCP1CON register. The remaining 8 MSB are 00111011. This is the 8-bit number that must be loaded into the CCPR1L register. To confirm that the work so far is OK, you will write a program to create this middle C note. This is shown in Listing 4-6.

Listing 4-6. The Code to Create the Note Middle C

```
1. #include <xc.h>
2. #include <conFigInternalOscNoWDTNoLVP.h>
3. #include <PICSetup.h>
4. void main ()
5. {
            i. initialise ();
            ii. OSCCON = 0b01010100;
            iii. T2CON = 0x06;
            iv. PR2 = 118;
6. CCP1CON = 0b00111100;
```

```
7. CCPR1L = 0X3B;
8. while (1);
9. }
```

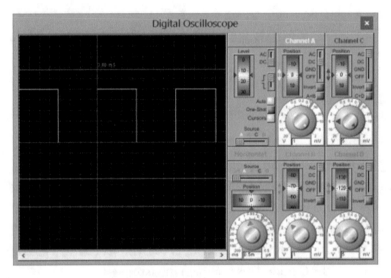

Figure 4-8. *The oscilloscope display of a simulation of the program*

Figure 4-8 shows the display on the oscilloscope of a simulation of the program. You can see that the time to complete one cycle is 3.8ms, which is the correct periodic time for the note middle C.

It is not showing a perfect 50/50 duty cycle due to the rounding errors in the calculations. An alternative approach, which maybe a better approach, to producing this middle C note is covered in Chapter 7.

Creating a Musical Keyboard

The algorithm for this program is as follows:

1. You need to save the settings for the CCP1CON register and the CCPR1L register for all of the musical notes you are going to make available.

2. You also need to allocate an input to each of the eight notes you will be using.

The program is shown in Listing 4-7.

Listing 4-7. The Code for the Musical Keyboard

```
1.  /*
2.  * File:    musicalNotesProg.c
3.  Author: hubert.ward
4.  *
5.  Created on 03 January 2019, 14:25
6.  */
7.  //Some include files
8.  #include <conFigInternalOscNoWDTNoLVP.h>
9.  #include <xc.h>
10. #include <PICSetUp.h>
11. #include <musicalNotes.h>
12. //some variables
13. unsigned char n;
14. //Some subroutines
15. void debounce ()
16. {
17. TMR0 = 0;
18. while (TMR0 < 100);
19. }
```

```
20. void main()
21. {
22. initialise ();
23. TRISB = OXFF;
24. TRISC = 0;
25. T2CON = OX06;
26. OSCCON = 0b01010100;
27. CCP1CON = 0b00001100;
28. while (1)
29. {
30. if (PORTAbits.RA0)
31. {
32. G3;
33. debounce ();
34. while (PORTAbits.RA0);
35. }
36. if (PORTAbits.RA1)
37. {
38. A3;
39. debounce ();
40. while (PORTAbits.RA1);
41. }
42. if (PORTAbits.RA2)
43. {
44. B3;
45. debounce ();
46. while (PORTAbits.RA2);
47. }
48. if (PORTAbits.RA3)
49. {
50. C4;
```

```
51. debounce ();
52. while (PORTAbits.RA3);
53. }
54. if (PORTAbits.RA4)
55. {
56. D4;
57. debounce ();
58. while (PORTAbits.RA4);
59. }
60. if (PORTAbits.RA5)
61. {
62. F4;
63. debounce ();
64. while (PORTAbits.RA5);
65. }
66. if (PORTAbits.RA6)
67. {
68. F4;
69. debounce ();
70. while (PORTAbits.RA6);
71. }
72. if (PORTAbits.RA7)
73. {
74. G5;
75. debounce ();
76. while (PORTAbits.RA7);
77. }
78. Nonote;
79. }
80. }
```

The Analysis Of Listing 4-7

I will restrict this to the new or more important instructions.

Line 11 #include <musicalNotes.h>

This includes a header file that defines phrases for the settings of the CCP1CON register and the CCPR1L register to create a range of different frequency square waves, one for each musical note you want to use. An example of one of the definitions is

```
#define C4 PR2 = 118, CCPR1L = 0X3B, CCP1CONbits.DC1B1 = 1,
CCP1CONbits.DC1B0 = 1;
```

These are the values that have been calculated for the note C4, which is middle C. Note that I am also including setting the two bits in the CCP1CON register. They are

```
CCP1CONbits.DC1B1 = 1, CCP1CONbits.DC1B0 = 1;
```

Note that CCP1CONbits.DC1B1 is actually Bit5 of the CCP1CON register and CCP1CONbits.DC1B0 is Bit4.

There is a small difference between this type of definition and the previous definitions you have used:

```
#define startbutton PORTAbits.RA0
```

The above definition for the startbutton does not end with a semicolon. However, the #define for the note C4 above does end with a semicolon.

This is because the #define C4 is listing a series of instructions and each instruction is separated by a comma but the last one uses the semicolon because it is the end of the list of instructions. There are four instructions for each definition of the note.

The #define startbutton PORTAbits.RA0 is really explaining to the compiler what the label startbutton stands for.

The full listing for this musicalNotes.h header file is given in Appendix 7.

Lines 15 to 19 create the debounce subroutine. The purpose of this subroutine was explained in Chapter 3.

Line 23 TRISB = 0XFF;

This is to load the TRISB register with all logic 1s. This sets all the bits in PORTB as inputs. You need this as the PICSetUp.h header file sets all of PORTB to outputs so you must override this.

Line 26 OSCCON = 0b01010100;

This overrides the setting the PICSetUp.h header file as you want to reduce the oscillator frequency to 2Mhz. This is needed because at 8Mhz the value calculated for the PR2 would be 472. This would be too big to go into an 8-bit register. You cannot divide the frequency any more so you need to reduce the frequency from 8Mhz to 2Mhz.

Lines 30 to 35 set out by asking if the switch connected to bit0 of PORTA has been pressed. If it has, the micro carries out the instructions to produce the note G3. It then calls the debounce subroutine and makes the micro wait until the switch has been released.

In this way, the PIC will play the note G3 for as long as the user keeps the button on Bit0 of PORTA pressed.

As soon as the user releases the button, the micro will move on to line 150.

Line 150 Nonote;

This makes the micro carry out the following series of instructions:

PR2 = 70, CCPR1L = 0X4F, CCP1CONbits.DC1B1 = 0, CCP1CONbits.DC1B0 = 1;

This is because the phrase Nonote is defined as that in the musicalnote.h header file.

What this does is make the mark time bigger than the period as set by the PR2 value. This will make the PIC send out a flat line on CCP1 instead of a square wave. Therefore, the frequency will be zero and no sound will be sent out.

The lines 36 to 149 simply ask if a button connected to one of the inputs has been pressed. If a button has been pressed, it sends out the appropriate note.

I hope this brief analysis helps you to understand how this program works.

Summary

In this chapter, you learned how to use the Capture Compare PWM module of the PIC to create different square waves. You also learned how to use those square waves to set the speed of a DC motor and how to create different musical notes.

You also learned about using the #define statement to create labels and a series of instructions.

In the next chapter, you will look at controlling and using two common types of DC motors, stepper motors and servo motors.

Answers to the Exercises

Exercise 4-1:

- Frequency = 48.999 Hz

- Frequency = 1046.502Hz

- Frequency = 2,200 Hz

Using

$$\lambda = \frac{v}{f}$$

when f = 48.999

$$\lambda = \frac{343}{48.999} = 7m$$

when f = 1046.502

$$\lambda = \frac{343}{1046.502} = 32.7cm$$

when f = 2,200

$$\lambda = \frac{343}{2200} = 15.59cm$$

Exercise 4-2: Square wave frequency = 2kHz. Therefore, the periodic time = 500µs.

First, you calculate the PR2 value using

$$PR2 = \frac{OCSFreq}{Frequency \times 4 \times TMR2Preset} - 1$$

To get the minimum values, try the highest TMR2Preset value first. If this doesn't produce a valid PR2 value, try the next TMR2Preset value. Therefore, start off with a TMR2Preset of 16.

$$PR2 = \frac{8E^6}{2E^3 \times 4 \times 16} - 1 = 63$$

This PR2 value is OK.

The 20/80 would give a mark time of 125µs. Therefore, using Equation 15, you have:

$$number = \frac{125E^{-6} \times 8E^{6}}{16} = 63$$

Converting 63 to a 10-bit binary number gets you 0000111111. The two least significant bits are 1,1 and they are stored in the CCP1CON register Bits 5 and 4. The remaining 8-bit number of 00001111 is what is stored in the CCPR1L register. You could use 0b00001111 or 0X0F or decimal 15.

CHAPTER 5

DC Motors

In this chapter, you will look at controlling two useful types of DC motors. They are

- The stepper motor

- The servo motor

You will learn how they work and how you can use the PIC micro to control them.

With reference to the servo motor, you will also look at using an analog input, such as a variable voltage, to control the position of the motor.

The Stepper Motor

The stepper motor is a DC motor that has a number of coils encased in the stator part of the motor. To make the rotor rotate, each of the coils in the stator are turned on sequentially so the rotor rotates in steps because it is attracted by the magnetic fields set up in the stator coils. The PIC program basically has to turn on these coils in a certain sequence to make the motor turn. In this way, the motor can turn through one revolution or just a few degrees of a revolution or through many revolutions.

The stepper motor I will use in this example is a very small motor, but it can be used for many applications. The actual motor is a 5V four-phase five-wire stepper motor and a picture of it is shown in Figure 5-1.

© Hubert Henry Ward 2020
H. H. Ward, *Intermediate C Programming for the PIC Microcontroller*,
https://doi.org/10.1007/978-1-4842-6068-5_5

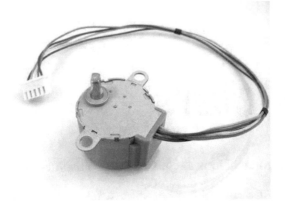

Figure 5-1. *The 5V four-phase stepper motor, 28BYJ-48*

There are five wires that can be connected to a driver circuit and they are

- Red connected to the +5V supply. This needs to be able to supply enough current to the motor, so it may need to be a different supply than the supply to the PIC. However, you should ensure all the 0V, or ground, of the supplies are connected together.

- Orange connected to coil 1

- Yellow connected to coil 2

- Pink connected to coil 3

- Blue connected to coil 4

The red lead supplies the 5V to all the coils. To energize the coils, the ground has to be connected to each coil to allow current to flow through them. If this is done in the correct sequence, the motor will turn in individual steps in either a clockwise or counterclockwise direction. The simplest way to switch the ground on to each coil is to use the ULN2004 driver I.C.. It has an array of seven Darlington NPN transistors. Each Darlington can sink up to 500mA, so they can easily cope with the current demanded from the coils of the stepper motor.

The sequence to make the motor move in a clockwise direction is stated in Table 5-1.

Table 5-1. *The Sequence to Rotate the Motor Clockwise*

Coil Number	Coil Colour
Coils 4 and 1	Blue and orange
Then coil 4	Blue
Then coils 3 and 4	Pink and blue
Then coil 3	Pink
Then coils 3 and 2	Yellow and pink
Then coil 2	Yellow
Then coils 1 and 2	Orange and yellow
Then coil 1	Orange

Note that clockwise is seen looking into the motor from the end of the shaft.

The sequence shown in Table 5-2 is how to make the motor rotate in a counterclockwise direction.

Table 5-2. *The Sequence for Rotating the Motor Counterclockwise*

Coil Number	Coil Colour
Coil 1	Orange
Then coils 1 and 2	Orange and yellow
Then coil 2	Yellow
Then coils 2 and 3	Yellow and pink
Then coil 3	Pink
Then coils 3 and 4	Pink and blue
Then coil 4	Blue
Then coils 4 and 1	Blue and orange

There should be a delay between changing from one step to the next step in the sequence. This delay must be long enough for the current in the coil to build up and so create the magnetic field that steps the motor round. However, the time constant of the coils is very short, so this delay can be short.

This stepper motor goes through 4096 of these individual steps to make one complete revolution. Therefore, each single step turns the stepper motor rotor through 0.08789 of a degree. As there are eight single steps in each sequence of steps, as shown in Tables 5-1 and 5-2, each sequence moves the motor through 0.70312 degrees. Therefore, it takes 360/0.70312 (i.e. 512 sequences of steps) to move the motor through 360 degrees or one complete revolution.

Using this information, you can determine how many steps, or sequences, are required to make the motor turn by any number of degrees.

The basic program for the stepper motor is shown in Listing 5-1.

Listing 5-1. The Basic Program for the Stepper Motor

```
1. // Program for a Stepping Motor
2. // Written By Mr Hubert Ward for the PIC18F4525
3. // Dated 02/07/19
4. // Configuration PIC18F4525
5. // OSC set to INTIO67
6. // WDT set to OFF
7. // LVP set to OFF
8. #include <conFigInternalOscNoWDTNoLVP.h>
9. #include <xc.h>
10. #include <PICSetUp.h>
11. // Some definitions
12. # define orange     PORTBbits.RB3
13. # define yellow     PORTBbits.RB2
14. # define pink       PORTBbits.RB1
15. # define blue       PORTBbits.RB0
16. //Global variables
17. unsigned char n, speed, clkcount;
18. unsigned int ck;
19. //some subroutines
20. void delay (unsigned char t)
21. {
22. while (clkcount < t)
23. {
24. TMR0 = 0;
25. while (TMR0 < 250);
26. clkcount ++;
27. }
28. }
```

```
29. void main()
30. {
31. initialise ();
32. T0CON = 0xC6;
33. speed = 50;
34. while (1)
35. {
36. if (PORTAbits.RA0) speed = 75;
37. if (PORTAbits.RA1) speed = 40;
38. if (PORTAbits.RA2) speed = 20;
39. ck = 0;
40. clockwise:    while (ck < 400)
41. {
42. orange = 1;
43. yellow = 0;
44. pink = 0;
45. blue = 1;
46. TMR0 = 0;
47. while (TMR0 < speed);
48. orange = 0;
49. yellow = 0;
50. pink = 0;
51. blue = 1;
52. TMR0 = 0;
53. while (TMR0 < speed);
54. orange = 0;
55. yellow = 0;
56. pink = 1;
57. blue = 1;
58. TMR0 = 0;
59. while (TMR0 < speed);
```

```
60. orange = 0;
61. yellow = 0;
62. pink = 1;
63. blue = 0;
64. TMRO = 0;
65. while (TMRO < speed);
66. orange = 0;
67. yellow = 1;
68. pink = 1;
69. blue = 0;
70. TMRO = 0;
71. while (TMRO < speed);
72. orange = 0;
73. yellow = 1;
74. pink = 0;
75. blue = 0;
76. TMRO = 0;
77. while (TMRO < speed);
78. orange = 1;
79. yellow = 1;
80. pink = 0;
81. blue = 0;
82. TMRO = 0;
83. while (TMRO < speed);
84. orange = 1;
85. yellow = 0;
86. pink = 0;
87. blue = 0;
88. TMRO = 0;
89. while (TMRO < speed);
90. ck ++;
```

```
 91. goto clockwise;
 92. }
 93. ck = 0;
 94. anticlockwise:    while (ck < 500)
 95. {
 96. TMRO = 0;
 97. while (TMRO < speed);
 98. orange = 1;
 99. yellow = 0;
100. pink = 0;
101. blue = 0;
102. TMRO = 0;
103. while (TMRO < speed);
104. orange = 1;
105. yellow = 1;
106. pink = 0;
107. blue = 0;
108. TMRO = 0;
109. while (TMRO < speed);
110. orange = 0;
111. yellow = 1;
112. pink = 0;
113. blue = 0;
114. TMRO = 0;
115. while (TMRO < speed);
116. orange = 0;
117. yellow = 1;
118. pink = 1;
119. blue = 0;
120. TMRO = 0;
121. while (TMRO < speed);
```

```
122. orange = 0;
123. yellow = 0;
124. pink = 1;
125. blue = 0;
126. TMR0 = 0;
127. while (TMR0 < speed);
128. orange = 0;
129. yellow = 0;
130. pink = 1;
131. blue = 1;
132. TMR0 = 0;
133. while (TMR0 < speed);
134. orange = 0;
135. yellow = 0;
136. pink = 0;
137. blue = 1;
138. TMR0 = 0;
139. while (TMR0 < speed);
140. orange = 1;
141. yellow = 0;
142. blue = 1;
143. TMR0 = 0;
144. while (TMR0 < speed);
145. ck ++;
146. goto anticlockwise;
147. }
148. clkcount = 0;
149. delay (16);
150. }
151. }
```

This program sets the stepper motor to turn clockwise with a slow speed. The speed can be varied by pressing one of the three buttons connected to Bits 0, 1, and 2 of PORTA.

The motor goes through 400 sequences in the clockwise direction. Then it goes through 500 sequences in the counterclockwise direction. There is then a short delay before the motor repeats the process. The figure of 400 sequences means the motor will turn through 281° in the clockwise direction. Then it will turn through 352° in the counterclockwise direction.

I hope there is no need to go through an analysis of every one of the instructions because there are no new instructions. However, I do think it would be useful to add an explanation for some of the instructions.

Line 18 unsigned int ck;

This sets up a 16-bit memory location named ck, made up of two 8-bit registers cascaded together, that can store positive values from 0 to 65535.

The variable ck needs to be an integer because it is used in lines 40 and 94 to control how many sequences the motor carries out in each direction, 400 and 500, respectively.

Line 42 orange = 1;

The label orange is defined in line 12 as Bit3 of PORTB. In this instruction, you are setting the bit to a logic 1. This sends 5V from the PIC to the input of the ULN2004. This turns the Darlington transistor inside the driver I.C. on this transistor and then switches the ground onto the orange coil in the motor. This then allows the current to flow though that coil and so sets up the magnetic field around it.

In this first step, the blue coil is also turned on in the same way as stated in line 45. The yellow and pink coils are turned off in lines 43 and 44 by setting the bits to a logic 0.

Line 46 TMR0 = 0;
Line 47 while (TMR0 < speed);

These two instructions create a small delay between each of the steps. The shorter this delay is (i.e. the smaller the value in the variable speed), the faster the motor will rotate. However, the delay must be long enough to allow the current to build up in the coils and so create the magnetic field that drags the rotor to them.

Stepper motors have many applications where precise movements are required, and printers are the most common application of stepper motors. The actual stepper motor used in this book can be used in many hobbyist projects. I have used it to control a four-story model lift and a turntable in a model railway.

Exercise 5.1

As an exercise, you explain what the following instruction, written on line 32, is doing:

TOCON = 0XC6;

Also, if the variable speed is loaded with 75, how long is the delay between switching the coils?

The Servo Motor

A servo motor is a motor that moves through a limited range of degrees. Typically it can move 90° in one direction and 90° in the opposite direction. It is normally controlled by sending a 50Hz frequency pulse train. The width of the pulse, the mark time, will vary from 1msec to 2msec. This variance of the pulse width will move the servo motor through its complete range of rotation. This movement can be described as going from -90° to $+90^\circ$, or going from 0° to 180° in one direction. The relationship between the changes in degrees to the change in pulse width is linear. Therefore, with a pulse width of 1msec, the servo motor would move to -90; with a pulse width of 1.5msec, it would move to 0; and finally, with a pulse width of 2msec, it would move to +90. Of course, any value of pulse width between 1ms and 2ms would produce the corresponding degrees of rotation from the servo motor.

To control the movement of the servo motor, you need to be able to produce an accurate pulse width at the required frequency of 50Hz.

Using the CCPM to Produce the Pulse Train Signal

In this first example of controlling the servo motor, you will continue the theme of using the CCP module discussed in Chapter 4.

The first thing to do is produce the 50Hz square wave. Chapter 4 explains how you can go about creating a square wave.

To keep the resolution of the rotation good, you'll use an oscillator frequency of 125kHz from the internal oscillator block. Therefore, to get a 50Hz frequency from this oscillator use Equation 5-1:

$$PR2 = \frac{PERIOD \times OscFreq}{4 \times TMR2Preset} - 1$$
$$\therefore PR2 = \frac{20E^{-3} \times 125E^{3}}{4 \times 4} - 1 \qquad \textbf{(Equation 5-1)}$$
$$\therefore PR2 = 155$$

This is the closest you can get to 155.25.

You should start off with the minimum pulse width of 1msec, which should correspond to turning the motor to -90°.

Note that I have chosen a TMR2 preset value of 4 because this will keep the number required to set the pulse width low. This number is calculated using Equation 5-2 as follows:

$$Number = \frac{MarkTime \times OscFreq}{TMR2\mathrm{Preset}}$$

$$\therefore Number = \frac{1E^{-3} \times 125E^{3}}{4}$$

$$\therefore Number = 31.25$$

(Equation 5-2)

Since this has to be converted into a 10-bit binary number, the value is rounded down to 31. In 10-bit binary, the number is 0b0000011111. This means that both Bit5 and Bit4 of the CCP1CON register must be set to logic 1 and the CCPRl1 register must be loaded with 0b00000111.

Using this concept, if you make the pulse width 1.5msec, the servo motor should be in the middle of its travel, which is 0°. To achieve a pulse width of 1.5msec, the number is 47 in decimal, which is 101111 in binary. This means Bit4 and Bit5 of the CCP1CON register must be set to logic 1 and 00001011 must be loaded into the CCPR1L register.

Figure 5-2 from PROTEUS shows the result of these settings.

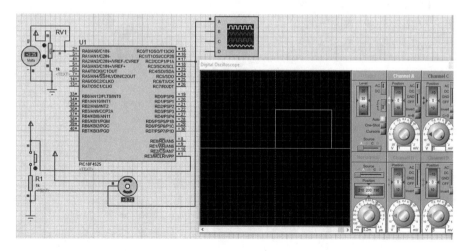

Figure 5-2. *The result of the 1.5msec pulse*

Controlling the Positions of the Servo Motor with a Variable Resistor

In this project, the position of the servo will be controlled via a potentiometer. This means the program will make use of one analog input, such as RA0, to take in the input from the potentiometer.

It will use the CCP1 output to output the 50Hz square wave and use the PWM module to vary the on pulse width from 1msec to 2msec and so control the position of the motor.

The program listing is shown in Listing 5-2.

Listing 5-2. Controlling the Servo Motor with a Variable Voltage

```
1.  #include <xc.h>
2.  #include <math.h>
3.  #include <conFigInternalOscNoWDTNoLVP.h>
4.  //some variables
5.  unsigned char n, button;
6.  //some subroutines
7.  void changeAngle ()
8.  {
9.  ADCONobits.GODONE = 1;
10. while (ADCONobits.GODONE);
11. CCPR1L = (7+round(ADRESH * 0.0314));
12. }
13. void  main ()
14. {
15. PORTA = 0;
16. PORTB = 0;
17. PORTC = 0;
18. TRISA = 0xFF;
19. TRISB = 0;
```

```
20. TRISC = 0;
21. ADCON0 = 0X01;
22. ADCON1 = 0X0E;
23. ADCON2 = 0B00100000;
24. OSCTUNE = 0;
25. OSCCON = 0x14;
26. T0CON = 0xC1;
27. T2CON = 0x05;
28. PR2 = 156;
29. CCP1CON = 0b00111100;
30. CCPR1L = 0x0E;
31. while (1)
32. {
33. changeAngle ();
34. }
35. }
```

The main working part of the program is the subroutine changeAngle. The main program simply calls this subroutine.

The width of the mark time of the 50Hz square wave is controlled via the value in the CCPR1L register. The value that the CCPR1L register needs to produce the minimum pulse of width of 1ms is 0b00000111, which is 7 in decimal. This value can be extended to 0b00001111, which is 15 in decimal, to produce the maximum pulse width of 2ms. This means that to start off with the minimum pulse width of 1ms, the CCPR1L must have the starting value of 7. Then, to get to the maximum pulse width of 2ms, the value in the CCPR1L should be increased by 8 to get to 15. This increase of 8 must come from the ADRESH. As the ADRESH changes from 0 to 255, in decimal, the potentiometer is moved from 0 to maximum. Dividing 8 by 255 gives the multiplying factor of 0.03137, hence the value used is 0.0314.

It is the instruction on line 11 that performs the function.

As an example of how this works, when the potentiometer is at 0V, the result of the ADC, stored in ADRESH, will be 0. Therefore, $7 + (0 \times 0.0314) = 7$. This creates a pulse width of 1ms.

When the potentiometer is at 5V, the ADRESH will go to 255. Therefore, you have $7 + (255 \times 0.0314) = 7 + 8.007 = 15$. The 0.007 is ignored as the instruction is making use of the "round" function. However, to use this "round" function you need to include the `math.h` header file, as is done in line 2 in Listing 5-2. This then will create the maximum pulse width of 2ms.

This is how the instruction on line 11, `CCPR1L = (7+round(ADRESH * 0.0314));`, works.

Again, I hope there is no need to give any further analysis of the instructions in the listing.

This then will enable the servo motor to move from -90 to +90 as the variable resistor, or potentiometer, is varied from 0 to its maximum. This variance of the pulse width is shown in Figures 5-3 and 5-4.

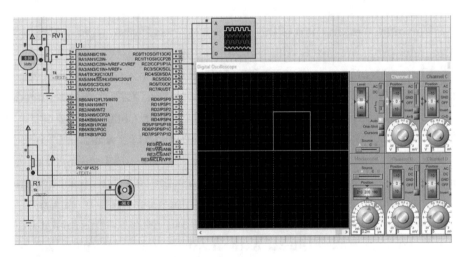

Figure 5-3. *The pulse width with 0V at the input*

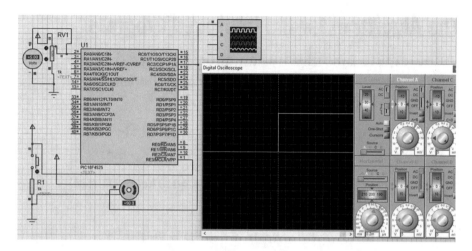

Figure 5-4. *The pulse width with 5V at the input*

Improving The Servo Motor Program

The issue with this simple program to control the servo motor is the definition. The pulse width can only vary by 1ms. With the current program, it is the value stored in the CCPR1L register that controls the actual pulse width of the signal. A value of 7 will produce the 1ms pulse width and this can be increased up to a value of 15 to produce the maximum 2ms pulse width. This gives a resolution of 125µs. This variation from 1ms to 2ms or from a value of 7 to a value of 15 could produce a 180° movement in the motor. This then gives a resolution of 22.5°. Not good enough really. Also, it would not produce a smooth movement of the motor.

A good resolution would be 1°. This would mean dividing this 1ms variance into 180 jumps, giving a resolution of 5.5µs. This degree of resolution, and better, can be achieved by taking a more simplistic approach to creating the 50Hz square wave and the pulse width. This is what the following program does.

215

The Algorithm for the Improved Program

- The basic concept is to turn an output on (i.e. set it high for at least 1ms and then keep it low for the remaining 19ms of the 50Hz period).

- The timing of these two periods is controlled by simply using a counter to count the required clock pulses.

- The program will use the basic timer0 to keep count of the clock pulses.

- The program will use Bit0 of PORTB to output the control signal.

- The program will use an analog signal from a variable voltage inputted to the PIC at bit0 of PORTA. This will be used to vary the pulse width from 1ms to 2ms. Note that when the pulse width is at 2ms, there will only be an 18ms time period for the output to stay low before starting the signal again.

- The signal starts with timer0 at a value of 0 and with the output on bit0 of PORTB high. Then 1ms, or up to 2ms, later the output will go low. The output will stay low for the remaining 19ms or 18ms, after which the cycle will repeat.

- The oscillator will be the 8Mhz signal from the internal oscillator block. This means the clock frequency will be 2MHz. Timer0 will be set to a divide rate of 2, which means it will count at a rate of 1Mhz. This means that each count will have a time span of 1µs. This means that timer0 will count as follows:

- 1000 to create a 1ms pulse

- 2000 to create a 2ms pulse

- 20000 to create a full 20ms time period

- This means that timer0 will have to be configured as a 16-bit counter, which can count up to 65535, which is more than enough for this purpose.

- The ADC result will be stored into the ADRESH and ADRESL registers. You will use the left justification, which means the ADRESH will store the eight most significant bits, and the two least significant bits will be stored in Bit7 and Bit6 of the ADRESL register. You could keep the programming simple by just using the ADRESH register as the value for the analogue input. However, this would mean that the maximum value would be 255. This would result in a resolution of 0.7°, which is pretty good but you can do better than that.

The essence of the program is as follows:

- Start timer0 counting from 0.

- At the same time, send Bit0 of PORTB high.

- Then create a variable for a waiting time from between 1ms to 2ms.

- Then send the output low.

- Then create a second variable for a waiting time of between 19ms to 18ms.

- During that second wait time, read the analog input value and store it to be used to vary the pulse width.

- Then, after the total 20ms has passed, repeat the cycle again.

- The various time periods will be created using timer0.

The complete program listing for this improved program is shown in Listing 5-3.

Listing 5-3. The Improved Program to Control a Servo Motor

```
1. /*A Program to control a servo motor
2. The 50Hz pulse train created with TMRO 16bit
3. Written by Mr H. H. Ward
4. For PIC 18f4525 dated 17/04/20*/
5. #include <xc.h>
6. #include <math.h>
7. #include <conFigInternalOscNoWDTNoLVP.h>
8. #define servoOut PORTBbits.RB0
9. //some variables
10. unsigned int rotate;
11. //some subroutines
12. void changeAngle ()
13. {
14. ADCONobits.GODONE = 1;
15. while (ADCONobits.GODONE);
16. rotate = 1000 +(round (((ADRESH << 2) + (ADRESL >>6)) * 0.95));
17. if (rotate > 1999) rotate = 1999;
18. }
19. void  main ()
20. {
21. PORTA = 0;
22. PORTB = 0;
23. PORTC = 0;
```

```
24. PORTD = 0;
25. TRISA = OxFF;
26. TRISB = 0;
27. TRISC = 0;
28. TRISD = 0;
29. ADCON0 = OX01;
30. ADCON1 = OXOE;
31. ADCON2 = 0B00100001;
32. OSCTUNE = 0;
33. OSCCON = 0b01110100;
34. T0CON = 0b10000000;
35. rotate = 1000;
36. while (1)
37. {
38. begin: TMR0 = 0;
39. servoOut = 1;
40. while(TMR0 < 2000)    if (TMR0 >= rotate)servoOut = 0;
41. while(TMR0 < 18500)    changeAngle ();
42. while (TMR0 < 20000);
43. goto begin;
44. }
45. }
```

There are no real new instructions but I will explain some of the more important instructions here.

Line 10 unsigned int rotate;

This simply creates a 16-bit register that will store the value that creates the variable pulse width. It needs to be a 16-bit number since it will store values greater than 255.

Line 16 rotate = 1000 +(round (((ADRESH << 2) + (ADRESL >>6)) * 0.95));

This instruction is part of the subroutine changeAngle. In this subroutine, you use the ADC to convert the variable voltage applied to Bit0 of PORTA into a 10-bit binary number. The PIC uses two 8-bit registers to store this 10-bit result since the PIC18f4525 only uses 8-bit registers. The two registers are called ADRESH and ADRESL. The letters ADRES stand for analog digital result, the H stands for high byte, and the L stands for low byte. This is because a 16-bit number, termed a word, can be split into two 8-bit numbers, termed a byte, which are termed the high byte for the upper 8 bits and the low byte for the lower 8 bits.

You are using left justification, which means the upper 8 bits of the ADC results are stored in the ADRESH register and the two remaining lower bits are stored in Bit7 and Bit6 of the ADRESL register, respectively.

You could use just the ADRESH register to obtain the value for the variable rotate, but this would reduce the resolution to 3.9µs or 0.7^O for a 180° swing. However, if you used all 10 bits of the ADC result, you could achieve a resolution of 1µs or 0.18703^O for a 180° swing.

To use all 10 bits, you must move a copy of both the ADRESH and the ADRESL into a 16-bit variable. The variable you will use is the rotate variable you created in line 10. However, this means that Bit7 of the ADRESH must be moved to Bit9 of the rotate variable. This is so that you can leave Bit0 and Bit1 of this 16-bit variable rotate for the two least significant bits of the result of the ADC conversion. This actually means that when you create the copy of the ADRESH in the variable rotate, you must first shift all the bits of the ADRESH two places to the left. This is done by including the C instruction << 2, as you do in line 16.

Now you need to add the 8 bits that have been stored in the ADRESL register. However, the two LSB bits of the ADC result were stored in Bits 7 and 6 of the ADRESL register. In those two positions, the bits will represent a value of 192, if they were both logic 1s, instead of 3, which is what they should represent because they would be Bits 1 and 0 of the ADC result.

This means you must move the two bits from Bit7 and Bit6 to Bit1 and Bit0 before you add them to the variable rotate. This is what the instruction >>6 does. It shifts the bits six places to the right.

In this way you make sure that the variable rotate has the actual 10-bit binary number that is the full result of the ADC conversion in the correct position in the variable rotate.

However, there is still one issue to deal with. It is the issue that the 10-bit result can go to a maximum of 1023, not the 1000 that you want. This is because 10 bits have a value of $2^{10} = 1024$. Therefore, to reduce this value, and also to make sure you don't create an increase in the pulse width greater than 1ms, you multiply the result of the addition by 0.95 before storing the result in the variable rotate. Note the use of brackets to split the instruction up into its different parts.

I know this is a very wordy description of how this instruction works, but it is quite a complex instruction. If you read through it a couple of times, I hope you will be able to follow it.

Line 17 if (rotate > 1999) rotate = 1999;

With this instruction you are trying to be super safe in making sure the value in rotate does not produce a pulse width that is greater than 2ms. With this instruction, if the value in the variable rotate exceeds 1999, then it will be changed to 1999.

Line 35 T0CON = 0b10000000;

This configures the Timer0 as follows:

- Setting Bit7 to a logic 1 turns the timer on.

- Setting Bit6 to a logic 0 makes it a 16-bit register.

- Setting Bit3 to a logic 0 allocates the prescaler, the divide rate to Timer0.

- Setting Bits 2, 1, and 0 to a logic 0 gives a divide rate of 2.

- Bits 5 and 4 are not really relevant here.

Line 41 while (TMR0 < 2000) if (TMR0 >= rotate) servoOut = 0;

This instruction controls when the signal to the servo goes low. The if test asks if the value in timer0 is greater than or equal to the value stored in the variable rotate. You cannot simply ask, is timer equal to rotate? This will only be true for one instant in time, and the test might miss that instant.

If the test is true, the micro will set the output on Bit0 of PORTB to a logic 0. Note the term servoOut means Bit0 of PORTB as defined in line 8.

The while (TMR0 < 2000) (i.e. is timer0 less than 2000?) is needed to trap the micro at this line until the value in Timer0 becomes greater than 2000. In this way, the micro will continually test if timer0 >= rotate until the test becomes true. If you didn't have this while part to line 41, then the micro would only carry out the if test once and then move on. Not what you want.

Line 42 while (TMR0 < 18500)   changeAngle ();

This traps the micro at this point in the program until the value in timer0 becomes greater than 18500. The value of 18500 in timer0 equates to 18500 x 1ms i.e. 18.5ms,

All the micro is asked to do while it is trapped here is call the subroutine changeAngle. In doing this, the micro will get the up-to-date position that the servo motor needs to take up. The call to the subroutine is at this point in the program because the micro is doing nothing while it waits for the 18.5ms period to complete.

It is important that the micro is not carrying out the instructions of the changeAngle subroutine when the 20ms time period comes to an end. This is important because if the micro was carrying out the changeAngle subroutine at this 20ms time period, then you might go over the 20ms period and so reduce the frequency of the pulse train. That is why the value for timer0 stipulated in the while test is 18500 not 20000. This is to ensure that the micro is not stuck inside the changeAngle subroutine during the last 1.5ms of the 20ms time period. You should appreciate that it will take at least 2.5µs for an ADC conversion to complete and there are other instructions in the changeAngle subroutine**.

It is not as easy as it was when writing programs in assembler to know exactly how long a C program instruction takes; therefore leave some leeway in your timing operations.

Line 42 while (TMR0 < 20000);

This makes the micro do nothing until the final 1.5ms has finished. This then is the end of the full 20ms period of the 50Hz pulse train. At the end of this period, the micro is forced to go back to the start of the sequence, at line 39, using the label begin as stated on line 43.

I downloaded the program using my prototype board to a practical servo motor. The movement of the motor was very smooth and the frequency of the pulse train was very stable at 50Hz. The pulse width did vary smoothly from 1ms to 2ms. Therefore I am much happier with this improved program than the first program that used the CCP module.

** To understand more of the ADC conversion routine, please read my first book, *C Programming for PIC Microcontrollers*.

Summary

In this chapter, you learned how to control two very useful types of motors, the stepper motor and the servo motor.

You also studied how the CCP module and the basic timer module can be used to control a servo motor.

You looked at how you can use some basic math tools in C programs and how to manipulate the bits of data in 8-bit registers to correctly align them in a 16-bit register.

Servo motors are widely used in industries with robotics, actuators, etc. and with hobbyist in remote cars, boats, and airplanes.

I hope this chapter has given you a fundamental appreciation of the two motors and the basis on which to use them in your own exciting projects.

In the next chapter, you will look at using a very exciting and useful aspect of all microcontrollers: the use of interrupts. You will also look at using the compare and capture aspect of the CCP module.

Solution to the Exercise

Exercise 5-1: The instruction T0CON = 0XC6; will load the SPF register T0CON with the following binary value:

11000110

This means Bit7 is a logic 1, which simply turns timer 0 on.

Also, Bit6 is a logic 1, which means the timer is an 8-bit timer.

Bit3 is a logic 0, which means the prescaler or divider is applied to timer0.

The last three bits are 110, which means that a divide rate of 128 is applied to the timer. This means the following:

- Osc = 8Mhz as set by the OSCCON register.

- The clock runs at a quarter of the oscillator, therefore it runs at 2Mhz.

- Time0 divides this by 128, therefore timer1 runs at 15.625kHz, so one count takes 64µS.

Loading the variable speed with 75 makes the micro wait until Timer0 has counted to a value of 75. As it takes Timer0 64µs to count once, it will take 75x64E-6 i.e. 4.8ms. This means the delay between switching the coils will be around 4.8ms. It will take some time for the micro to complete the instructions in the delay and this will add a bit more to the delay but this would be very small, in the order of a couple of microseconds.

CHAPTER 6

Interrupts

In this chapter, you are going to look at interrupts. You will look at the importance of the fetch and execute cycle and the program counter.

Also, as stated in Chapter 4, you will use the compare aspect of the CCP module to create a square wave.

After reading this chapter, you will know what the program counter (PC) is and its importance. You will also learn what interrupts are, what they can be used for, and how to use them. You will appreciate what the compare aspect of the CCP module can do.

What Are Interrupts?

Interrupts are a very useful aspect of a microcontroller. Consider the situation where a microcontroller is monitoring a fire alarm system and other everyday tasks such as word processing or email. Hopefully the fire alarm will not go off. However, if it does, the microcontroller will stop your word processing and turn on the fire alarms and maybe some sprinklers and send out a call to the local fire station.

One way of making sure this will happen is for the program to examine the fire alarm switch to see if it has been pressed. The question is how often should it examine the switch: once every five minutes, once a minute, every second? This type of monitoring is termed "software polling." However, 99% of the time it is a waste of effort, as hopefully,

© Hubert Henry Ward 2020
H. H. Ward, *Intermediate C Programming for the PIC Microcontroller*,
https://doi.org/10.1007/978-1-4842-6068-5_6

in this case, the fire alarm has not gone off. Also, there may be a delay in realizing the fire alarm switch was pressed because it was pressed between the polling of the switch. It's not a very efficient method.

This is where interrupts can be used. This is a process whereby the microcontroller simply lets you carry on with mundane tasks but if an emergency happens, such as the fire alarm being pressed, the microcontroller will automatically interrupt the normal sequence of your program and force the controller to carry out the required action of the emergency. The monitoring of the fire alarm itself does not need any program instructions. What to do if the fire alarm goes off is written as a special type of subroutine called an interrupt service routine, or ISR.

This seems ideal since there is no wasted time polling the switch and there is no possibility of missing the emergency call. In reality, it is really a very efficient method of software polling, but, apart from writing to some SFRs, you don't have to write it into your program; it happens automatically. Also, there is no chance of you missing a call.

To appreciate how this concept works, you need to take a brief look at the fetch and execute cycle of the microcontroller.

The Fetch and Execute Cycle

All microprocessor systems have to go through this type of cycle every time they carry out an instruction. The actual approach may vary but in essence it has to be something along these lines.

The Program Counter

You have to appreciate that all of the instructions for any program the micro is doing must be stored in the memory of the system, and the micro has to know where to go to in this memory to find the next instruction.

For the PIC to run a program, the micro must go to its program memory area to find the instructions of the program. All the memory locations in the PIC's memory have their own address. How then does the micro know which address in memory it needs to go to so that it can get the instructions? A special register called the program counter (PC) does this job. With respect to the PIC18F4525, the PC is a 21-bit register that is made up of three 8-bit registers. When the PIC is first turned on, the housekeeping firmware loads the PC with the address of the first instruction in the program. This relates to the main loop that all C programs must have. From then on the PC is automatically incremented in the fetch and execute cycle, so that it is always pointing to the location in memory where the micro can get the next instruction in the program.

The fetch and execute cycle goes along following lines:

1. The micro examines the program counter to find out where it has to go to in the memory to find the next instruction. At the start of the program, this is the first instruction. The micro will then go to that address and get the instruction. This is the fetch part.

2. The next step, BEFORE the micro even looks at the instruction, is to increment the contents of the PC so that it is always pointing to the memory location of the next instruction. Note that because the instruction might be in two parts called the opcode and the operand, the information in the next memory location may not be an opcode; it may be the operand. However, this concept is not too important for this analysis.

3. This next step is the important step, and it may occur as I will describe it now or with some micros it may occur later in the cycle. However, it must occur in the fetch and execute cycle. The step is that the micro will check the interrupt flag. This is a flag that will be set if an event has occurred that demands the micro stops what it is doing, whatever it is, and deal with the emergency that triggered the interrupt flag. If this interrupt flag is set, the micro goes through the following steps:

    a. It stores the contents of the PC onto an area in memory called the stack.

    b. It then goes to a special memory location called the interrupt vector to find out where it has to go to carry out the sequence of events to deal with the emergency that triggered the interrupt flag.

    c. It must then carryout the instructions of the ISR (the interrupt service routine).

    d. Then, on returning from the ISR, it will reload the PC with the memory address it stored on the stack when it started the response to the interrupt in Step a.

    e. The micro can then complete the fetch and execute cycle.

4. If the flag is not set, the micro moves onto Step 5.

5. The next step in the cycle is to examine the instruction it has just retrieved from memory. If the micro needs more info before it can carry out the instruction, it looks at the contents of the PC to find out where in memory it must go and goes there to get the info. This means the cycle goes back to Step 1 and the micro goes through Steps 2 and 3 as before. This means it must check the interrupt flag again.

6. If the instruction does not need any more info, then the micro can carry out the instruction. This is the execute part of the cycle. Then the cycle starts back again at Step 1.

I am not guaranteeing that this is an exact description of the cycle. Indeed, the whole sequence is a complex procedure and it is not my intention to explain it in this book. However, it is correct in the essence of what must happen every time the micro gets an instruction or data from memory. It is important to realize that the micro must check this interrupt flag.

In this way, it is a kind of software polling except that the programmer does not have to write any program instruction to make this happen. It is done by what is known as the firmware of the PIC.

The benefit of using this approach is that you can never miss an interrupt call and you don't have to waste time, and instructions, continually asking if an interrupt has occurred.

However, what you do have to understand is how to make the PIC make use of this interrupt flag. I will explain this in the next section.

The Sources of Interrupts

The PIC18F4525 has a number of different sources that can be used to trigger this interrupt flag.

- There are external interrupt sources and the PIC18F4525 has three, which are

    - INT0 on Bit0 of PORTB

    - INT1 on Bit1 of PORTB

    - INT2 on Bit2 of PORTB

- There is also the use of change on PORTB as an external interrupt; this uses Bits 7, 6, 5, and 4 of PORTB.

- There is a wide range of internal interrupts, known as peripheral interrupts, which come from a range of peripheral devices, such as timers, the ADC, the UART, etc.

In general, there are three bits for each of the different interrupt sources that are used to control their operation. They are

1. The enable bit that simply enables the source to cause an interrupt.

2. The interrupt flag for that source. This is used to identify which source caused the interrupt.

3. The interrupt priority bit. This is used to signify if this interrupt can interrupt other interrupts that are already running.

There are 10 registers that are associated with interrupts and you will look at them as you go through an interrupt exercise.

The Process for a Simple Interrupt with No Priorities

The PIC18F4525 can apply two levels of interrupt priorities, which are simply high or low priorities. To start, you will look at using interrupts with no priorities. This implies that there is a way of enabling or disabling the priority interrupts. Indeed, there is and it is Bit7 of the RCON register. This is called the IPEN (interrupt priority enable) bit. If you reset this bit to a logic 0, you will have disabled the interrupt priority function of the PIC. This is what you will do now. You will look at using interrupt priorities later in this chapter.

The process of an interrupt is as follows:

- A source will set the interrupt flag that is checked in the fetch and execute cycle.

- The current contents of the PC are stored on the stack. This is so the micro can find out where it needs to go back to in the main program when the interrupt service routine has been completed.

- The PC is then loaded with the address 0X0008 if the high-priority interrupts are being used or address 0X0018 if there are no high-priority interrupts being used. These two addresses are termed "interrupt vector addresses." In this case, since you are not using priority interrupts, the PC is loaded with 0X0018.

- The micro then goes to the interrupt vector address where it loads the PC with the address that is stored there. This will be the address of the ISR, which, in the download operation, the housekeeping firmware stores in that vector.

- The micro can now go to this ISR where it polls the interrupt flags of the sources that are being used to determine which source caused the interrupt.

- The micro then carries out the instructions of that particular interrupt after which it returns back from the interrupt.

- In doing so, the PC is reloaded with the address from the stack and the micro can then carry on with the fetch and execute cycle.

To help explain how this works, let's write a program that will use two of the external interrupt sources, those of INT0 on Bit0 of PORTB and INT2 on Bit2 of PORTB, to cause an interrupt.

It will also use a peripheral interrupt source that associated with timer 2, TMR2.

Setting Up the PIC to Respond to the Interrupts

Now you can now go about setting up the PIC to respond to the two external interrupts: INT0, which is the external interrupt connected to PORTB Bit0, and INT2, which is the external interrupt connected to PORTB Bit2 and the TMR2 peripheral interrupt.

The first control register you will look at is the INTCON register. The names of the individual bits of the INTCON are detailed in Table 6-1.

Table 6-1. *The INTCON Register*

Bit7	Bit6	Bit5	Bit4	Bit3	Bit2	Bit1	Bit0
GIE/GIEH	PEIE/GIEL	TMR0IE	INT0IE	RBIE	TMR0IF	INT0IF	RBIF[1]

The operation of the bits is described as follows:

Bit7, GIE/GIEH (global interrupt enable/global interrupt enable priority high)

This bit has two uses. The uses for this bit depend upon the setting of the IPEN bit, which is Bit7 of the RCON register. Don't worry; it's not as confusing as it looks. The IPEN bit is simply the interrupt priority enable bit. This is a function that can allow an interrupt to be interrupted by another interrupt that has been given a higher priority than the one currently running. The programmer can allow this to happen by enabling the function. This is done by setting this bit, the IPEN bit, to a logic 1. If, as you will be doing, you set this bit to a logic 0, you won't enable any interrupts to have a higher priority.

When the IPEN bit is a logic 0, the action for Bit7 is

- A logic 1 will enable all unmasked interrupts

- A logic 0 will disable all interrupts.

When the IPEN bit is a logic 1, the action for bit 7 is

- A logic 1 will enable all high-priority interrupts.

- A logic 0 will disable all interrupts.

This means that if you are to use any interrupts, external or peripheral, no priority or use priority, this bit must be set to a logic 1. The term "global" means it can enable or disable external and or peripheral interrupts.

Bit6, PEIE/GIEL (peripheral interrupt enable/global interrupt low priority enable)

This bit also has two sets of actions which depend on the setting of the IPEN bit in the RCON register.

When the IPEN bit is a logic 0, the action for Bit6 is

- A logic 1 will enable all unmasked peripheral interrupts.

- A logic 0 will disable all peripheral interrupts.

When the IPEN bit is a logic 1, the action for Bit6 is

- A logic 1 will enable all low priority interrupts.

- A logic 0 will disable all the low priority peripheral interrupts.

Since this program is going to use one of the peripheral interrupts, this bit must set to a logic 1.

Bit 5, TMR0IE (timer0 overflow interrupt enable bit)

There is an interrupt flag associated with timer0. When timer0 gets to its maximum value, a further increment will cause it to roll over back to 0; this is termed "roll over." When this happens, the TMR0IF, timer0 interrupt flag, will be set to tell the micro this has happened. To allow this action to instigate an interrupt, you have to set this Bit5 of the INTCON register.

A logic 1 in Bit5 of the INTCON register will enable this interrupt.

A logic 0 in Bit5 of the INTCON register will disable this interrupt.

However, even though the interrupt action is disabled, the TMR0IF, Bit 2 of this INTCON register, will be set the first time timer0 rolls over. But this action will not set the interrupt flag, which is checked within the fetch and execute cycle.

You will not be using this interrupt, so you set this to logic 0.

Bit 4, INT0IE (external INT0 enable bit)

A logic 1 will enable the INT0 interrupt.

A logic 0 will disable the INT0 interrupt.

Therefore, as you are using INT0, this bit must be set to a logic 1.

Bit 3, RBIE (PORTB change interrupt enable bit)

A logic 1 will enable this interrupt.

A logic 0 will disable this interrupt.

Note that this interrupt is activated when one of the inputs on Bit7, Bit6, Bit5, and Bit4 of PORTB change their logic state.

You will not be using this interrupt, so you set this to logic 0.

Bit 2, TMR0IF (the timer0 interrupt flag)

This is the actual flag that the TMR0 sets when the timer rolls over. Note this flag has to be cleared or reset (i.e. set back to a logic 0) by the software program.

A logic 1 indicates that timer0 has rolled over. This bit must be cleared in software so that the micro can set it again the next time timer0 rolls over.

The programmer can monitor this bit to detect when timer0 rolls over even if this action is not going to initiate an interrupt. Indeed, the programmer can monitor most interrupt flags in this fashion.

Bit 1, INT0IF (INT0 external interrupt flag)

This is the actual flag that the INT0 interrupt sets when the INT0 causes an interrupt. In the ISR, you can ask the micro to check this flag to see if it was INT0 that caused the interrupt.

A logic 1 indicates that an interrupt on INT0 has occurred. This bit must be cleared in software.

Bit 0, RBIF (PORTB change interrupt flag)

A logic 1 means at least one of Bit7 to Bit4 on PORTB has changed state. This bit must be cleared in software.

In the ISR, you can ask the micro to check this flag to see if it was a change of state on PORTB that caused the interrupt.

You should now be able to determine what logic you must write to each of these bits in the INTCON register.

As you are going to use an interrupt, be it external or peripheral, you will have to enable all unmasked interrupts and so you must set Bit7 to a logic 1. Note that the IPEN bit in the RCON register will be set to a logic 0 since you won't be using any high-priority interrupts.

You will need to enable the peripheral interrupts because you are using the TMR2 peripheral interrupt. Therefore you must set Bit6 the PEN, peripheral enable bit, to a logic 1.

You are not using the TMR0 interrupt, so you can set Bit5 to a logic 0.

You are going to use the INT0 interrupt, therefore Bit4 must be set to a logic 1.

You are not going to the use the change on PORTB interrupt, therefore Bit3 can be set to a logic 0.

Bits 2, 1, and 0 are actual flags that if they are used, the micro will set. Therefore at this present time, set them to a logic 0.

This means that the 8-bit number for the INTCON register will be as shown in Table 6-2.

Table 6-2. *The Data to Be Written to INTCON Register*

Bit7	Bit6	Bit5	Bit4	Bit3	Bit2	Bit1	Bit0
GIE/GIEH	PEIE/GIEL	TMR0IE	INT0IE	RBIE	TMR0IF	INT0IF	RBIF1
1	1	0	1	0	0	0	0

The instruction to do this is

INTCON = 0b11010000;

This enables all global interrupts and peripheral interrupts. It also enables the INT0 interrupt.

You now need to enable the other two interrupts, the INT2 and TMR2 match interrupts. The control register that controls the INT2 external interrupt is INTCON3. INTCON1 and INTCON2 control other interrupts that you are not using. Therefore, these two control registers can be left at their default settings of zero.

The names of the bits of the INTCON3 8-bit register are shown in Table 6-3.

Table 6-3. *The TNTCON3 Register*

Bit7	Bit6	Bit5	Bit4	Bit3	Bit2	Bit1	Bit0
INT2IP	INT1IP	Not Used	INT2IE	INT1IE	Not Used	INT2IF	INT1IF

As you are not using any interrupt priority, Bits 7 and 6 can be set to logic 0.

As you are using the external interrupt INT2, Bit4 must be set to a logic 1 since this is INT2IE (interrupt 2 interrupt enable bit).

As you are not using INT1, Bit3 must be set to a logic 0.

Note that Bits 1 and 0 are flags or signals to the program that the appropriate interrupt has occurred. Therefore, at this point in time, they will be set to a logic 0.

Therefore, the 8-bit number that has to be written to this control register is 0b00010000. This is done with the following instruction:

```
INTCON3 = 0b00010000;
```

Just as a point of interest, I'll explain why we use the term "flag." This is because in the United States and some other countries, people sometimes have boxes at their garden gate where they get mail. To signify to the mailman that there is mail in the box that needs posting, the owner flips up a flag-shaped lever on the side of the can. This is seen as a logic 1. The mailman will get the post and flip the flag down, a logic 0. If there is no outgoing mail, this flag will be left down. Hence we use the term flag to represent a signal source.

The PIE1 Register

This is the peripheral interrupt enable 1 register. It is an 8-bit register that allows us to enable some of the peripheral interrupts; the TMR2 interrupt is one of them. There are so many peripheral interrupts that the PIC18F4525 has two PIE registers. The names of the bits of the PIE1 are shown in Table 6-4.

Table 6-4. *The PIE1 Register*

Bit7	Bit6	Bit5	Bit4	Bit3	Bit2	Bit1	Bit0
PSPIE[1]	ADIE	RCIE	TXIE	SSPIE	CCP1IE	TMR2IE	TMR1IE

The 8 bits control the PIC in the following manner:

Bit7, PSPIE (parallel slave port read/write interrupt enable bit)

1 = Enables the PSP read/write interrupt

0 = Disables the PSP read/write interrupt

Bit6, ADIE (A/D converter interrupt enable bit)

1 = Enables the A/D interrupt

0 = Disables the A/D interrupt

Bit5, RCIE (EUSART receive interrupt enable bit)

1 = Enables the EUSART receive interrupt

0 = Disables the EUSART receive interrupt

Bit4, TXIE (EUSART transmit interrupt enable bit)

1 = Enables the EUSART transmit interrupt

0 = Disables the EUSART transmit interrupt

Bit3, SSPIE (master synchronous serial port interrupt enable bit)

1 = Enables the MSSP interrupt

0 = Disables the MSSP interrupt

Bit2, CCP1IE (CCP1 interrupt enable bit)

1 = Enables the CCP1 interrupt

0 = Disables the CCP1 interrupt

Bit1, TMR2IE (TMR2 to PR2 match interrupt enable bit)

1 = Enables the TMR2 to PR2 match interrupt

0 = Disables the TMR2 to PR2 match interrupt

Bit0, TMR1IE (TMR1 overflow interrupt enable bit)

1 = Enables the TMR1 overflow interrupt

0 = Disables the TMR1 overflow interrupt

Since you want to use the TMR2 interrupt, you must set Bit1 to a logic 1. All of the other bits can be set to a logic 0.

Therefore, the data to be written to the PEI1 control register is 0b00000010. This is done with the following instruction:

```
PEI1 = 0b00000010;
```

The Algorithm for the Interrupt Test Program

The main section of the program will either turn off all LEDs on PORTC if Bit4 of PORTB is momentarily pressed or turn on LEDs 1 and 2 of PORTC if Bit5 of PORTB is momentarily pressed.

The three interrupts will force the PIC to do the following:

- Light up the first four LEDs connected to Bits 0, 1, 2, and 3 of PORTC. This will happen if the INT0 external interrupt is activated. This will happen when Bit0 of PORTB is momentarily pressed.

- Light up the three LEDs connected to Bits 2, 3, and 5 of PORTC. This will happen if the INT2 external interrupt is activated. This will happen when Bit2 of PORTB is momentarily pressed.

- The LED connected to Bit0 of PORTD will light up the first time the value in timer2 matches the value in the PR2 register.

- The next time the value in timer2 matches the value in the PR2 register, the LED will turn off.

- From then on, the LED will continue to turn on and turn off when the value in timer 2 matches the value in the PR2 register. This is the action of the TMR2 match interrupt. Every time the value in timer2 matches the value in the PR2 register, the TMR2 match interrupt will occur.

Compiler Software Version Issue

There is an issue I have come across when using interrupts. There seems to be a problem of which compiler version to use with interrupts. I have noticed that the later versions of the XC8 compiler seem to have a problem with keyword Interrupt. However, I don't have this problem when I use version 1.35. Therefore, to ensure the program compiles correctly, you should select version 1.35 when asked to select the compiler in the project creation process. If you have already created your project, you can change the compiler program by holding the right mouse button on the name of the project in the project tree. A flyout menu will appear, so select the properties option that appears at the bottom of the menu. You will see the window shown in Figure 6-1. You can now change the complier software to the earlier version 1.35, as I have done. The program will now compile correctly.

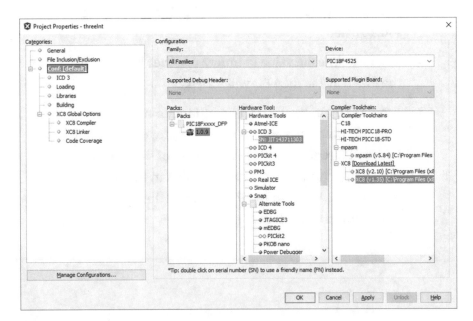

Figure 6-1. *The Project Properties window*

This is a very strange issue. I have tried to find a solution on the Internet but I have found nothing that makes sense of this. What is even stranger is that if you now change the compiler back to the version 2.10, the program will compile correctly. I think this is another example of *change is not always for the best.* I do prefer using the XC8 compiler version 1.35 for my projects.

The complete code for this program that tests the operation of these three interrupts is shown in Listing 6-1.

Listing 6-1. The Code for the Three Interrupt Sources

```
1. /*This is simple program to investigate interrupts
2. It uses three interrupt sources which are
3. INTO and INT2 two external interrupts
4. TMR2 match interrupt an internal peripheral interrupt
5. INTO and INT2 will effect the display on PORTC
6. The TMR2 match will effect bit0 on PORTD
7. The program is written for the PIC 18F4525
8. Written by H H Ward Dated 07/06/15
9. */
10. #include <xc.h>
11. #include <conFigInternalOscNoWDTNoLVP.h>
12. #include <PICSetUp.h>
13. void interrupt ISR ()
14. {
15. if (INTCONbits.INTOIF == 1)
16. {
17. INTCONbits.INTOIF= 0;
18. PORTC = 0xOF;
19. }
20. else if(INTCON3bits.INT2IF == 1)
21. {
```

```
22. INTCON3bits.INT2IF= 0;
23. PORTC = 0x2C;
24. }
25. else if (PIR1bits.TMR2IF == 1)
26. {
27. PIR1bits.TMR2IF = 0;
28. if (PORTDbits.RD0 == 0) PORTDbits.RD0 = 1;
29. else PORTDbits.RD0 = 0;
30. }
31. }
32. main ()
33. {
34. initialise ();
35. TRISBbits.RB0 = 1;
36. TRISBbits.RB2 = 1;
37. TRISBbits.RB4 = 1;
38. TRISBbits.RB5 = 1;
39. TRISD = 0;
40. INTCON = 0b11010000;
41. INTCON2 = 0b0000000;
42. INTCON3 = 0b00010000;
43. PIE1 = 0b00000010;
44. RCONbits.IPEN = 0;
45. OSCCON = 0b00010100;
46. T2CON = 0b00000111;
47. PR2 = 250;
48. PORTC = 0;
49. while (1)
50. {
51. if (PORTBbits.RB4 == 1) PORTC = 0;
```

```
52. else if (PORTBbits.RB5 == 1)  PORTC = 6;
53. }
54. }
```

The Analysis of Listing 6-1

Lines 1 to 9 are simply my comments for this program.

Line 10 #include <xc.h>

This is the main include file.

Line 11 #include <conFigInternalOscNoWDTNoLVP.h>

This is the header file you created before.

Line 12 #include <PICSetUp.h>

This is the header file you created before. However, there are certain aspects you will have to change. They are changed later in the program.

Line 13 void interrupt ISR ()

This is the first step in creating a special subroutine. It is termed the interrupt service routine ISR. That is why you have the keyword interrupt after the keyword void. When the IDE loads the program down to the PIC, the firmware will load the interrupt vector address 0X0018 with the memory location of where the first instruction of this ISR can be found in the PIC's program memory.

The keyword void means that the ISR will not be sending any data back to the main program.

Line 14 {

This is simply the opening curly bracket of the ISR.

Line 15 if (INTCONbits.INTOIF == 1)

There are three possible interrupt sources that may have set the interrupt flag that was checked during the fetch and execute cycle. The first thing you must do in the ISR is determine which interrupt source caused the interrupt. You do this by testing each of the interrupt flags that belong to the sources. This uses the *if this, then do that, else do something else* test. In this case, check the next interrupt flag. In line 15, you check to see if the INT0IF (INT0 interrupt flag, that is Bit1 of the INTCON register) has been set. If it has, this means that it was the external interrupt INT0 that caused the interrupt. If it isn't set, then you must check the other interrupt flags.

Line 16 {

Since there is more than one instruction to carry out with this test, you have to envelope the instructions inside a set of curly brackets. This is the opening curly bracket for the instructions associated with INT0.

Line 17 INTCONbits.INT0IF = 0;

This will turn the INT0 Interrupt Flag off. This must be the first thing you do or the INT0 interrupt will continue to cause an interrupt even though Bit0 of PORTB has gone back to a logic 0. Note you would have let go of the momentary switch connected to Bit0 of PORTB by now.

Line 18 PORTC = 0x0F;

This is what should happen if the INT0 interrupt is made to happen. The first four bits on PORTC should go to a logic 1 and the remaining bits go to a logic 0.

Line 19 }

This is the closing curly bracket of the first if, the test for the INT0 interrupt. If it was INT0 that caused the interrupt, then the micro will ignore all the other instructions in the ISR and return back to the main program from here.

Line 20 else if (INTCON3bits.INT2IF == 1)

This is the else part of the first if test. If the test on line 15 was untrue, then the micro will carry out this test. This tests to see if the INT2IF is set. This would mean that the INT2 caused the interrupt.

Line 21 {

Again, this test is a multiple-line instruction and so the instructions are enclosed in a set of curly brackets. This is the opening curly bracket for this test.

Line 22 INTCON3bits.INT2IF = 0;

Again, you must turn off the interrupt flag that caused the interrupt so that it doesn't continually cause an interrupt. In this, case it was INT2 that caused the interrupt so set its flag, IN2IF, to a logic 0.

Line 23 PORTC = 0x2C;

This is what should happen if the INT2 interrupt is made to happen.

Line 24 }

This is the closing curly bracket of the second if, the test for the INT2 interrupt.

Line 25 else if (PIR1bits.TMR2IF == 1)

Here you are checking to see if it was the third source that caused the interrupt. This is the TMR2 interrupt, which is an internal peripheral interrupt. This does not require any action from the user of the program. This interrupt will happen automatically every time the value in timer2 matches the value stored in the PR2 register. This PR2 register is a special register that is used in conjunction with timer2.

Line 26 {

This is the opening curly bracket for this if test.

Line 27 PIR1bits.TMR2IF = 0;

Again, the first thing you must do is turn off the TMR2 interrupt flag.

Line 28 if (PORTDbits.RD0 == 0) PORTDbits.RD0 = 1;

Here you are creating an if test that tests to see if Bit0 of PORTD is at a logic 0. If it is a logic 0, then set it to a logic 1. Note that this is a single-line if test, so you don't need the curly brackets.

Line 29 else PORTDbits.RD0 = 0;

This is what the PIC must carry out if the test on line 28 was untrue (i.e. if Bit0 of PORTD was actually at a logic 1, then reset the bit to logic 0). Note that because you are using the *if this, then do this, else do that* type of function with lines 28 and 29, if the test on line 28 was true, the micro would simply skip this else instruction on line 29. The micro would only carry out the instruction on line 29 if the test on line 28 was untrue.

This is the difference between this type of instruction and simply listing a series of if test after if test. With the if test after if test, the micro must look at each if test whether or not the pervious test was true. This is a very subtle difference, but an important one.

In this way, lines 28 and 29 will make the logic on Bit0 of PORTD alternate between logic 1 and logic 0 every time the TMR2 interrupt happens. In this way, you make an LED connected to this bit flash at a rate controlled by timer2 and the value stored in the PR2 register.

Line 30 }

This is the closing curly bracket of the third if test.

Line 31 }

This is the closing bracket of the ISR.

Line 32 void main ()

This is the creation of the main loop.

Line 33 {

This is the opening curly bracket of the main loop.

Line 34 initialise ();

This is a subroutine call to force the PIC to go to the subroutine called initialise. This subroutine is in the file you created in the PICSetup.h header file and it will set up the PIC as you normally want it.

Line 35 TRISBbits.RB0 = 1;

To understand this line, you must remember that in the PICSetup.h header file you made all the bits in PORTB outputs. However, in this program you will need Bits 0, 1, 4, and 5 to be inputs. Therefore, you must change those bits in the TRISB to a logic 1. This is what this instruction does to Bit0 in TRISB.

Line 36, 37, and 38 do the same but for Bits 1, 4, and 5.

Line 39 TRISD = 0;

Here you are setting all the bits in TRISD to a logic 0. This makes all the bits on PORTD outputs. You need this because you will connect at least one LED to Bit0 of PORTD. Again, you should recall that in the PICSetup.h header file you set PORTD to all inputs.

Line 40 INTCON = 0b11010000;

This turns on all global and peripheral interrupts and enables the INT0 interrupt.

Line 41 INTCON2 = 0b00000000;

You are not using any interrupts associated with this control register. Note that you don't really need this instruction as it defaults to zero.

Line 42   INTCON3 = 0b00010000;

This enables the INT2 interrupt.

Line 43 PEI1 = 0b00000010;

This enables the TMR2 peripheral interrupt.

Line 44 RCONbits.IPEN = 0;

This disables the interrupt priority facility. You don't really need this instruction as the bit defaults to logic 0 at start-up.

Line 45 OSCCON = 0b00010100;

This sets the oscillator frequency to 125kHz and makes it stable.

Line 46 T2CON = 0b00000111;

This turns timer2 on and sets the divide rate at 16. This means timer2 counts at the following frequency:

oscillator = 125kHz

The clock is a quarter of the oscillator (i.e. = 31.25kHz).

timer2 divides this by 16, therefore frequency = 1.953kHz.

This means one tick of timer2 takes 512μs.

Since the PR2 is set to 250, it takes 250x512μs before the LED on PORTD will come on and a further 250x512μs before it turns off. Therefore, the LED will flash on for 128ms and off for 128ms.

Note that Bit0 of the T2CON register could be set to a logic 0 and nothing would change. This is because the T2CON register doesn't care what logic is on this bit when selecting the TMR2 Preset to 16. This is signified by the x on the datasheet.

Line 47 PR2 = 250;

This simply loads 250 into the PR2 register. This is the value timer2 must count up to before it sets the interrupt.

As an exercise, change the value in the PR2 to 125. What do you think will happen?

Line 48 PORTC = 0;

This simply sets all bits on PORTC to logic 0 and so turns everything connected to PORTC off.

Line 49 while (1)

This sets up a forever loop to make the micro carry out the instructions within the curly brackets forever.

Line 50 {

The opening curly bracket for the forever loop.

Line 51 if (PORTBbits.RB4 == 1) PORTC = 0;

This tests to see if the logic on Bit4 of PORTB has gone to a logic 1. If it has, then it sets all bits on PORTC to logic 0 (i.e. turns everything connected to PORTC off).

Line 52 else if (PORTBbits.RB5 == 1) PORTC = 6;

If Bit4 of PORTB is not a logic 1, then test to see if Bit5 of PORTB has gone to a logic 1. If it has, load PORTC with the value 6. This will turn on Bits 1 and 2 of PORTC. Note, if the test on line 51 is true, then the micro will skip this instruction on line 52. The micro will only carry out this instruction if the test on line 51 is untrue.

Line 53 }

This is the closing bracket of the forever loop.

Line 54 }

This is the closing bracket of the main loop.

When you run this program, you should see that an LED on Bit0 of PORTD will continually flash at a frequency of 3.9Hz. This frequency is controlled by the value in the PR2 register. You should appreciate that there is nothing in the main loop of the program that makes this happen, apart from loading the PR2 with the value 250. This happens purely because of the peripheral interrupt of TMR2 match with the PR2.

A simulation of the program is shown in Figure 6-2.

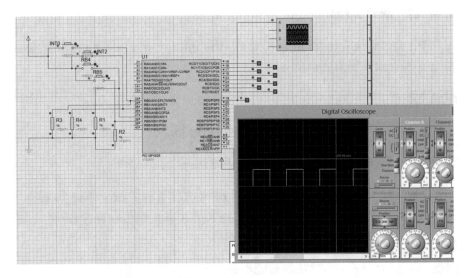

Figure 6-2. *Simulation of the program*

Exercise 6.1

If Bit6 of the INTCON register was set to a logic 0, explain what would change and why it would change.

Explain how you could keep the logic at Bit6 of the INTCON register a logic 1, but still achieve the same result.

Using the Compare Function of the CCP Module

This function links into the use of interrupts. You will use it as the alternative method of producing a square wave, as mentioned in Chapter 4. In Chapter 4, you created the square wave using the PWM firmware of the CCP module in the PIC. This was because you were primarily creating square waves to use the PWM to set the speed of a DC motor. If all you want to do was produce a square wave, then perhaps this next method will be more efficient.

The principle behind this operation is that the compare function of the CCP compares the value of the CCPRX register with either the TMR1 or TMR3 registers. Note that these three registers can be used as simple 8-bit registers or 16-bit registers. To make them into 16-bit registers, they use two 8-bit registers cascaded together.

Exercise 6-2

Briefly explain the advantage of cascading two 8-bit registers together, like this, to make a 16-bit register.

This means that each of the registers has a low byte (the CCPRXL) and a high byte (the CCPRXH), both of which can be accessed separately.

You use the x because there is CCPR1 and CCPR2. Note that by writing CCPR1 and CCPR2 you are addressing the complete 16-bit register. Writing CCPR1L means you are only addressing the low byte 8-bit register.

With the compare operation the CCPRX is compared with either the TIMR1 of TIMER3. When the values in the two registers are the same, you can control what happens to the CCPX pin on the PIC. There are three possible actions that can happen when the comparison finds a match between the two registers:

- The CCPX can be driven high.

- The CCPX can be driven low.

- The CCPX can toggle; that is if, it is high, it goes low, or if it is low, it goes high.

It is the third option that can be used to create a square wave on the CCPX pin (i.e. on the CCP1 or CCP2 pin).

It is Bit6 and Bit3 of the T3CON register, the control register for timer3, that allow the programmer to decide which timer register is compared with the value in the CCPRX register. The two bits control this selection, as shown in Table 6-5.

Table 6-5. *The Control of the Clock Sources for the Capture/Compare Mode of the CCP Modules*

Bit 6	Bit 3	Operation
0	0	Timer 1 is the capture/compare clock source for the CCP I/O
0	1	Timer 1 is the capture/compare clock source CCP1 I/O Timer 3 is the capture/compare clock source CCP2 I/O
1	0	Timer 3 is the capture/compare clock source for the CCP I/O
1	1	Timer 3 is the capture/compare clock source for the CCP I/O

For this program, you will set both bits to logic 0. This sets timer1 as the clock source for both the CCP I/O.

To test this concept, the following program will be created.

The Algorithm for the Compare Function

- The main program will simply make an LED connected to Bit0 of PORTB flash at 0.5 seconds on and 0.5 seconds off (i.e. flash with a frequency of 1Hz).

- The CCP module will compare the low byte of the CCPR1 register with the low byte of the timer1 register and, when they match, it will toggle the output of the CCP1 bit on PORTC. This will produce a square wave output on the CCP1 output. The frequency will be controlled by the value stored in the CCPR1 register.

- The frequency of square wave is controlled as follows:

  - The CCP1 output toggles from low to high when the value in the timer1 register equals the value stored in the CCPR1 register. At the same time, the value in timer1 will be reset to 0.

  - The CCP1 output will then toggle from high to low when the value in timer1 next equals the value in the CCPR1 register.

  - The process will repeat and the CCP1 output will toggle from low to high when the timer1 equals the CCPR1 register.

- This means the square wave will have a 50/50 duty cycle and the periodic time will be twice the time taken for the value in the timer1 register to equal the value in the CCPR1 register.

- To appreciate how long it will take for this to happen, you have to understand the setting of the timer1 control register T1CON.

- This will be loaded with the value 0b00110001 in line 30 of the program. This makes the timer1 register an 8-bit register with a divide rate of 8. (I made it an 8-bit register simply because my PROTEUS only supports 8-bit registers.)

- Knowing that the clock runs at a quarter of the oscillator and the oscillator was set to 8Mhz in the PICSetup.h header file, the clock will run at 2Mhz.

- As you are using a divide rate of 8, then timer1 will count at a frequency of 250khz (i.e. 2,000,000 divided by 8).

- This means one count will take 4µs as this is the periodic time for a frequency of 250kHz.

- You will load the CCPR1 register with 250 and so the mark time and the space time will be 250 x 4µs = 1ms. This means that the periodic time for the square wave will be 2ms, which gives a frequency of 500Hz.

- The production of this 500Hz square wave is all done with the use of the CCP1 interrupt. This interrupt is triggered when the value in the CCPR1 register is matched by the value in the timer1 or timer3 register. You are using the timer1 register. This means you need to enable the CCP1 interrupt.

The program to test this process is shown in Listing 6-2.

Listing 6-2. The CCP1 Interrupt Program

```
1. /* File:    variableFreqProg.c
2. Author: H. H. Ward
3. Using only 8 bit register therefore use TMR1L, CCPR1L
```

```
4. Created on 01 February 2019, 16:36
5. */
6. #include <xc.h>
7. #include <conFigInternalOscNoWDTNoLVP.h>
8. #include <PICSetUp.h>
9. unsigned char n;
10. void interrupt ISR ()
11. {
12. PIR1bits.CCP1IF = 0;
13. if (TMR1L >= CCPR1L) TMR1L = 0;
14. }
15. void delay (unsigned char t)
16. {
17. for (n = 0; n < t; n ++)
18. {
19. TMR0 = 0;
20. while (TMR0 < 255);
21. }
22. }
23. void main ()
24. {
25. initialise ();
26. INTCON = 0XC0;
27. PIE1 = 0X04;
28. TRISC = 0x00;
29. PORTC = 0;
30. T1CON = 0b00110001;
31. TMR0 = 0;
32. CCP1CON = 0b00000010;
33. CCPR1L = 250;
34. while (1)
```

```
35. {
36. PORTBbits.RB0 =(PORTBbits.RB0 ^ 1);
37. delay (15);
38. }
39. }
```

The Analysis Of Listing 6-2

I hope lines 1 to 9 need no analysis because you have used them before.

Line 10 void interrupt ISR ()

This is creating the interrupt service routine for this program.

Line 11 {

Simply the opening curly bracket for the ISR.

Line 12 PIR1bits.CCP1IF = 0;

This clears the CCP1 interrupt flag. You need to do this now to stop the CCP1 from continually interrupting the program.

Line 13 if (TMR1L >= CCPR1L) TMR1L = 0;

This line checks to see if the value in the TMR1L register is equal to or greater than the value on the CCPR1L register. If it is, then reset the value in the timer1 register back to 0.

The important thing to notice about this is that you are only using the low byte of the timer1 and the CCPR1 registers, hence the reference to TMR1L and CCPR1L. Also, you know the two registers will be equal to each other because that occurrence has caused the interrupt in the first place. However, you cannot ask if the two registers are equal, or use

```
if (TMR1L = CCPR1L) TMR1L = 0;
```

This is because by the time the micro gets to this instruction, the value in timer1 will be greater than the value in the CCPR1L register.

One last thing I should mention is that you have no need to ask this question at all, because the match must have happened already since the interrupt has occurred. This means you could replace this instruction with TMR1L = 0; and not use the if statement.

However, I wanted to show how and why you could use the >= the greater than or equal instruction. The program would work in just the same way. Try it and see.

Line 14 }

This is the closing curly bracket of the ISR.

Lines 15 to 22 create your variable delay subroutine from before.

The majority of the remaining lines you have used before. The new lines are

Line 26 INTCON = 0XC0;

This sets Bit7 and Bit6 of the INTCON register. This is to enable all of the global and peripheral interrupts. Note that the CCP1 interrupt is a peripheral interrupt.

Line 27 PIE1 = 0X04;

This sets Bit2 of the peripheral interrupt enable 1 register. This then enables the CCP1 interrupt.

Line 32 CCP1CON = 0b00000010;

This puts the CCP module into the compare mode. See Table 4-2 in Chapter 4.

Line 33 CPR1L = 250;

This loads the CCPR1L register with the value 250 in decimal. It is this value, linked with the frequency of timer1, that controls the mark and space and so the frequency of the square wave output on the CCP1 pin.

Line 36 PORTBbits.RB0 =(PORTBbits.RB0 ^ 1);

This is a new instruction. What it does is perform a logical EXOR operation with Bit0 of PORTB and the logic value 1. The ^ symbol simply stands for the EXOR logic instruction.

The truth table for the logical EXOR (i.e. Exclusive OR) is shown in Table 6-6.

Table 6-6. *The Truth Table for the EXOR Function*

B	A	F
0	0	0
0	1	1
1	0	1
1	1	0

This shows that the output F will be a logic 1 if A OR B are a logic 1. When the logic in both inputs are the same, the output F will be a logic 0. This is really a True OR function, as the output F will only be a logic 1 when either input A OR input B is a logic 1. The OR gate sets the output F to a logic 1 if A OR B is a logic 1, but also if A AND B are a logic 1. This is why the OR gate is sometimes called, or should be called, the inclusive OR since it includes the AND function. Note that EXOR stands for exclusive OR since it excludes the AND function.

What this means is that if Bit0 of PORTB is a logic 0, then when you EXOR it with a logic 1, the results is that bit0 goes to a logic 1. However, the next time you EXOR it with a logic 1, the two would be the same and Bit0 of PORTB is forced back to a logic 0.

This makes the logic at Bit0 of PORTB simply toggle on and off. It is a very neat way of toggling an output.

Line 37 delay (15);

This simply calls a 0.5 second delay between each EXOR operation.

These two instructions make the LED at Bit0 of PORTB oscillate on and off at a frequency of 1 Hz.

A simulation of the program to create the 500Hz square wave is shown in Figure 6-3.

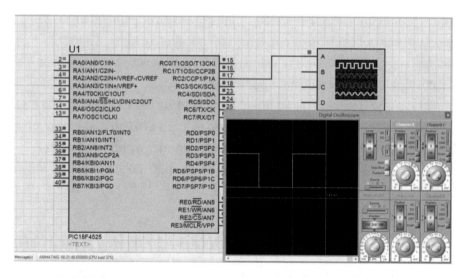

Figure 6-3. *The square wave using the compare function of the CCP module*

Using Priority Enabled Interrupts

Since the PIC can handle a large number of interrupts in one program, there may be a time when an interrupt is more important than the one that is running at present. In this case, the more important interrupt should be able to safely interrupt the current one and make the micro carry out its instructions of the ISR and then return to complete the instructions of the interrupt it overrode.

To enable this to happen, you can give interrupts a level of priority so that the PIC can say one interrupt is more important than another interrupt. With the PIC 18F4525, there are only two levels of priority: low priority and high priority. Other PICs may offer more levels of priority; indeed, the 32-bit PICs offer up to seven levels of priority.

The high-level interrupt can override a low-priority one but a low-priority interrupt cannot override a high-priority interrupt. Also, an interrupt cannot override an interrupt of the same priority. The PIC 18f4525 only has two levels of priority, which is not very extensive, but it is an attempt to provide a useful application.

To show you what you can do with the priority interrupts with the PIC 18F4525 I have written a program that incorporates a high and low level interrupt. It will use INT1 as the low priority interrupt and INT2 as the high priority interrupt. To keep the analysis simple, these will be the only interrupts used.

The Algorithm for the High/Low Priority Program

- The first change is to set the IPEN bit, which is Bit7 of the RCON register. This is needed to enable the priority function of the interrupts.

- Next, you need to set the priority level for the two interrupts you are going to use.

- INT1 can be set to either low or high priority. This is controlled by the INT1IP (interrupt1 interrupt priority bit), which is Bit6 of the INTCON3 register. To set this to low priority, you simply set this bit to a logic 0.

- INT2 can be set to either low or high priority. This is controlled by the INT2IP (interrupt2 interrupt priority bit), which is Bit7 of the INTCON3 register. To set the INT2 to high priority, this bit must be set to a logic 1.

- You must enable these two interrupts and their interrupt enable pins are Bit4 for INT2 and Bit3 for INT1 of the INTCON3 register. These two bits must be set to a logic 1 to enable the two external interrupts.

- This means that the data to be written to the INTCON3 register is 0b10011000. This is done using the instruction INTCON3 = 0b10011000;.

- You also need to enable the global high priority interrupts, which means Bit7 of the INTCON register must be set to a logic 1.

- As the IPEN bit is set to a logic 1 and you are using low-priority interrupts, you need to set Bit6 of the INTCON register, since now Bit6 is used to enable all low-priority interrupts.

- This means that the data to be written to the INTCON register is 0b11000000. This is done using the instruction INTCON = 0b11000000;.

- Since you are using both high- and low-priority interrupts, you need to write two interrupt service routines, one for the high priority and one for the low priority. Note that the PIC has two vector locations in

the program memory area; this is shown in Figure 6-4.
The high priority vector is at address 0008h and the
low priority vector address is at 0018h. It is at these
two addresses where the housekeeping software of the
PIC stores the address of the two respective interrupt
service routines. When the PIC is called to go to the
ISR, it goes to the respective vector address to find the
address it needs to load into the program counter for
the respective ISR. These vector locations are shown in
the program memory map in Figure 6-4.

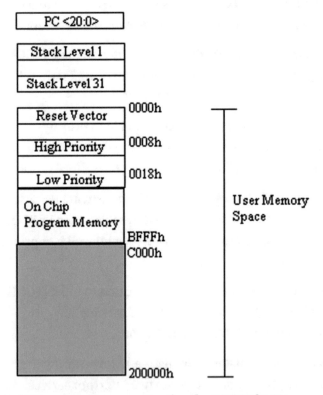

Figure 6-4. The user memory map for the PIC18f4525

Again, because of the uncertainty of the keyword interrupt, you should use the XC8 v1.35 compiler software when creating the project.

I downloaded this program to my prototype board and it worked perfectly.

The program for the high and low priority interrupts is shown in Listing 6-3.

Listing 6-3. The Code For the High/Low Priority Interrupts

```
1. /*This is  simple program to investigate interrupt high an
   low priority
2. It uses two external interrupt sources which are
3. INT1 and INT2 two external interrupts
4. INT1 and INT2 will effect the display on PORTB
5. The main program simply makes an led on PORTD flash
6. The program is written for the PIC 18F4525
7. Written by H H Ward Dated 07/06/15
8. */
9. //some include files
10. #include <xc.h>
11. #include <conFigInternalOscNoWDTNoLVP.h>
12. //some variables
13. unsigned char n;
14. //some subroutines
15. void delay (unsigned char t)
16. {
17. for (n = 0; n < t; n ++)
18. {
19. TMR0 = 0;
20. while (TMR0 < 255);
21. }
22. }
```

```
23. void interrupt HP_int ()
24. {
25. if (INTCON3bits.INT2IF == 1)
26. {
27. INTCON3bits.INT2IF= 0;
28. PORTC = 0x0F;
29. while (!PORTBbits.RB4);
30. PORTC = 0;
31. }
32. }
33. void interrupt low_priority LP_int ()
34. {
35. INTCON3bits.INT1IF = 0;
36. PORTC = 0x2C;
37. while (!PORTBbits.RB5);
38. PORTC = 8;
39. }
40. void main ()
41. {
42. TRISB = 0xFF;
43. TRISC = 0;
44. TRISD = 0;
45. RCON = 0b10000000;
46. INTCON = 0b11000000;
47. INTCON3 = 0b10011000;
48. ADCON1 = 0x0F;
49. OSCCON = 0b01110100;
50. T0CON = 0b11000111;
51. PORTD = 0;
52. PORTC = 0x01;
53. while (1)
```

```
54. {
55. PORTDbits.RD0 = 1;
56. delay (30);
57. PORTDbits.RD0 = 0;
58. delay (30);
59. }
60. }
```

Analysis of Listing 6-3

Lines 1 to 9 are just some normal comments about the program. Lines 10 and 11 are the two major include files. I did not include the PICSetUp.h header file because I want to remind you about some important control registers.

Lines 15 to 22 set up the usual variable delay subroutine that you have used before.

Line 23 void interrupt HP_int ()

This is how you set up the high-priority interrupt service routine.

Line 24 {

This is the normal opening curly bracket.

Line 25 if (INTCON3bits.INT2IF == 1)

There is no real need for this instruction since there is only one high-priority interrupt. I am only adding this instruction to show how you would accommodate the use of more than one high-priority interrupt.

Line 26 {

This is the normal opening curly bracket of the test in line 25. Again, this is not really needed in this program.

Line 27 INTCON3bits.INT2IF = 0;

This resets the INT2 interrupt flag back to a logic 0. This is very important here as with priority interrupts the global interrupt enable bit, Bit7 of the INTCON register, is not temporarily set to a logic 0, which would temporarily disable all interrupts. This means that if you left the INT2IF flag at a logic 1, the PIC would constantly trigger the interrupt service routine. Try commenting this instruction out by putting two forward slashes (//) in front of it and see what happens.

Line 28 PORTC = 0X0F;

This just lights up the first four bits on PORTC. This is just something for the PIC to do in this ISR.

Line 29 while (!PORTBbits.RB4);

This makes the PIC wait until the switch connected to Bit4 of PORTB goes to a logic 1. This is because while the logic on the bit is a logic 0, signified by the ! (or NOT) symbol, the PIC will do nothing.

This is just so that the PIC is trapped in this ISR, giving you time to try to interrupt it with INT1. However, since INT1 is a low-priority interrupt and INT2 is a high-priority one, INT1 should not be able to interrupt this ISR.

Line 30 PORTC = 0;

This turns everything connected to PORTC off. This is just to signify that you have completed the last instruction of this ISR for INT2 and the PIC can return to the main program or to the interrupt it may have interrupted.

Line 31 }

The closing bracket of the if test on line 25.

Line 32 }

The closing bracket of the ISR.

Line 33 void interrupt low_interrupt LP_int ()

This is how you set up the low-priority ISR.

Line 34 {

This is the opening curly bracket of the low-priority ISR.

Line 35 INTCON3bits.INT1IF = 0;

This resets the INT1F to logic 0 to prevent it continually triggering the interrupt. Note also that you have not had to test which interrupt triggered the ISR since there is only one low-priority interrupt.

Line 36 PORTC = 0x2C;

This turns on anything connected to Bits 5, 3, and 2 of PORTC. Just something for this ISR to do.

Line 37 while (!PORTBbits.RB4);

This gets the PIC to wait until the switch connected to Bit4 is switched to a logic 1. This is done to trap the PIC here, giving you time to try to interrupt the ISR with INT2. Since INT2 is of a higher priority than INT1, it should interrupt the ISR.

Line 38 PORTC = 8;

This will set Bit3 of PORTC to a logic 1. This is to let you know the PIC has carried out the last instruction of the low-priority ISR.

Line 39 }

The normal closing bracket of the low priority ISR.

Line 40 void main ()

This sets up the important main loop of the program.

Line 41 {

The opening curly bracket of the main loop.

I have now gone through some setup instructions that are really in the PICSetUp.h header file. I have done this to remind you that these instructions are needed for every program and that you may have to tailor them to the specific program.

Line 42 TRISB = 0XFF;

This sets all the bits in the special function register TRISB to a logic 1. This sets all bits on PORTB to inputs.

Line 43 TRISC = 0;

This simply sets all the bits in TRISC a logic 0. This then sets all the bits on PORTC as outputs.

Line 44 TRISD = 0;

This does the same but with TRISD and so sets all bits on PORTD as outputs.

Liane 45 RCON = 0b10000000;

This sets Bit7 of the RCON register to a logic 1. This is the IPEN bit that turns on the interrupt priority function of the PIC.

Line 46   INTCON = 0b11000000;

This sets Bit7 and Bit6 to a logic 1. As the IPEN bit is a logic 1, this enables all high and low priority interrupts.

Line 47   INTCON3 = 0b10011000;

This sets INT2 to high priority, Bit7 is a logic 1. It also sets INT1 to low priority, Bit6 is a logic 0. It also enables INT2 and INT1; Bit4 and Bit3 respectively are set to logic 1.

Line 48 ADCON1 = 0X0F;

This sets Bits 3, 2, 1, and 0 to a logic 1. This then makes all 13 bits that could be analog set to digital.

This is required because Bits 0, 1, 2, 3, and 4 of PORTB can be used as analog but you need them to be digital. You could have loaded the ADCON1 register with 0X07 but since you are not using the ADC you made them all digital.

Line 49 OSCCON = 0b01110100;

This sets the internal oscillator to produce a stable 8Mhz frequency.

Line 50 T0CON = 0b11000111;

This turns on timer0, sets it to an 8-bit register, and gives it a maximum divide rate. In this way timer0 counts at a frequency of 7812.5Hz.

Line 51   PORTC = 0X01;

This just sets bit 0 of PORTC to a logic 1.

The remaining lines of the program just set up a forever loop with Bit0 of PORTD simply flashing one second on and one second off.

Explanation of How the High/Low Priority Program Works

The main program just makes Bit0 of PORTD flash on and off. If you momentarily press the switch on Bit1 of PORTB, you will initiate the INT1 interrupt. The PIC will get the address of the low-priority ISR from the low-priority vector at location 0018h. The PIC will then go to the low-priority ISR where it will carry out the instruction to reset the INT1 interrupt flag. If it didn't do this, the PIC would continually think the INT1 interrupt had been caused and you could not move on. This is because, unlike the situation with non-priority interrupts, the PIC does not turn off all interrupts by temporarily setting Bit7 of the INTCON register to a logic 0 whenever an interrupt is initiated. This is because with priority interrupts you need all interrupts to be still enabled so that a higher priority interrupt can override the current interrupt.

The PIC then carries out the instruction PORTC = 0X2C;. Bit0 of PORTD will stop flashing as long as the PIC is carrying out the instructions of the ISR for INT1. This is because the PIC will not be looking at the instructions in the main program.

The PIC then waits for the user to momentarily press the switch on Bit5 of PORTB. This is to give you time to activate INT2. If you do activate INT2, then, because it has a higher priority than INT1, the PIC will break out of the low-priority ISR and go to the high-priority ISR.

The first thing it does after resetting the INT2 interrupt flag, neglecting the test to see if it was the INT2 interrupt, is to carry out the instruction PORTC = 0X0F. This will overwrite what was in PORTC. This is so that you know the PIC is now running the high-priority ISR.

Now the PIC waits for you to momentarily press the switch on Bit4 of PORTB. This is to give you time to try to activate the INT1 interrupt. However, because INT1 is a low-priority interrupt, it cannot override the INT2 ISR.

Now when you send Bit4 momentarily to a logic 1, the PIC can move onto the next instruction in the high-priority ISR. This is where it loads PORTC with the value 0. This will set all of the bits on PORTC to a logic 0.

Now, if the INT2 had interrupted the low-priority interrupt INT1, the PIC would have gone back to the instruction on line 37 of `if (!PORTBbits.RB5);` where it is waiting for you to momentarily press the switch connected to Bit5. You should be able to appreciate that the PIC has gone back to this instruction because Bit0 of PORTD is still not flashing. If you now momentarily press the switch on Bit5 of PORTB, you should see Bit0 of PORTD start to flash again.

I hope this analysis helps you to understand how the high and low priority interrupts on the PIC18f4525 work. The principle is the same for most PICs. There is a simulation of the program shown in Figure 6-5.

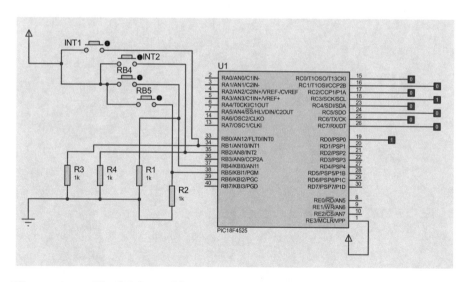

Figure 6-5. *The high and low priority interrupts*

Summary

In this chapter, you learned what interrupts within the microcontroller are and why you have them. You studied how to set them up and use them. You learned the difference between high and low priority interrupts and how to set up the priority interrupts and use them.

You had a brief look at the fetch and execute cycle that all micros must go through when carrying out an instruction. You also looked at the important special function register called the program counter.

I hope you have found this chapter useful. In the next chapter, you will look at the capture aspect of the CCP module and the use of the EEPROM in the PIC.

CHAPTER 7

Frequency Measurement and the EEPROM

In this chapter, you are going to look at the final function of the CCP module. This is the capture module. You will learn what it captures and how to make use of it.

You will also look at the EEPROM function of the PIC. You will learn what the EEPROM is and how to use in within the PIC 18F4525.

Using the Capture Function of the CCP

You have already learned that the CCP is actually three modules within the PIC. The control register that allows you to select the one of the three modules you want to use is the CCPXCON register. The X is there because there are two sets of control registers and two outputs that the CCP module controls. The X is simply replaced with the numbers 1 or 2 for the respective module.

© Hubert Henry Ward 2020
H. H. Ward, *Intermediate C Programming for the PIC Microcontroller*,
https://doi.org/10.1007/978-1-4842-6068-5_7

Setting the CCP to the Capture Mode

To set the respective CCP module, you will use CCP1, and you will write the control byte to the respective CCPXCON register. In this example, you will use the CCP1CON register. Note that it is the four least significant bits (Bits 3, 2, 1, and 0) that control the operation of the CCP module; see Table 4-3 in Chapter 4. However, there are four different modes for the capture function of the CCP. To appreciate why there are four modes and how to decide which mode to use, here's an overview of what the capture mode does and what it can be used for.

What the CCP Captures in the Capture Mode

In this example, you will use the CCP1 module. If you use CCP2, simply replace the 1 with a 2.

In the capture mode, the CCP uses the register pair CCPR1H and CCPR1L, the high byte and low byte, respectively, to form a 16-bit register. This register can be accessed as the 16-bit CCPR1 register. It can be used to capture, or record, the current value present in the timer registers, TMR1 or TMR3, at the instant a certain event happens at the CCP1 input. There are four possible events that will trigger this capture:

- Every time the input goes from high to low, termed a falling edge

- Every time the input goes from low to high, termed a rising edge

- Every fourth rising edge

- Every sixteenth rising edge

This is why there are four modes for the capture function of the CCP; see Table 4-3 in Chapter 4.

When a capture is made, the CCP1IF flag will be set (i.e. go to a logic 1) and this can be used to trigger an interrupt or it can be simply monitored so that it can be used to signal when a capture has occurred and the program should go through a process. The program you will be using uses the latter interpretation since you don't want to use interrupts. Note that the CCP1IF must be reset to logic 0 after you have responded to it, so that the it can be set to a logic 1 the next time the desired event at the input occurs.

The selection of one of the four modes is controlled by Bits 1 and 0 of the CCP1CON register as long as Bit2 is set to a logic 1; see Table 4-3 in Chapter 4.

When using the CCP in this capture mode, you must do the following:

1. Set the respective CCP pin to input. This is done by setting the relevant bit in the TRISC register. However, you should remember that the CCP2 pin can be set to be on PORTC Bit2 or PORTB Bit3. This is controlled by the configuration words. So be sure you set the correct pin to input.

2. Set the respective timer register to 16-bit.

3. The timer that is to be used, timer1 or timer3, must be set in either timer mode or synchronized counter mode.

The use of the capture mode is best explained with an example. In this example, you will use the CCP module to determine the frequency of a square wave inputted to CCP1 on the PIC. You will also use the CCP module, in PWM mode, to create the square wave. In this way, you will know what the frequency of the square wave should be and thus be able to check the accuracy of the process.

The Algorithm for the Frequency Measurement Program

- You will set the CCP1 module to capture mode. And you will set it to capture the value at every fourth rising edge. This means the CCP1CON register must be loaded with 0b00000110; see Table 4-3 in Chapter 4

- You must set bit2 of PORTC to input since this is the CCP1 pin. This is done using the TRICbits.RC2 = 1; instruction.

- The concept behind the program is to monitor the CCP1IF (i.e. the CCP1 interrupt flag).

- When it goes to a logic 1, load a count value with the data that has been copied from the timer register into the CCPR1. This will be count 1.

  - Note that you don't need to enable any interrupts. This flag will automatically go to a logic 1 when a capture is made even though you are not using it to cause a real interrupt (i.e. set the interrupt flag that is examined during the fetch and execute cycle).

- The CCP1IF flag must be reset to a logic 0 so that it can signal when the next capture occurs.

- At the next capture, the current value of the timer will be copied as before into a variable, this time called count2.

- In this way, the count value between the two events can be calculated as count value = count2 – count 1.

- Depending on how the desired event has been set up using the CCP1CON register, this count value will be for 1, 4, or 16 cycles of the wave form inputted to the PIC. This means you must divide this count value by 1, 4, or 16. In your case, you will divide it by 4.

- Knowing the rate at which the timer counts, this count value can be converted into a time period by multiplying the count value by the periodic time for the timer.

- You will use timer1 to count the time slots.

- You will set timer1 to be a 16-bit register with a divide rate of 8.

  - Since you set the crystal to 8Mhz, as normal, the clock will run at 2MHz. This means timer1 will count at 250kHz, making one count equal 4µs.

- Putting this together means that an expression to determine the frequency, using the label Hertz, as these are the units for frequency, can be put together as shown in Equation 7-1.

$$Hertz = \frac{4}{(count2 - count1) \times 4E^{-6}} \qquad \textbf{(Equation 7-1)}$$

The 4 in the numerator is because you will set the compare to happen after every fourth rising edge of the signal. This means setting the least four bits of the CCP1CON register to 0110.

The $4E^{-6}$ is there because this is the periodic time of the timer frequency.

The count2 – count1 will produce the value representing the count between the four cycles of the input signal.

- This equation will then load the variable Hertz with a binary number that is the actual frequency of the input signal.

- However, this presents another problem. How do you display this binary number as a decimal number you can read on the LCD display?

  - If you fully understand the problem, then you should understand how you can solve the problem.

Example Frequency Measurement

To help you understand the problem, consider the measurement of a 500Hz square wave at the input.

You need to appreciate how the value of timer1 will respond to this input signal. Note it does not really matter what value timer1 has at the beginning as long as the final value of timer1 does not exceed its maximum value of 65535.

Therefore, simply to prevent this occurrence, ensure that the value of timer1 is set back to 0. This will be count1.

Knowing that one tick or count with timer1 takes 4µs, and the periodic time of the square wave input at 500Hz is 2ms, you can determine what the value of timer1, after one cycle, will be. This is shown in Equation 7-2.

$$timer1 = \frac{2E^{-3}}{4E^{-6}} = 500 \qquad \textbf{(Equation 7-2)}$$

As the program will recorded the value after four cycles, the value of timer1 will be 2000. This will be stored in count2. These two values will become the values stored in count1 and count2. Putting all this into Equation 7-3 you have

$$Hertz = \frac{4}{(2000 - 0) \times 4E^{-6}} = 500 \qquad \textbf{(Equation 7-3)}$$

This will be stored as a 16-bit binary number, which is 0b0000000111110100 or 0X01F4.

This example might help you see why you use hexadecimal numbers to represent binary numbers.

However, the problem now is how to use that binary number, for that is how the PIC will store this value in the variable Hertz, to produce a display of 00500Hz on the display.

There is an open source function that can convert this binary number to the correctly formatted ASCII to be displayed on the LCD. However, I firmly believe that you should understand how the code you use works. Also, because the open source function has to be much more versatile, you can make a subroutine that has much less code in it. Therefore, let's create a subroutine that will convert the binary number stored in the variable Hertz and correctly display it on the LCD. I will explain how it works when I analyses the program instructions.

To help explain the principle of how the program captures the time period of the input signal, see the diagram shown in Figure 7-1.

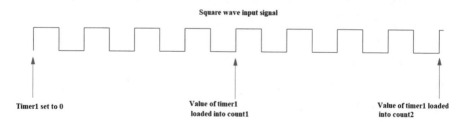

Figure 7-1. *The input square wave. The times timer1 value is loaded into count1 and count2*

Figure 7-1 should help explain the process. The value represented by count2 – count1 will be the count value for four cycles of the input waveform.

The Program to Measure the 500Hz Square Wave

The actual program to complete this task is shown in Listing 7-1.

Listing 7-1. The Program Using the binToDec Subroutine

```
1. /*
2. * File:    captureProg.c
3. Author: Hubert Ward
4. *
5. Created on 21 April 2020, 12:06
6. */
7. #include <xc.h>
8. #include <conFigInternalOscNoWDTNoLVP.h>
9. #include <4bitLCDPortb.h>
10. #include <PICSetUp.h>
11. #include <math.h>
12. unsigned int freq, bitres, Hertz, p, ucol,
    tensp,hunsp,thoup, count1, count2;
13. unsigned char tthou, thou, huns, tens, units, ttn, tn, hn,
    ten, un, dn;
14. //some subroutines
15. void binToDec()
16. {
17. tthou = Hertz/10000;
18. for (ttn = 0; ttn < 10; ttn ++)
19. {
```

```
20. if (tthou == ttn)
21. {
22. lcdData = (0x30 + ttn);
23. lcdOut ();
24. thoup = (Hertz-(ttn*10000));
25. }
26. }
27. thou = thoup/1000;
28. for (tn = 0; tn < 10; tn ++)
29. {
30. if (thou == tn)
31. {
32. lcdData = (0x30 + tn);
33. lcdOut ();
34. hunsp = (thoup-(tn*1000));
35. }
36. }
37. huns = hunsp/100;
38. for (hn = 0; hn < 10; hn ++)
39. {
40. if (huns == hn)
41. {
42. lcdData = (0x30 + hn);
43. lcdOut ();
44. tensp = (hunsp-(hn*100));
45. }
46. }
47. tens = tensp/10;
48. for (ten = 0; ten <10; ten++)
49. {
50. if (tens == ten)
51. {
```

```
52. lcdData = (0x30 + ten);
53. lcdOut ();
54. units = (tensp-(ten*10));
55. }
56. }
57. for (un = 0; un <10; un++)
58. {
59. if (units == un)
60. {
61. lcdData = (0x30 + un);
62. lcdOut ();
63. }
64. }
65. lcdData = 0xA0;
66. lcdOut ();
67. lcdData = 0x48;
68. lcdOut ();
69. lcdData = 0x7A;
70. lcdOut ();
71. }
72. void main ()
73. {
74. initialise ();
75. CCP1CON = 0b00000110;
76. T0CON = 0XC7;
77. T1CON = 0b10110001;
78. T2CON = 0X06;
79. T3CON = 0;
80. PR2 = 249;
81. CCP2CON = 0b00111100;
82. CCPR2L = 0X7D;
83. TRISCbits.RC2 = 1;
```

```
84. setUpTheLCD ();
85. writeString ("The Frequency is");
86. while (1)
87. {
88. line2 ();
89. PIR1bits.CCP1IF = 0;
90. CCPR1 = 0;
91. TMR1 = 0;
92. while (!PIR1bits.CCP1IF );
93. count1 = CCPR1;
94. PIR1bits.CCP1IF = 0;
95. while (!PIR1bits.CCP1IF );
96. count2 = CCPR1;
97. PIR1bits.CCP1IF = 0;
98. Hertz = (4/((count2-count1)*0.000004));
99. binToDec ();
100. }
101. }
```

Analysis of Listing 7-1

I should point out that in the header file, 4bitLCDPortb.h, I have now
included the subroutine for the writeString. This is because I would
normally use this subroutine with the LCD. This then means that I have
added the following subroutine to the header file that was described in
Chapter 3; the listing for the writeString subroutine is;

```
void writeString (const char *words)
{
while (*words)
{
lcdData = *words;
```

```
lcdOut ( );
*words ++;
}
}
```

Of course you could leave it out of the header file if you whished. However, if you did that you would need to add it to the program listings in this chapter as the instructions that write a string to the LCD use this subroutine. The explanation for how this subroutine works has been given in Chapter 3.

Lines 1 to 11 are the normal comments and includes.

Line 12 creates the various unsigned integers that are required in the program. You use unsigned integers since you need full 16-bit registers to store some of the values.

Line 13 creates some unsigned chars since you will need some simple 8-bit registers to control the loops in the program. If you only need an 8-bit variable, use chars and not ints because this will save memory.

Line 14 is just a way of splitting up the listing into different sections.

Line 15 creates the subroutine to convert 16-bit binary numbers so that they can be displayed on the LCD.

Line 16 is the opening curly bracket of the subroutine. To help understand how this subroutine works, you will look at how the LCD would display 65535 because this is the highest decimal value the 16-bit variable Hertz can store. This is made up of five columns: a ten thousand, a thousand, a hundred, a tens, and a units column. Each column can hold a value from 0 to 9. This means the LCD display must be split into these five columns, which can each display the values 0 to 9. What the subroutine does is look at the ten thousand column first to see what value it has to display in this column. The program then looks to see what digit it must display in the next column. It repeats this process until it has finished with the units column. The program then displays a space followed by the letters Hz.

Line 17 tthou = Hertz/10000;

Here's an unsigned char variable named tthou. The program will store the actual ASCII value for the digit, from 0 to 9, which represents how many tens of thousands there are in the number Hertz. In this case, it's 6 since the value in Hertz is 65535.

In this instruction you are dividing the value in Hertz by 10000; this would normally produce 6.5535, which would require a float in C to store it. However, you are trying to store the result in an unsigned char, which can only store a whole value or integer. This will make the micro discard any value after the decimal point. Therefore, tthou stores the value of 6, which is what you want. If you used the round function that is in included in the header file math.h, the micro would have rounded the result up to 7 and stored 7 in the variable tthou, which is not what you want.

Line 18 for (ttn = 0; ttn < 10; ttn ++)

This sets up a for do loop, which is controlled by the variable ttn. What this loop does is determine what digit should be sent to the LCD. The loop starts off by loading the variable ttn with zero. Then in line 20 it ask if tthou is the same a ttn, which at this point it isn't since tthou is 6 and ttn is 0. If it was the same, the program would have gone on to send this to the LCD. As tthou was loaded with 6, at line 17, then the micro goes through the for do loop again. After the fifth loop, the ttn will also be loaded with 6, in line 18. Then, when you ask again is tthou = tnn, at line 20, the answer would be yes. This means that the micro then goes to line 22 via line 21.

Line 22 lcdData = (0x30 + ttn);

This loads the variable lcdData with the sum of 0x30 and what is in ttn. The number 0x30 will set the high nibble of the variable lcdData to 3. This puts you in the third column of the ASCII data sheet. In this column, it is the low byte that can be used to locate the actual ASCII for the character you want to display. It starts with the low byte = 0000 for the ASCII for 0, which is 0X30 or 0b00110000 in full 8 bits. It then goes on through to 1001 (i.e. 9 in binary). This means that the ASCII for 9 is 0X39 or 0b00111001 in 8-bit binary. The full ASCII for the ten digits to be displayed in each column is shown in Table 7-1.

Table 7-1. *The ASCII for Digits 0 to 9*

Digit	High Nibble (Hex)	Low Nibble (Hex)
0	0011 (03)	0000 (00)
1	0011 (03)	0001 (01)
2	0011 (03)	0010 (02)
3	0011 (03)	0011 (03)
4	0011 (03)	0100 (04)
5	0011 (03)	0101 (05)
6	0011 (03)	0110 (06)
7	0011 (03)	0111 (07)
8	0011 (03)	1000 (08)
9	0011 (03)	1001 (09)

As ttn is 6 (00000110 in binary), the value loaded into lcdData is 00110000 + 00000110 = 00110110 or 0X36.

Line 23 lcdOut ();

This calls the subroutine lcdOut to send the ASCII data in lcdData to the LCD.

Note that lcdData is a variable created in the 4bitLCDPortb.h header file for the LCD. The subroutine lcdOut is a subroutine in the same header file for the LCD.

Line 24 thoup = (Hertz-(ttn*10000));

The variable thoup is an unsigned char that will be passed onto the next section of the subroutine to determine what the digit for the thousands column will be. What this instruction does is load the variable, thoup, with a value that is equal to what is in Hertz – ttn*10000. To appreciate what this does, you will use the example that Hertz = 65535 and ttn = 6. That means that the value loaded into thoup = 65535 – 6x10000 = 65535 – 60000. Therefore, thoup = 5535.

What this instruction does is decrease the value that is in Hertz by the ten thousands that is in Hertz. In this way, the variable that is used in the next section of the subroutine will just have the correct number of thousand, hundreds, tens, and units, which is what you want for the next column on the LCD display. That variable is thoup.

Lines 25 and 26 are just the closing brackets for the if and for do loops opened on lines 19 and 21.

Lines 27 to 36 do the same process but now for the thousands column.

Lines 37 to 46 do the same process but now for the hundreds.

Lines 47 to 64 do the same but for the tens and units.

These loops ensure that the correct ASCII for the correct digit is displayed in the correct columns on the LCD display. The only thing I would like to improve is to not display any unnecessary zeros as in 00500 when displaying 500Hz. It would be good to make this subroutine work for any format of numbers such as decimal numbers. However, for this program that is not a requirement and so that is for another program.

Line 65 lcdData = 0xA0;

This loads the variable lcdData with the ASCII for a blank or space.

Line 66 lcdOut ();

This calls the subroutine lcdOut to send the character to the display.

Lines 68 to 70 do the same but for the characters H and z. Line 71 is the closing bracket for the binToDec subroutine. This subroutine will take any 16-bit binary integer and convert it to the correct ASCII in the correct columns ready to be displayed on the LCD. If you want to deal with decimal numbers and negative numbers, there is a bit more work to do. I will do it at some point.

Lines 72 to 75 are fairly straightforward.

Line 75 CCP1CON = 0b00000110;

This sets the CCP1 module into capture mode but also where it is the fourth rising edge of the input signal on CCP1 that will instigate the capture. At that occurrence, the value in either timer1 or timer3 will be copied into the CCPR1 16-bit register.

Line 76 is simply setting up timer0 as you normally do.

Line 77 T1CON = 0b10110001;

This turns timer1 on and sets it to a 16-bit register. It also sets it to divide the clock by 8, making it count at a rate of 250kHz. This makes the time for one tick = 4µs.

Line 78 T2CON = = 0X06;

This turns timer2 on and sets the timer preset to 4.

Line 79 T3CON = 0;

This turns timer3 off but more importantly it sets Bits 6 and 3 to logic 0. This makes timer1 the clock for the CCP modules; see Table 6-3 in Chapter 6.

Line 80 PR2 = 249;

This loads the PR2 register with the value 249. This makes the frequency of the square wave outputted on CCP2 as 500Hz. This is the signal that will be measured on the input CCP1.

Line 81 CCP2CON = 0b00111100;

This loads the control register for the CCP2 module with 0b00111100. Bits 3 and 2 set it into PWM mode while Bits 5 and 4 hold the two least significant bits of the mark time number for a 50/50 duty cycle.

Line 82 CCPR2L = 0X7D;

This loads the low byte of the CCPR2 register with the value 0X7D. This is the most significant bits of the number to create the 50/50 duty cycle.

Line 83 TRISCbits.RC2 = 1;

This makes sure that this bit is an input. This bit is what the input CCP1 is connected.

Line 89 PIR1Bits.CCP1IF = 0;

The PIR1bits are the peripheral interrupt request 1 bits that could request an interrupt for the PIC. This instruction makes sure that the CCP1IF is at a logic 0; if it was a logic 1, you would not be able to distinguish when the next capture has taken place. Now, when the next capture takes place, the PIC will automatically set this bit and you can test for that happening.

Lines 90 and 91 just make sure that the two registers are at zero.

Line 92 while (!PIR1bits.CCP1IF);

This tests to see if the CCP1IF, CCP1 interrupt flag, is still a logic 0. If it is, the PIC will keep on testing this until the test becomes untrue when the CCP1IF bit goes to a logic 1. This will indicate that a capture has occurred. This means that the current value in timer1 has been copied into the register CCPR1.

Line 93 count1 = CCPR1;

This copies the value that has just been copied into the CCPR1 from timer1 into the variable count1.

Line 94 PIR1Bits.CCP1IF = 0;

This resets this flag back to zero so that you can tell when the next capture has taken place.

Line 95 while (!PIR1bits.CCP1IF);

This makes the PIC wait for the next capture.

Line 96 count2 = CCPR1;

This copies the second value into count2.

Line 97 PIR1Bits.CCP1IF = 0;

This resets this flag back to zero so that you can tell when the next capture has taken place.

Line 98 Hertz = (4/((count2-count1)*0.000004));

This loads the variable Hertz with the number that represents the frequency of the signal inputted on CCP1. Note that this is the square wave that is created with the CCP2 output. If this calculation produced a decimal result, any digits after the decimal point would be lost since the variable Hertz is an unsigned int.

Line 99 binToDec ();

This calls the subroutine that converts the binary number in Hertz to the correct format to display on the LCD.

Line 100 and 101 simply close the respective brackets.

There is quite a bit to this program as it is quite complicated. However, I hope that I have described the process well and after maybe a few readings you will find it useful. Certainly the ability to measure the frequency of signals can be useful. In speed, control is usual to create a pulse chain that is proportional to the speed of the motor. Therefore, if you had a program that could determine the frequency of that pulse train, you could determine the speed of the motor. You could then, using PWM, vary the voltage applied to the motor to either speed it up or slow it down.

One issue is that this program can only measure frequencies up to 65.535kHz. You could use a 32-bit PIC to try to overcome this but that's for another book. You could also use a ready-made function that would simply allow you to display a floating point value on the LCD but I prefer to explain to you how the code works. The sprintf(str, "%.2f", dp) function, which is included in the stdio.h header file, is a function that will take a variable named dp, which is a float, and display it correctly on the LCD. This would do the job fine but again it would take up a lot more memory. Also, since it uses floating point numbers and a lot of programming, I am not going to explain how it works in this book. I have written the program, shown in Listing 7-2, that uses this approach and Figure 7-4 shows the program working. It is entirely up to you which approach you choose to use. Listing 7-2 does look smaller but a lot of code will be added with the sprinf function when the program compiles.

Listing 7-2. The Frequency Program Using The sprintf Function.

```
1. /*
2. * File: captureProg.c
3. Author: Hubert Ward
4. *
5. Created on 21 April 2020, 12:06
6. */
7. #include <xc.h>
8. #include <conFigInternalOscNoWDTNoLVP.h>
9. #include <4bitLCDPortb.h>
10. #include <PICSetUp.h>
11. #include <math.h>
12. #include <stdio.h>
```

```
13. unsigned int freq, bitres, ucol, tensp,hunsp,thoup, count1,
    count2;
14. unsigned char tthou, thou, huns, tens, units, ttn, tn, hn,
    ten, un, dn;
15. float Hertz;
16. //some subroutines
17. void displayFreq(float dp)
18. {
19. sprintf(str, "%.2f", dp);
20. writeString(str);
21. writeString(" Hz");
22. }
23. void main ()
24. {
25. initialise ();
26. CCP1CON = 0b00000110;
27. T0CON = 0XC7;
28. T1CON = 0b10110001;
29. T2CON = 0X04;
30. T3CON = 0;
31. PR2 = 15;
32. CCP2CON = 0b00001100;
33. CCPR2L = 0X08;
34. TRISD = 0;
35. TRISCbits.RC2 = 1;
36. setUpTheLCD ();
37. writeString ("The Frequency is");
38. while (1)
39. {
40. line2 ();
41. PIR1bits.CCP1IF = 0;
42. CCPR1 = 0;
```

```
43. TMR1 = 0;
44. while (!PIR1bits.CCP1IF );
45. count1 = CCPR1;
46. PIR1bits.CCP1IF = 0;
47. while (!PIR1bits.CCP1IF );
48. count2 = CCPR1;
49. PIR1bits.CCP1IF = 0;
50. Hertz = (4/((count2-count1)*0.000004));
51. displayFreq(Hertz);
52. }
53. }
```

The main difference is that the binToDec subroutine has been removed. However, the sprintf function and the studio.h header file have to be added; see line 12. Also, the variable Hertz has been changed to a float; see line 15. The final difference is that line 53 calls the subroutine displayFreq with the variable Hertz, which is now a float, being passed up to the subroutine. It is really up to you which approach you use.

Line 19 sprintf (str, "%.2f", dp);

I thought I should explain what the %.2f in this instruction does. It simply defines how many decimal places are shown in the display. In this case, the 2 defines that two decimal places are displayed.

Figures 7-2 and 7-3 are a series of pictures showing the PIC to create and measure the frequency of some square waves using Listing 7-1.

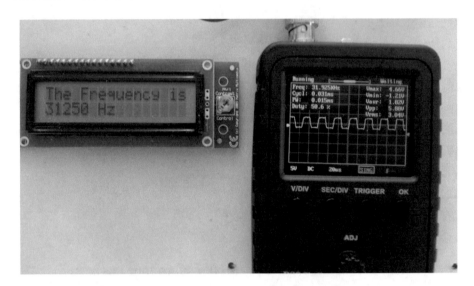

Figure 7-2. *The display of a 31.25kHz square wave*

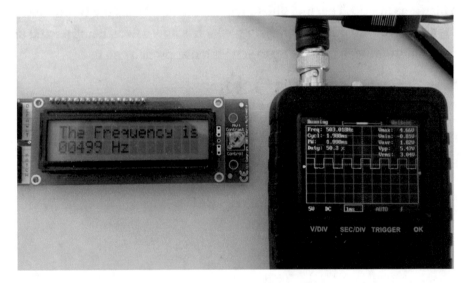

Figure 7-3. *The display of a 500Hz square wave*

Both figures show the calculated value of the frequency from the program and the measured signal from the PIC on the oscilloscope. Both displays show very similar values. This should indicate that the square wave generation by the PIC and the frequency measurement by the PIC are fairly accurate.

Figures 7-4 and 7-5 are a series of pictures showing the PIC to create and measure the frequency of some square waves using Listing 7-2.

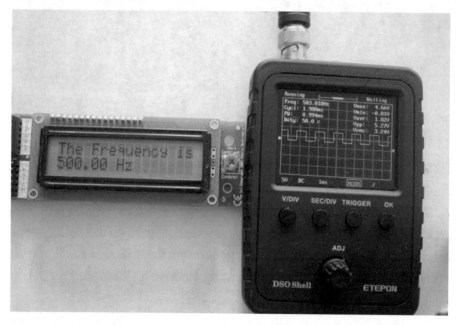

Figure 7-4. *The 500Hz measurement using the sprintf function*

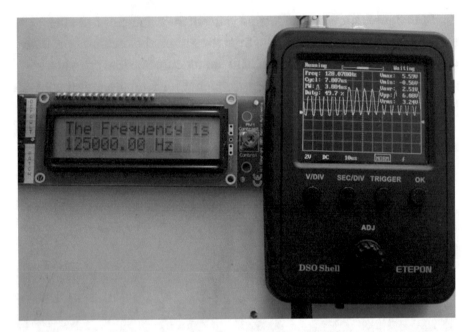

Figure 7-5. *The 125kHz measurement using the sprintf function*

The two examples do work well. One interesting observation is that the 125kHz-generated signal is not much of a square wave on the oscilloscope. This is because of the time period in generating the square wave. It may be a problem with the PIC or the rather inexpensive oscilloscope.

Using the EEPROM Inside the 18f4525

First, it would be useful to explain what the EEPROM is. The phrase EEPROM, which is really a set of initials, stands for electrically erasable programmable read-only memory. It has origins in PROM, which stands for programmable read-only memory. PROM is where computer designers stored housekeeping programs such as the BIOS. BIOS stands for basic input/output system. The users could not modify these programs.

However, since designers often needed to modify these programs, they created erasable PROMs (i.e. EPROMs) so that they could change the programs stored in the PROM. To erase the EPROM they would have to expose the chip to ultraviolet light. They could then erase the old program and update the chip with the new housekeeping programs.

However, as the technology advanced, the method of erasing the EPROM was improved so that they could be erased by applying the correct electrical voltages. This gave birth to the EEPROM. However, the idea that it would be read-only is gone since it can be written to as well as read from, but the name has stuck.

So how does EEPROM differ from ordinary RAM, or random access memory, which can also be written to and read from? Well, it is the fact that all along, from PROM, then EPROM, and now EEPROM, the type of memory used is what is called non-volatile memory, whereas RAM is volatile. The difference is that volatile memory loses its contents when the power is removed whereas non-volatile keeps its contents when the power is removed. This means that any EEPROM memory can be used to store any important data that a program does not want to lose even if the power is removed. This is indeed a useful aspect of the EEPROM.

You must not confuse EEPROM with battery-backed RAM. With this type of RAM, a battery provides power to the RAM if the main power source is lost for a period of time.

Some microcontrollers can have an EEPROM device externally connected to the micro using some serial connection. A common way of communicating with this external EEPROM is via the SPI module.

The 18f4525, like a lot of PIC micros, has an internal area of its memory that acts like an EEPROM, in that it is non-volatile memory and you can write to it and read from it. In this chapter, you are going to discover how to write to and read from the internal EEPROM inside the PIC 18F4525. To do this, you must use the following registers:

- EECON1

- EECON2

- EEDATA

- EEADR

- EEADRH

The EEADRH register is used to store the high byte of the address in the EEPROM you want to either write to or read from and the EEADR register is used to store the low byte.

The EECON1 register uses its 8 bits to control the different aspects of the EEPROM. The important bits are

- Bit7, the EEPGD bit. This is used to set where the data being used is stored. A logic 1 in this bit means the data goes to the normal program memory, whereas a logic 0 means it will go to the EEPROM. Therefore, before writing data to the EEPROM, this bit must be set to a logic 0. I feel I should point out that the program memory area of the PIC is also non-volatile. This is evident since the program instructions remain on the PIC even when the power has been removed. However, the program may use some data memory to store some variables. This data memory is volatile memory. With this EEPGD bit you can decide where the information is to be written to, the EEPROM area or the program area.

- Bit6, the CFGS bit. This is used in a similar fashion to the EEPGD in that a logic 1 in this bit directs the data to the configuration memory and a logic 0 directs the data to the flash program memory or the EEPROM memory. Since you want to access the EEPROM memory, this bit also needs to be set to a logic 0.

- Bit5 is not used.

- Bit4 is used to enable an erase operation.

- Bit3 is a signal to let the programmer know there has been an error with the write operation.

- Bit2 must be set to a logic 1 to enable a write operation.

- Bit1 is used to start the write operation by setting it as logic 1. This will automatically return to a logic 0 when the write cycle is complete, so you can use this action to determine that the write operation has completed.

- Bit0 is used to initiate a read operation. This bit must be set to a logic 1 when you need to read from the EEPROM. It needs to be set to a logic 0 in software.

The complete list of the bits in the EECON1 register is shown in Table 7-2.

Table 7-2. *The Bits of the Control Register EECON1*

Bit7	Bit6	Bit5	Bit4	Bit3	Bit2	Bit1	Bit0
EEPGD	CFGS		FREE	WRERR	WREN	WR	RD

BIT7	EEPGD Flash Program or Data EEPROM Memory Select Bit
	Logic 1 means access flash program memory
	Logic 0 means access data EEPROM memory
Bit6	CFGS flash program/data EEPROM or configuration select bit
	Logic 1 means access the configuration registers
	Logic 0 means access flash program or data EEPROM memory
Bit5	Not used read as 0
Bit4	FREE flash row erase enable bit
	Logic 1 means erase the program memory row addressed by TBLPTR
	Logic 0 means perform write only
Bit3	WRERR Flash Program/Data EEPROM Error bit
	Logic 1 means a write operation is prematurely terminated
	Logic 0 means the write operation has completed
Bit2	WREN flash program/data EEPROM write enable bit
	Logic 1 allows write cycles to flash program/data EEPROM
	Logic 0 inhibits write cycles to flash program/data EEPROM
Bit1	WR write control bit
	Logic 1 means a data EEPROM erase/write or a program erase/write cycle
	Logic 0 means write cycle to the EEPROM is complete
Bit0	RD read control bit
	Logic 1 initiates an EEPROM read
	Logic 0 does not initiate an EEPROM read

The EECON2 register is used to make sure the user does not write to the EEPROM accidentally. This is because for a write operation to the EEPROM to be successful, you must write 0X55 to this register followed by 0XAA every time you want to write to the EEPROM. If this does not happen, the write operation will not be successful.

To help explain how this can be done, Listing 7-3 contains a program that gets the main section of the program to write data to the EEPROM. The program then reads that data back from the EEPROM and displays it on an LCD connected to the PIC.

Listing 7-3. The Program to Test Writing to and Reading from the EEPROM

```
1. /*
2. * File:    18FEepromShort.c
3. Author: hward
4. *
5. Created on 19 October 2017, 17:39
6. */
7. #include <xc.h>
8. #include <conFigInternalOscNoWDTNoLVP.h>
9. #include <PICSetUp.h>
10. #include <4bitLCDPortb.h>
11. //some definitions
12. #define readEEPROM      0b00000011
13. #define writeEEPROM     0b00000010
14. #define wren            0b00000110
15. #define wrdi            0b00000100
16. #define rdsr            0b00000101
17. #define wrsr            0b00000001
18. #define pe              0b01000010
19. #define se              0b11011000
```

```
20. #define ce              0b11000111
21. #define rdid            0b10101011
22. #define dpd             0b10111001
23. //some variables
24. unsigned char t;
25. char str[80];
26. unsigned char *seg2Pointer;
27. unsigned char ndata [39], ndatapointer;
28. unsigned char seg2 [39] =
29. {
30. 0x41,    //ASCII for 'A'
31. 0x6E,    //ASCII for 'n'
32. 0x6E,    //ASCII for 'n'
33. 0x2C,    //ASCII for ','
34. 0x57,    //ASCII foe 'W'
35. 0x61,    //ASCII for 'a'
36. 0x72,    //ASCII for 'r'
37. 0x64,    //ASCII for 'd'
38. 0x32,    //ASCII for '2'
39. 0x31,    //ASCII for '1'
40. };
41. void main ()
42. {
43. initialise ();
44. setUpTheLCD ();
45. seg2Pointer = seg2;
46. writeString ("Using The EEPROM");
47. line2 ();
48. while (1)
49. {
50. EEADRH = 0x00;
51. EEADR = 0x00;
```

```
52. EECON1bits.EEPGD = 0;
53. EECON1bits.CFGS = 0;
54. EECON1bits.WREN = 1;
55. for (t = 0; t<10; t++)
56. {
57. EEDATA = *seg2Pointer;
58. EECON2 = 0x55;
59. EECON2 = 0x0AA;
60. EECON1bits.WR = 1;
61. while (EECON1bits.WR);
62. EEADR ++;
63. seg2Pointer ++;
64. }
65. EECON1bits.WREN = 0;
66. EEADRH = 0x00;
67. EEADR = 0x00;
68. for (t = 0; t<10; t++)
69. {
70. EECON1bits.RD = 1;
71. while (EECON1bits.RD);
72. ndata[t] = EEDATA;
73. lcdData = ndata [t];
74. lcdOut ();
75. EEADR ++;
76. }
77. EECON1bits.EEPGD = 1;
78. n = 0x22;
79. PORTC = n;
80. wait: goto wait;
81. }
82. }
```

Analysis of Listing 7-3

Lines 1 to 9 are the standard type comments and the standard `include` files.

Line10 #include <4bitLCDPortb.h>

This includes the header file created earlier to use the LCD on the first four bits of PORTB.

Lines 11 to 22 set up some definitions to create some labels that represent the commands required to use the EEPROM.

Lines 23 to 27 set up the variables, arrays, and pointers used in the program.

Line 28 unsigned char seg2 [39] =

This is setting up an array that uses 39 memory locations, with the first 10 locations being loaded now with the values listed between the following curly brackets.

Line 29 {

This is the opening bracket of the list of values to be stored in the first 10 locations of the array.

Lines 30 to 39 are the 10 values to be loaded into the first 10 locations in the array. The data is actually the ASCII values for each of the characters listed after the comment's forward slashes. In this way the 10 locations spell out the phrase Ann,Ward21. This will be written the EEPROM memory by the PIC. It will then read back from the EEPROM by the PIC and displayed on line 2 of the LCD.

Line 40};

This is the closing bracket of the list of values to be stored in the array. Note also the semicolon. This indicates that lines 28 to 40 are really an instruction for the PIC. Note also the comma after each ASCII code in the list.

Line 41 void main ()

This sets up the main loop of the program.

Line 42 {

The opening curly bracket of the main loop.

Line 43 initialise ();

This calls the subroutine that is written in the PICSetUp.h header file. This sets up the PIC in the standard way as before.

Line 44 setUpTheLCD ();

This calls the subroutine to set up the LCD. This subroutine is written in the 4bitLCDPortb.h header file.

Line 45 seg2pointer = seg2;

This loads the pointer seg2pointer with the address of the first memory location in the array seg2.

Line 46 writestring ("Using The EEPROM");

This calls the subroutine writestring, which is written in the 4bitLCDPortb.h header file. This instruction sends the characters, written inside the normal brackets between the quotation marks, to the LCD.

Line 47 line2 ();

This calls the subroutine line2, which sends the cursor to the beginning of the second line on the LCD screen.

Line 48 while (1)

This sets up the forever loop.

Line 49 {

This is the opening curly bracket that contains the instructions that the PIC must now do forever.

Line 50 EEADRH = 0x00;

This sets the 8 bits in the EEADRH register to 0.

Line 51 EEADR = 0x00;

This sets the 8 bits in the EEADR register to 0.

The EEPROM on the PIC18F4525 has 1024 locations. This requires 10 address lines to address each location. The number of memory address locations that can be addressed by a number of address lines is set by the following expression:

$$memory\ locations = 2^n$$

where n is the number of address lines.

If n was 10, then the number of memory locations that can be addressed is

$$memory\ locations = 2^{10} = 1024$$

This means that you need 10 address lines to address the 1024 locations in the EEPROM memory area. Each address line can hold one bit of data. This means that you need a 10-bit binary number to address 1024 memory locations. Since the PIC18F4525 is an 8-bit micro, it will take two memory locations to store the 10-bit number to address these 1024 memory locations. The EEADRH stores the two MSB bits of this 10-bit number. They are stored in Bit0 and Bit1 of the EEADRH register. The remaining six bits (Bits 2, 3, 4, 5, 6, and 7) are left at logic 0 and are not used.

The eight lower bits of the address are stored in the EEADR 8-bit register.

This means that the instructions on lines 50 and 51 load the two registers with address of the first memory location in the EEPROM memory area (i.e. address 0X0000 in hexadecimal format).

Line 52 EECON1bits.EEPGD = 0;

This sets Bit7 of the EECON1 register to a logic 0.

This tells the micro that the following data is to go to the EEPROM memory area.

Line 53 EECON1bits.CFGS = 0;

This sets Bit6 of the EECON1 register to a logic 0. This is to make sure the data does not go to the configuration words.

Line 54 EECON1bits.WREN = 1;

This sets Bit2 of the EECON1 register to a logic 1. This is to enable a write operation. Note that it does not initiate a write operation.

Line 55 for (t = 0; t<10; t++)

This sets up a for do loop to control the number of times the following instructions are carried out.

Line 56 {

The opening curly bracket for the for do loop.

Line 57 EEDATA = *seg2Pointer;

The EEDATA is the 8-bit register that holds the data waiting to be written to the EEPROM memory location specified by the EEADRH and EEDAR register pair. With this instruction you are making a copy of the data in the memory location in the seg2 array, as pointed to by the seg2pointer, into the EEDATA register.

Line 58 EECON2 = 0x55;
Line 59 EECON2 = 0XAA;

These two instructions write the data to the EECON2 register in the specific order to ensure that you, as the programmer, intend to write the data that is in EEDATA register to the EEPROM. It is a type of security check, and if it is not done in exactly this way, the data will not be written to the EEPROM memory.

Line 60 EECON1bits.WR = 1;

This is required to initiate a write operation. The PIC will now write the data stored in the EEDATA register to the EEPROM memory. When the write operation is complete, the PIC will automatically reset this bit back to a logic 0.

Line 61 while (EECON1bits.WR);

This makes the PIC do nothing while the logic on this bit is a logic 1. Therefore, it waits for the write operation to complete.

Line 62 EEADR ++;

This simply increments the value stored in the EEADR register. This is the low byte of the address that the EEADRH and EEADR register pair are holding. This means they will be pointing to the next memory location in the EEPROM memory. Note that if you want to write more than 256 bytes of data to the EEPROM, you must manipulate the EEADRH register as well.

Line 63 *seg2pointer ++;

This adds one to the value in the seg2pointer. This means that the pointer will now be pointing to the next address in the seg2 array.

Line 64 }

This is the closing bracket of the for do loop started in line 55. This loop is carried out 10 times and it will fill the first 10 memory locations in the EEPROM memory with the 10 ASCII codes stored in the seg2 array.

Line 65 EECON1bits.WREN = 0;

This loads this bit in the EECON1 register with a logic 0. It is used to disable the write to the EEPROM function since you no longer want to write data to the EEPROM memory.

Line 66 EEADRH = 0x00;

This is not really needed since you have not changed the value in this register. It is a just an extra measure.

Line 67 EEADR = 0x00;

This resets the value in this register, which by now has gone to 0X0B (i.e. 11 in decimal) back to 0. These two instructions make sure the address that the EEADRH and EEADR registers are pointing to is the first address in the EEPROM memory.

Line 68 for (t = 0; t<10; t++)

This sets up another for do loop that is executed 10 times.

Line 69 {

The opening curly bracket of the for do loop.

Line 70 EECON1bit.RD = 1;

This starts the operation that gets the PIC to read the data stored in the address that is pointed to by the contents of the register pair EEADRH and EEADR.

Line 71 while (EECON1bits.RD);

This makes the PIC do nothing while the logic on the pin EECON1bit. RD is a logic 1. This pin will stay at a logic 1 until the read operation, started on line 70, has been completed. When the read completes, the PIC will automatically reset the logic on this PIN to a logic 0. This then will allow the PIC to move onto the next instruction.

The data that is read from the EEPROM during this read operation is automatically stored in the EEDATA register.

Line 72 ndata[t] = EEDATA;

This loads the memory location in the ndata array with the value currently stored in the EEDATA register. The actual memory location in the array ndata is controlled by the value of the variable t, which starts off at zero. Note the value for the variable t will increase by one every time the PIC goes through the for do loop. Each time you go through the loop, you increment the EEADR register so that when the next read operation is executed, it is the value in the next memory location in the EEPROM that is written into the EEDATA register.

Line 73 lcdData = ndata [t];

This loads the variable lcdData with the value stored in the first location in the array ndata.

Line 74 lcdOut ();

This calls the subroutine lcdOut and sends the value in lcdData to the LCD.

Line 75 EEADR ++;

This simply increments the value stored in the EEADR register ready to load the value in the next memory location in the EEPROM in the next read operation.

Line 76 }

The closing bracket of the for do loop.

Line 77 EECON1bits.EEPGD = 1;

This sets the logic on this bit back to a logic 1. This is because you have finished writing to the EEPROM. This may not be required because if you don't use the two security bytes and the write control bits, no data will be written to the EEPROM or the configuration words; therefore, it must go to the flash program memory. You could check this by commenting out this instruction by writing the two forward slashes in front of the text on this line.

Line 78   n = 0x22;

This loads the variable n with the value 0X22 ready to send this data to PORTC.

Line 79 PORTC = n;

This loads PORTC with the value stored in the variable n. This is just to check that you are no longer using the EEPROM.

Line 80 wait: goto wait;

This sets up a label termed wait. Then it gets the PIC to goto this label wait. There the PIC will find the instruction to make the PIC go to the label wait. In this way, you get the PIC to constantly go around in this trapped circle, so the program halts at this point in the program.

This program simply writes data to the EEPROM memory area. The data comes from an array called seg2. The data is the ASCII characters to write out the following text: Ann,Ward21.

The program will then read the data from the EEPROM memory and display it on the second line of the LCD display.

The program then writes the value 0X22 into the variable n and loads PORTC with that value.

Simulation of the EEPROM Program Using MPLABX

If you choose the simulator in the select tool window, as shown in Figure 7-6, when you create the project, you can run a simulation of the program within MPLABX. This will allow you to look at the EEPROM memory area and confirm that the specified data is written to the EEPROM. If you have already created the project, you can change the tool to simulator by right-clicking the project name in the project tree and selecting the Properties option from the bottom of the flyout menu that appears.

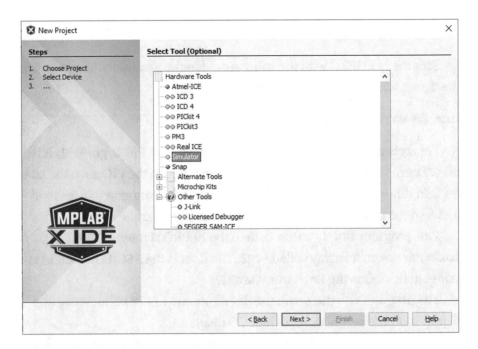

Figure 7-6. *The Select Tool window*

Having changed the tool to simulator, you can run the simulation of the program by clicking the Debug Main Project option in the main menu bar, as shown in Figure 7-7.

Figure 7-7. *The Debug Main Project option*

When you click this option, the program should build and show as a user program running in the output window. You can then select the Windows option from the main menu bar. Then select the Target Memory Views from the dropdown menu that appears. Finally, select EE Data Memory from the flyout menu that appears. Figure 7-8 should help explain what to do.

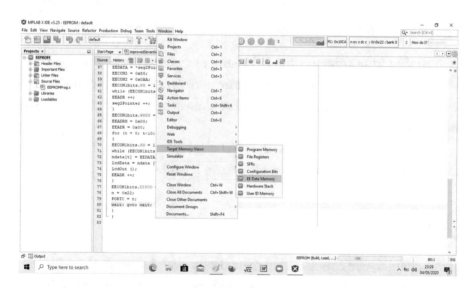

Figure 7-8. *Selecting the EE data memory*

When you select this option, the EE data memory will be displayed in a window at the bottom of the MPLABX screen. This is shown in Figure 7-9.

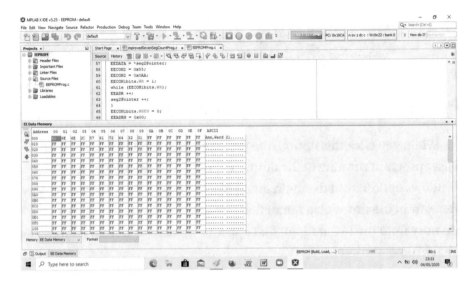

Figure 7-9. *The window showing the data in the EE data memory*

You should see that the first 10 memory locations have been filled with the ASCII characters as the program carries out the instructions. You should also see a window at the side that shows the actual characters that the data represents.

Unfortunately you can't see the LCD display but the simulation does go a long way to confirming that the program works.

Summary

In this chapter, you concentrated on two very useful aspects of the PIC: the capture mode of the CCP module and the EEPROM memory of the PIC. You learned how to use the capture mode to determine the frequency of an input signal. In this exercise, you learned how to write your own code to display a 16-bit binary integer correctly on the LCD screen. You then considered the use of the sprintf function in the stido.h header file to display a floating point binary number of the LCD screen.

You then looked at what EEPROM is and how to use it to store data and read that data from it. You also looked at using the simulation within MPLABX to confirm that your programs work.

This is the last chapter in this, my second book on controlling the PIC micro. I hope you have found it both interesting and useful. I will be writing a third book in this series of books and it will look at communication with the PIC18F4525. Thanks again for reading my book(s) on the PIC microcontroller.

APPENDIX 1

Some Useful Definitions

Here are some useful definitions. This table covers bit operators:

Operator	Description
&	AND each bit
|	OR each bit (inclusive OR)
^	EXOR each bit (exclusive OR)
<<n	Shift left n places
>>n	Shift right n places
~	One's compliment (invert each bit)

© Hubert Henry Ward 2020
H. H. Ward, *Intermediate C Programming for the PIC Microcontroller*,
https://doi.org/10.1007/978-1-4842-6068-5

Example: If 'x' = 1111 1111, then

Operation	Result
x & 0X0F	0000 1111
x I 0X0F	1111 1111
x^0X0F	1111 0000
x = x<<2	1111 1100
x = x>>4	0000 1111
x = ~x	0000 0000

APPENDIX 2

Mathematical and Logic Operators

Here are some common operators.

Operator	Description
+	Leaves the variable as it was
-	Creates the negative of the variable
++	Increments the variable by 1
--	Decrements the variable by 1
*	Multiplies the two variables, y = a*b
/	Divides y = a/b
%	Used to get the remainder of a division of two variables, m = a%b
<	Less than, so (y < a) means is y is less than a
<=	Less than or equal to, so (y < =a) means is y is less than or equal to a
>	Greater than, so (y > a) means is y is greater than a
>=	Greater than or equal to, so (y > =a) means is y is greater than or equal to a

(*continued*)

© Hubert Henry Ward 2020
H. H. Ward, *Intermediate C Programming for the PIC Microcontroller*,
https://doi.org/10.1007/978-1-4842-6068-5

Operator	Description
=	Makes the variable equal to, so y = 3. After this, y takes on the value of 3.
!	This is the NOT operator. For example if (!PORTBbits.RB0) is a test to see if the logic on bit0 of PORTB is a logic '0'. If it is the test is true.
&&	Whole register AND
||	Whole register OR
?	This is a test operator. For example, y = (a>0) ? a : -1; This is a test to see if 'a' is greater than 0. If it is then y becomes equal to 'a'. If it is not then y = -1.

APPENDIX 3

Keywords

Here are some common keywords and what they do.

Keyword	What It Does
typedef	This allows the programmer to define any phrase to represent an existing type.
#ifndef	This checks to see if a label you want to use has not been defined in any include files you want to use. If it has, it does not allow you to define it now. If it hasn't, you are allowed to define it now
#define	You can define what your label means here.
#endif	This denotes the end of your definition after the #ifndef code.
Sizeof	This returns the size in number of bytes of a variable.

Global variables are variables that, once declared, can be read from or written to anywhere from within the program.

© Hubert Henry Ward 2020
H. H. Ward, *Intermediate C Programming for the PIC Microcontroller,*
https://doi.org/10.1007/978-1-4842-6068-5

APPENDIX 4

Data Types

This table shows data types.

Type	Size	Minimum Value	Maximum Value
char	8 bits	-128	127
unsigned char	8 bits	0	255
int	16 bits	-32,768	32,767
unsigned int	16 bits	0	65,535
short	16 bits	-32,768	32,767
unsigned short	16 bits	0	65,535
short long	24 bits	-8,388,608	8,388,607
unsigned short long	24 bits	0	16,777,215
long	32 bits	-2,147,483,648	2,147.483,647
unsigned long	32 bits	0	4,294,967,295
float	32 bits		

© Hubert Henry Ward 2020
H. H. Ward, *Intermediate C Programming for the PIC Microcontroller*,
https://doi.org/10.1007/978-1-4842-6068-5

This table shows floating point numbers.

Type	Size	Minimum Exponent	Maximum Exponent	Minimum Normalized	Maximum Normalized
float	32	-126	128	2^{-126}	2^{128}
double	32	-126	128	2^{-126}	2^{128}

APPENDIX 5

The ASCII Character Set

This table shows some of the most useful code from the ASCII character set.

High Nibble	0000		0010	0011	0100	0101	0110	0111
Low Nibble	CG.Ram Location							
xxxx 0000	1			0	@	P	\	p
xxxx 0001	2		!	1	A	Q	a	q
xxxx 0010	3		"	2	B	R	b	r
xxxx 0011	4		#	3	C	S	c	s
xxxx 0100	5		$	4	D	T	d	t
xxxx 0101	6		%	5	E	U	e	u

(*continued*)

© Hubert Henry Ward 2020
H. H. Ward, *Intermediate C Programming for the PIC Microcontroller*,
https://doi.org/10.1007/978-1-4842-6068-5

xxxx 0110	7	&	6	F	V	f	v
xxxx 0111	8	'	7	G	W	g	w
xxxx 1000	1	<	8	H	X	h	x
xxxx 1001	2	>	9	I	Y	i	y
xxxx 1010	3	*	:	J	Z	j	z
xxxx 1011	4	+	;	K	[	k	{
xxxx 1100	5	'	<	L		l	|
xxxx 1101	6	-	=	M	]	m	}
xxxx 1110	7	.	>	N	^	n	
xxxx 1111	8	/	?	0	_	o	

APPENDIX 6

Numbering Systems Within Microprocessor-Based Systems

As will become evident in the study to come, microprocessor-based systems use the binary number system. This is because the binary number system can only have one of two digits, either a 0 or a 1. These states are called logic 0 or logic 1, as in electronic devices. Note also that all of the logic operations such as AND, OR, NAND, NOR, NOT, and EXOR work using the binary format. The binary format can be used to mimic the logic states of TRUE or FALSE precisely, and best of all, they can be represented by voltage(i.e. 0V for logic 0 and +5V for logic 1).

Therefore, it is essential that the modern engineer gains a full understanding of the binary number system. This appendix is aimed at teaching you all you need to know about binary numbers.

© Hubert Henry Ward 2020
H. H. Ward, *Intermediate C Programming for the PIC Microcontroller*,
https://doi.org/10.1007/978-1-4842-6068-5

Binary Numbers

Binary numbers are a series of 0s and 1s that represent numbers. With respect to microprocessor-based systems, the numbers they represent themselves represent code for instructions and data used within microprocessor-based programs. We, as humans, cannot easily interpret binary numbers because we use the deanery number system. The deanery number system uses the base number 10, which means all the columns we put our digits in to form numbers are based on powers of 10. For example, the thousand column is based on 10^3 and the hundreds column is based on 10^2. The tens column is based on 10^1 and the ones column is based on 10^0. Try putting 10^0 in your calculator using the x^y button and you will find it equals 1; in fact, any number raised to the power 0 will equal 1.

Converting Decimal to Binary

Probably the first step to understanding binary numbers is in creating them (i.e. converting decimal to binary). There are numerous ways of doing this but I feel the most straightforward is to repeatedly divide the decimal number by 2, the base number of binary. This is shown here:

Convert 66 to binary.

The remainders

2	66	0
2	33	1
2	16	0
2	8	0
2	4	0
2	2	0
	1	

1 0 0 0 0 1 0
The MSB   The LSB

NB you must use the last 1 from
the divide 2 by 2 or 3 by 2

Simply keep on dividing the number by 2, putting the answer underneath as shown, with the remainder to the side. You should note that all the remainders are either **0** or **1**. These digits actually make up the binary number. Note also that the last division always results in an answer of **1**; we stop there so no more dividing.

To create the binary number, we take the top of the remainders, as shown, and put it into the least significant bit (LSB), or column, for the binary number. The other remainder digits follow on, thus making up the complete seven-digit number.

Converting from Binary to Decimal

It would be useful to determine if the binary number shown does actually relate to 66 in decimal. This is done by converting the binary number 1 0 0 0 0 1 0 back into decimal. To do this, you must realize that numbers are displayed in columns. The columns are based on the base number of the system used. With binary numbers, the base number is 2, therefore the columns are based on powers of 2. This is shown in this table:

Base Number	2^7	2^6	2^5	2^4	2^3	2^2	2^1	2^0
Decimal equivalent	128	64	32	16	8	4	2	1
Binary number		1	0	0	0	0	1	0

To complete the conversion, you simply sum all the decimal equivalents where there is a 1 in the binary column.

In this case, the sum is 64+2 = 66.

Now, let's convert 127 to binary and check the result.

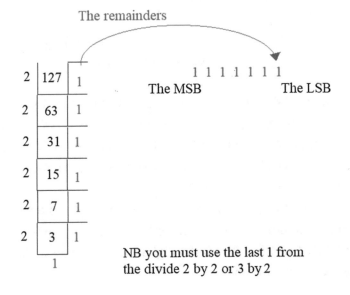

The remainders

1 1 1 1 1 1 1
The MSB   The LSB

NB you must use the last 1 from the divide 2 by 2 or 3 by 2

Base Number	2^7	2^6	2^5	2^4	2^3	2^2	2^1	2^0
Decimal equivalent	128	64	32	16	8	4	2	1
Binary number	0	1	1	1	1	1	1	1

To complete the conversion, simply sum all the decimal equivalents where there is a 1 in the binary column.

In this case, the sum is $64 + 32 + 16 + 8 + 4 + 2 + 1 = 127$.

Now you try it. Convert the following numbers to binary and check your results by converting back to decimal:

99

255

137

Adding and Subtracting Binary Numbers

Adding and subtracting numbers is perhaps the most basic operation we can carry out on numbers. Binary numbers follow the same rules as decimal, but there are only two allowable digits. Also, computers don't actually subtract numbers, as the following will show.

Add the following decimal numbers in 8-bit binary notation and check your answers:

$23 + 21, 35 + 123, 125 + 75$

Worked example:

Remember binary numbers have only two digits: 0 or 1.

Add 23 to 21 in 8-bit binary.

Method:

Convert to 8-bit binary and add. Remember the following four rules:

$0+0 = 0$

$0+1 = 1$

$1+0 = 1$

$1+1 = 0$ with 1 to carry

23 in 8 bit binary is

0 0 0 1 0 1 1 1 Note that you must state all 8 bits because it is an 8-bit binary.

By the same process, 21 in binary is 0 0 0 1 0 1 0 1.

Therefore, the sum is 0 0 0 1 0 1 1 1

+ 0 0 0 1 0 1 0 1

_____

0 0 1 0 1 1 0 0

_____

To check your, answer put the result into the look-up table and then add the decimal equivalent.

Power	2^7	2^6	2^5	2^4	2^3	2^2	2^1	2^0
Decimal equivalent	128	64	32	16	8	4	2	1
Binary number	0	0	1	0	1	1	0	0

The sum is 32 + 8 + 4 = 44.

Subtracting Binary Numbers

Microprocessor-based systems actually subtract numbers using a method which is addition. This involves using the 2's compliment of a number and it is best explained by the following example.

Subtract the following decimal numbers using the 8-bit binary 2's compliment and check your answers:

128 - 28, 79 - 78, 55 - 5, 251 - 151

Worked example:

Convert the two numbers to binary using the method shown in previously.

128 in 8-bit binary is 10000000. **NOTE that you MUST use ALL 8 bits.**

28 in 8-bit binary is 00011100.

Take the 2's compliment of 00011100 since this is the number that you are subtracting from 128.

Only create the 2's compliment of the subtrahend, the number you are subtracting with.

NOTE that you must use a full 8-bit number, putting an extra 0 in where needed.

To take the 2's compliment, first take the compliment and then add binary 1 to the compliment. The compliment of the binary number is found by simply flipping all the bits, so a 0 becomes a 1 and a 1 becomes a 0.

The compliment of 00011100 is 1 1 1 0 0 0 1 1.

Add binary 1 + 0 0 0 0 0 0 0 1.

---

1 1 1 0 0 1 0 0

Now add the 2's compliment to the first binary number as shown:

1 0 0 0 0 0 0 0

+ 1 1 1 0 0 1 0 0

The result is 0 1 1 0 0 1 0 0.

NOTE THAT THE LAST CARRY INTO THE NINTH DIGIT IS DISCARDED BECAUSE THERE CAN ONLY BE THE SPECIFIED NUMBER OF DIGITS, EIGHT IN THIS CASE. Don't forget that you added 1 so you should give it back.

The binary result converts to 100 in decimal. This is the correct result.

Check your answers in the usual way.

Note that computers subtract in this method because we can only create an adder circuit in logic.

The Hexadecimal Number System

A microprocessor-based system can only recognize data that is in the binary format. In its most basic form, this means that all data inputted at the keyboard should be in binary format. This is quite a formidable concept. Just think if every letter of every word must be inputted as a binary number. It takes at least four binary digits to represent a letter, so typing words into a computer would be very difficult indeed. Thankfully, word processing programs use ASCII characters to represent the letters you press at the keyboard.

With the type of programs we will be writing into microcomputers we will actually be typing in two characters to represent the code for the instructions or data of the programs we will write. If we were to type these in as binary numbers, it would take 8 binary bits to make each code. This would be very time-consuming and difficult to avoid errors. To make things easier, we will use the hexadecimal numbering system. This system has 16 unique digits: 0 1 2 3 4 5 6 7 8 9.

We cannot use 10 because it uses two digits, a 1 and a 0. Therefore, we must use six more unique digits. To do this, we use the first six letters of the alphabet. Therefore, the full 16 digits are

0 1 2 3 5 6 7 8 9 A B C D E F.

Remember, we are going to use the hexadecimal number to represent binary digits and this revolves round the idea that one hexadecimal digit represents four binary digits as the four binary bits in decimal go from 0 to 15 (i.e. 16 numbers). Therefore, every 8-bit binary number can be represented by two hexadecimal digits. This makes typing in the code for programs much quicker and more secure than using the full binary numbers that computers use. Note that to accommodate the user typing inputs as hexadecimal digits, there is a program in the micro's ROM to convert the hexadecimal to binary for us. However, we will look at converting binary to hexadecimal.

Convert the following 8-bit binary numbers to hexadecimal:

10011110, 10101010, 11111111, 11110000, 00001111, and 11001101

Worked example

Method: Split the 8 bits into two 4-bit numbers. Convert each 4-bit into the decimal equivalent and then look up the hexadecimal for the decimal equivalent in the look-up table. **NOTE: Treat each four binary bits as a separate binary number.**

Convert 1 0 0 1 | 1 1 1 0

Dec 9 | 14

Hex 9 | E

Answer 10011110 in Hex is 9E

In this way, 8-bit binary numbers can be converted into two hexadecimal digits.

APPENDIX 7

The musical notes header file:

```
/*Definitions for most of the musical notes
 Written by Mr. H. H. Ward dated 14/10/13*/
#define B0  PR2 = 253,  CCPR1L = 126
#define C1s PR2 = 226,  CCPR1L = 113
#define C1  PR2 = 239,  CCPR1L = 119
#define D1  PR2 = 213,  CCPR1L = 106
#define D1s PR2 = 201,  CCPR1L = 100
#define E1  PR2 = 190,  CCPR1L = 95
#define F1  PR2 = 179,  CCPR1L = 89
#define F1s PR2 = 167,  CCPR1L = 85
#define G1  PR2 = 160,  CCPR1L = 80
#define G1s PR2 = 150,  CCPR1L = 75
#define A1  PR2 = 142,  CCPR1L = 71
#define A1s PR2 = 134,  CCPR1L = 67
#define B1  PR2 = 127,  CCPR1L = 63
#define C2  PR2 = 119,  CCPR1L = 60
#define C2s PR2 = 113,  CCPR1L = 56
#define D2  PR2 = 106,  CCPR1L = 53
#define D2s PR2 = 100,  CCPR1L = 50
#define E2  PR2 = 95,   CCPR1L = 47
#define F2  PR2 = 89,   CCPR1L = 45
#define F2s PR2 = 85,   CCPR1L = 42
#define G2  PR2 = 80,   CCPR1L = 40
#define G2s PR2 = 75,   CCPR1L = 38
#define A2  PR2 = 71,   CCPR1L = 36
```

© Hubert Henry Ward 2020
H. H. Ward, *Intermediate C Programming for the PIC Microcontroller*,
https://doi.org/10.1007/978-1-4842-6068-5

```
#define A2s PR2 = 67,    CCPR1L = 34
#define B2  PR2 = 63,    CCPR1L = 32
#define C3  PR2 = 60,    CCPR1L = 30
#define C3s PR2 = 56,    CCPR1L = 28
#define D3  PR2 = 53,    CCPR1L = 27
#define D3s PR2 = 50,    CCPR1L = 25
#define E3  PR2 = 47,    CCPR1L = 24
#define F3  PR2 = 45,    CCPR1L = 22
#define F3s PR2 = 42,    CCPR1L = 21
#define G3  PR2 = 40,    CCPR1L = 20
#define G3s PR2 = 38,    CCPR1L = 19
#define A3  PR2 = 35,    CCPR1L = 18
#define B3  PR2 = 31,    CCPR1L = 16
#define C4  PR2 = 29,    CCPR1L = 15
#define C4s PR2 = 28,    CCPR1L = 14
#define D4  PR2 = 27,    CCPR1L = 13
#define D4s PR2 = 25,    CCPR1L = 12
#define E4  PR2 = 24,    CCPR1L = 12
#define F4  PR2 = 22,    CCPR1L = 11
#define F4s PR2 = 21,    CCPR1L = 10
#define G4  PR2 = 20,    CCPR1L = 10
#define G4s PR2 = 19,    CCPR1L = 9
#define A4  PR2 = 18,    CCPR1L = 9
#define A4s PR2 = 17,    CCPR1L = 8
#define B4  PR2 = 16,    CCPR1L = 8
#define C5  PR2 = 15,    CCPR1L = 7
#define C5s PR2 = 14,    CCPR1L = 7
#define D5  PR2 = 13,    CCPR1L = 7
#define D5s PR2 = 12,    CCPR1L = 6
#define E5  PR2 = 11,    CCPR1L = 6
```

APPENDIX 8

The Frequency and Wavelength of the Main Musical Notes

Here are the frequencies and wavelengths of the main musical notes. The wavelength of the frequency is the distance the wave travels in one cycle. The wavelength can be calculated using $\lambda = \dfrac{v}{f}$ where λ is the wavelength, v is the speed of sound 343m/s, and f is the frequency in Hertz.

So, for example, the musical note D3# has a frequency of 155.5 Hertz. Therefore the wavelength is

$$\lambda = \frac{343}{155.56} = 2.2049 m \, or \, 220.49 cm$$

Musical Note	Frequency, Hertz	Wavelength, m
C_0	16.35	20.97859
$C^\#_0$ or D^b_0	17.32	19.8037
D_0	18.35	18.6921
$D^\#_0$ or E^b_0	19.45	17.63496

(continued)

© Hubert Henry Ward 2020
H. H. Ward, *Intermediate C Programming for the PIC Microcontroller*,
https://doi.org/10.1007/978-1-4842-6068-5

Musical Note	Frequency, Hertz	Wavelength, m
E_0	20.60	16.65049
F_0	21.83	15.71232
$F^{\#}_0\ G^b_0$	23.12	14.83564
G_0	24.50	14
$G^{\#}_0$ or A^b_0	25.96	13.21263
A_0	27.50	12.47273
$A^{\#}_0$ or B^b_0	29.14	11.77076
B_0	30.87	11.11111
C_1	32.70	10.4893
$C^{\#}_1$ or D^b_1	34.65	9.89899
D_1	36.71	9.343503
$D^{\#}_1/E^b_1$	38.89	8.819748
E_1	41.20	8.325243
F_1	43.65	7.857961
$F^{\#}_1$ or G^b_1	46.25	7.416216
G_1	49.00	7
$G^{\#}_1$ or A^b_1	51.91	6.60759
A_1	55.00	6.236364
$A^{\#}_1/B^b_1$	58.27	5.886391
B_1	61.74	5.555556
C_2	65.41	5.243847
$C^{\#}_2$ or D^b_2	69.30	4.949495
D_2	73.42	4.671752

(*continued*)

APPENDIX 8   THE FREQUENCY AND WAVELENGTH OF THE MAIN MUSICAL NOTES

Musical Note	Frequency, Hertz	Wavelength, m
$D^{\#}_2$ or E^b_2	77.78	4.409874
E_2	82.41	4.162116
F_2	87.31	3.928531
$F^{\#}_2/G^b_2$	92.50	3.708108
G_2	98.00	3.5
$G^{\#}_2/A^b_2$	103.83	3.303477
A_2	110.00	3.118182
$A^{\#}_2$ or B^b_2	116.54	2.943195
B_2	123.47	2.778003
C_3	130.81	2.622124
$C^{\#}_3$ or D^b_3	138.59	2.474926
D_3	146.83	2.336035
$D^{\#}_3$ or E^b_3	155.56	2.204937
E_3	164.81	2.081184
F_3	174.61	1.964378
$F^{\#}_3/G^b_3$	185.00	1.854054
G_3	196.00	1.75
$G^{\#}_3$ or A^b_3	207.65	1.651818
A_3	220.00	1.559091
$A^{\#}_3$ or B^b_3	233.08	1.471598
B_3	246.94	1.389001
C_4	261.63	1.311012
$C^{\#}_4$ or D^b_4	277.18	1.237463

(*continued*)

Musical Note	Frequency, Hertz	Wavelength, m
D_4	293.66	1.168017
$D^{\#}_4/E^b_4$	311.13	1.102433
E_4	329.63	1.040561
F_4	349.23	0.982161
$F^{\#}_4$ or G^b_4	369.99	0.927052
G_4	392.00	0.875
$G^{\#}_4/A^b_4$	415.30	0.825909
A_4	440.00	0.779545
$A^{\#}_4$ or B^b_4	466.16	0.735799
B_4	493.88	0.694501
C_5	523.25	0.655518
$C^{\#}_5/D^b_5$	554.37	0.61872
D_5	587.33	0.583999
$D^{\#}_5$ or E^b_5	622.25	0.551225
E_5	659.25	0.520288
F_5	698.46	0.49108
$F^{\#}_5/G^b_5$	739.99	0.46352
G_5	783.99	0.437506
$G^{\#}_5$ or A^b_5	830.61	0.41295
A_5	880.00	0.389773
$A^{\#}_5$ or B^b_5	932.33	0.367895
B_5	987.77	0.347247
C_6	1046.50	0.327759

(continued)

Musical Note	Frequency, Hertz	Wavelength, m
$C^{\#}_6/D^{b}_6$	1108.73	0.309363
D_6	1174.66	0.291999
$D^{\#}_6$ or E^{b}_6	1244.51	0.27561
E_6	1318.51	0.260142
F_6	1396.91	0.245542
$F^{\#}_6/G^{b}_6$	1479.98	0.23176
G_6	1567.98	0.218753
$G^{\#}_6$ or A^{b}_6	1661.22	0.206475
A_6	1760.00	0.194886
$A^{\#}_6$ or B^{b}_6	1864.66	0.183948
B_6	1975.53	0.173624
C_7	2093.00	0.16388
$C^{\#}_7$ or D^{b}_7	2217.46	0.154681
D_7	2349.32	0.146
$D^{\#}_7$ or E^{b}_7	2489.02	0.137805
E_7	2637.02	0.130071
F_7	2793.83	0.122771
$F^{\#}_7$ or G^{b}_7	2959.96	0.11588
G_7	3135.96	0.109376
$G^{\#}_7$ or A^{b}_7	3322.44	0.103237
A_7	3520.00	0.097443
$A^{\#}_7$ or B^{b}_7	3729.31	0.091974
B_7	3951.07	0.086812

(continued)

Musical Note	Frequency, Hertz	Wavelength, m
C_8	4186.01	0.08194
$C^{\#}_8$ or D^b_8	4434.92	0.077341
D_8	4698.63	0.073
$D^{\#}_8/E^b_8$	4978.03	0.068903
E_8	5274.04	0.065036
F_8	5587.65	0.061385
$F^{\#}_8$ or G^b_8	5919.91	0.05794
G_8	6271.93	0.054688
$G^{\#}_8$ or A^b_8	6644.88	0.051619
A_8	7040.00	0.048722
$A^{\#}_8$ or B^b_8	7458.62	0.045987
B_8	7902.13	0.043406

Index

© Hubert Henry Ward 2020
H. H. Ward, *Intermediate C Programming for the PIC Microcontroller*,
https://doi.org/10.1007/978-1-4842-6068-5

Printed in the United States
By Bookmasters